TEXAS GOVERNMENT

Third Edition

TEXAS GOVERNMENT
Politics and Economics

Kim Quaile Hill
Kenneth R. Mladenka

Texas A&M University

Wadsworth Publishing Company
Belmont, California
A Division of Wadsworth, Inc.

Texas Marketing Representatives: *Dean Allsman,*
  Tom Fallath, Rusty Johnson,
  Doni Marquart, Diana Morgan,
  Ragu Raghavan, Jim Smith
Political Science Editor: *Peggy Adams*
Editorial Assistant: *Soeun Park*
Production Editor: *Gary Mcdonald*
Managing Designer: *Cloyce Wall*
Print Buyer: *Barbara Britton*
Art Editor: *Donna Kalal*
Permissions Editor: *Robert Kauser*
Designer: *Wendy Calmenson*
Copy Editor: *Rosemary Sheffield*
Photo Researcher: *Photosearch*
Technical Illustrator: *Kathryn W. Werhane*
Cover: *Cloyce Wall*
Compositor: *Graphic World Inc.*
Printer: *Fairfield Graphics*

Acknowledgments

Ch. 2, pp. 17 and 23, Figures 2-1 and 2-2 from "The Imprint of the Upper and Lower South on Mid-Nineteenth Century Texas," by T. G. Jordan, *Annals of the Association of American Geographers,* 1967, 57 (December): 668. Reprinted by permission.

Ch. 3, p. 37, quote from *Imperial Texas: An Interpretative Essay in Cultural Geography,* by D. W. Meinig. © 1969 by D. W. Meinig. Reprinted by permission of the University of Texas Press.

P. 39, quotes from *American Civics,* by W. H. Hartley and W. S. Vincent. © 1970 by Harcourt Brace Jovanovich, Inc. Reprinted by permission of the publisher.

Pp. 44–45, Fig. 3-1 from *American Federalism: A View from the States,* 3rd Edition, by D. J. Elazar. © 1984 by Harper & Row, Publishers, Inc. Reprinted by permission of HarperCollins Publishers.

Ch. 6, pp. 120–121, newspaper article copyright 1986, *The Houston Post.* Reprinted by permission.

P. 122, quote from *There Also Shall Be a Lieutenant Governor,* by J. Davis, pp. 18–19. © 1967 by the University of Texas Institute for Public Affairs. Reprinted by permission.

Ch. 7, pp. 144–145, Table 7-1, from *Politics in the American States: A Comparative Analysis,* 4th Edition, by V. Gray, H. Jacob, and K. N. Vines (Eds.), pp. 458–459. © 1983 by Virginia Gray, Herbert Jacob, and Kenneth N. Vines. Reprinted by permission of HarperCollins Publishers.

Ch. 8, pp. 172–173, column by Molly Ivins © 1992 *The Fort Worth Star Telegram.* Reprinted by permission of the publisher.

Chapter Opening Photos

Chs. 1, 7, © Kevin Vandivier/Viesti Associates, Inc.
Ch. 2, Archives Division–Texas State Library
Ch. 3, © Larry Kolvoord/Viesti Associates, Inc.
Chs. 4, 5, 6, 9, 10, 11, 12, 13, © Bob Daemmrich Photos
Ch. 8, Courtesy J. Griffis Smith/Texas Department of Transportation
Ch. 14, © Joe Viesti/Viesti Associates, Inc.

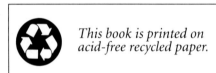

This book is printed on acid-free recycled paper.

© 1993 by Wadsworth, Inc. All rights reserved. No part of this book may be reproduced, stored in a retrieval system, or transcribed, in any form or by any means, without the prior written permission of the publisher, Wadsworth Publishing Company, Belmont, California 94002.

1 2 3 4 5 6 7 8 9 10—97 96 95 94 93

Library of Congress Cataloging-in-Publication Data

Hill, Kim Quaile, 1946–
  Texas government : politics and economics / Kim Quaile Hill,
Kenneth R. Mladenka. — 3rd ed.
   p. cm.
  Mladenka's name appears first on the earlier editions.
  Includes bibliographical references and index.
  ISBN 0-534-20058-3 (alk. paper)
  1. Local government—Texas. 2. Texas—Politics and government.
I. Mladenka, Kenneth R., 1943– II. Title.
JK4816.H547 1993
320.9764—dc20   92-35974

Preface ix

1 The Political Economy of Texas — 1

The Current Character of the Texas Economy 2
The Declining Importance of the Oil and Gas Industries 3
The Prominence of High-Tech Industries 5
The Future of the Texas Economy 9
Conclusion 10
References 12

2 The Population of Texas — 15

The History of Population Growth in Texas 15
The Future of Population Growth in Texas 24
Major Demographic Characteristics 24
Conclusion 33
References 34

3 The Political Cultures of Texas — 37

The Concept of Political Culture 38
The Patterning of America's Political Cultures 41
Political Subcultures in Texas 46
Conclusion 51
Note 52
References 53

4 The Texas Constitution

55

The Functions of State Constitutions 55
The History of the Texas Constitution 58
Revising the Constitution 62
Impacts of the 1876 Constitution 68
Conclusion 70
References 72

5 Elections in Texas: Political Parties, Public Participation, and Interest Groups

75

Political Parties in a Democratic Polity 75
Formation of the One-Party System in Texas 76
Consequences of the One-Party System 79
Weakening of the One-Party System 82
Reasons for Low Voter Turnout in Texas 88
Obstacles to Two-Party Competition 90
Interest Groups in a Democratic Polity 94
Checks on Interest Group Power 95
Interest Group Power in Texas 98
Interest Groups and Elections 99
Conclusion 100
References 101

6 The Legislature

105

The Image of the Texas Legislature 105
The Functions of Legislatures 106
The Reality of the Texas Legislature 111
The Legislators Themselves 124
Special Interest Groups and the Legislature 130
Conclusion 133
References 134

7 The Governor

137

The Image of the Governor 137
The Functions of Governors 139
The Reality of the Texas Governor's Powers 143
The Governor's Staff 149
The Governor's Informal Powers 150
The Governors Themselves 152

Contents   vii

Conclusion   156
Notes   157
References   157

8   The Executive Branch of State Government   161

The Role of the Bureaucracy in a Democratic Society   162
The Evolution of the Bureaucratic Role   165
The Power of the Bureaucracy   165
The State Agencies   167
The Size of the Executive Branch   173
Fragmentation in the Executive Branch   175
Reorganizing the Texas Bureaucracy   175
Sunset Review of State Agencies   181
Conclusion   183
References   184

9   The Court System   187

The Functions of State Court Systems   187
The Role of the Courts in the Public Policy Process   188
The Image of the Court System   189
Organization of the Texas Court System   190
The Work Load of Texas Courts   197
The Judges Themselves   203
Conclusion   207
Notes   208
References   208

10   The Political Economy of the Metropolis   211

Metropolitan Texas   212
Federal Aid and the Development of the Metropolis   214
Fragmented Government   216
Annexation   218
State–City Relations   219
The Policy Priorities of Texas Cities   219
Conclusion   221
References   222

11   Government and Policy in Texas Cities   225

City and State Governments Compared   225

viii Contents

Forms of City Government   227
Does the Form Really Matter?   229
Who Governs Texas Cities and Other Local Governments?   230
Participation in City Politics   231
City Budgets   238
Conclusion   240
References   241

12 Counties and Special Districts · 243

Legal Responsibilities of County Government   243
Constitutional Provisions   244
Offices of County Government   245
The Problems with County Government   248
The Policy Priorities of Texas Counties   248
Special Districts   252
School Districts   255
Conclusion   260
References   261

13 Taxation and Spending · 263

The Level of State and Local Taxes   263
Sources of Tax Revenues   264
Current Controversies About the Texas Tax System   269
The Level of State and Local Spending   270
Federal Aid in Texas   273
Distribution of Benefits and Burdens   276
Conclusion   279
Notes   281
References   281

14 The Future of Government and Public Policy in Texas · 285

A Time of Change and Challenge   285
History, Tradition, and Traditional Attitudes Toward
    Government   286
Contemporary Attitudes Toward Government   289
The Future of Public Policy   292
Contemporary Governmental Realities   294

Index · 297

Preface

This new edition of *Texas Government: Politics and Economics* maintains the central themes that guided its predecessors. We begin with a consideration of how economic forces and debates over current economic concerns affect state and local governments. We argue that economic concerns are of particular relevance in Texas today, shaping the politics and policies of the state more than any other force. The interplay of economics and politics is one of the major themes of the book.

The character of the state's population is another factor that greatly influences Texas politics. Chapter 2 explores the history of population growth in the state, recent patterns of urbanization and suburbanization, the likely future of population growth, and the unique social and economic positions of the state's three major ethnic groups. These population characteristics determine a number of the state's major policy concerns, and we refer to them throughout the book.

Among these population-based concerns, the political consequences of urbanization get particular attention. Compared to other texts on Texas government, this book offers relatively lengthy and thorough discussions of the political consequences of that process, the governing of the state's large metropolitan areas, and the various entities of local government that are on the front lines of the latter effort. And we are preoccupied with these matters because of their centrality for so many of the state's policy problems.

At the same time, a state's population is more than just numbers of people, whether it is the number living in cities versus small towns, the number in poverty, the number in each major ethnic group, and so on. Individuals and identifiable groups of Texans have particular attitudes toward government and the role they wish it to have in their state. They have what is called in Chapter 3 distinctive *political cultures*. Thus that chapter discusses such attitudes held by major groups of Texans, and it explains how those attitudes influence the politics of the state.

x

Preface

The effects of political culture can be seen in many different areas of the state's political life; we return to this matter in other chapters of this book.

We are conscious, as well, of how the past determines much of the future. We discuss the history of the major political institutions and processes in the state. As one example, the state's political culture could be very quickly summarized without elaboration. But to understand how that particular culture arose and how it might be evolving, one must know some of the history of migration to the state and the different historical experiences of major groups of migrants. We discuss those matters to give the reader a richer sense of how culture is important for politics. Similarly, the state's constitution, adopted in 1876, has a powerful influence on the character of contemporary state government. We explain that influence in Chapter 4, but we do so in the context of a discussion of why the constitution was written as it was. By knowing the motivations of the authors of the constitution, we can better understand how and why it affects state government today. These examples illustrate how one can often understand present-day political realities far better if he or she knows their history. We give great weight and consideration to history throughout the book.

We are concerned with the quality of the democratic process in the state. Every Texan knows that this state and this nation are democracies. But what, indeed, is the role of the general public in the making of state and local government policy? What are the major avenues by which democracy is supposedly ensured? How well do those avenues function in Texas? Are some Texans, or groups of Texans, more politically powerful than others? We address these questions in virtually every chapter.

This third edition of *Texas Government* also profits from the inclusion of an especially large amount of new material. A number of chapters have been almost wholly rewritten. All of them have been subjected to thorough updating to take into account recent political events and scholarship. Equally important, there is a considerable amount of new material on specific, contemporary political and policy problems. We discuss at some length the decline of the crude oil and natural gas industries and the political consequences of that decline, the rise of the Republican Party in the state, the role of Political Action Committees (PACs) in recent state politics, the increasingly prominent role of state and federal courts in policy decisions, efforts to revise the state tax system, and the Texas lottery. We have added most of this material to offer more examples of current, everyday political affairs that illustrate the general themes of this book.

Other changes from earlier editions are also worthy of note. We have considerably expanded the discussion of the executive branch of state government, and that revision draws upon the work of the Texas Performance Review carried out by the state comptroller in 1991. We have also considerably revised the order and content of the chapters on urbanization and local government. In particular, there is a good deal of new material and detail on the structures and policies of cities, counties, special districts, and school districts. And the final chapter now offers a deliberate summary and conclusion for the entire book. That chapter includes, as well, some prognostications for the political future of the state.

We are now particularly conscious of how this book has evolved because of the advice and comments of a host of other professors of Texas government—going back even to the first edition. We are pleased to acknowledge here the assistance of all those individuals. For the first edition they included Carl Burney, San Jacinto College; Jill Clark, University of Texas at Arlington; David Fairbanks, University of Houston–Downtown; Michael Flavin, Midwestern State University; William Hoffman, Del Mar College; Lucille Meismer-Dukes, El Paso Community College; Lynette Perkins, University of St. Thomas; Wayne Pryor, Brazosport College; Roland Smith, Texas Tech University; and M. T. Waddell, Galveston College.

For the second edition they were Thomas Clay Arnold, University of Texas at Arlington; Jeremy Curtoys, Tarleton State University; E. Larry Dickens, Sam Houston University; Jim Dukes, Richland College; Patricia Caperton Parent, Southwest Texas State University; and Larry Pool, Mountain View College.

For this third edition they were Weston Agor, University of Texas at El Paso; Jill Clark, University of Texas at Arlington; Jim Enelow, University of Texas at Austin; and Candy Stevens-Smith, Texarkana Community College.

Kim Quaile Hill
Kenneth R. Mladenka

About the Authors

Kim Quaile Hill was born in Arkansas, but his family moved to Beaumont, Texas, when he was one year old. He grew up in Beaumont and then attended Rice University to earn both his bachelor's and doctoral degrees. He taught at the University of Houston–Clear Lake before joining Texas A&M University where he is a professor of political science and Director of the Graduate Program in Public Administration. Professor Hill's current research is concerned primarily with the democratic process in state government policy making.

Kenneth R. Mladenka was born in Moulton, Texas, and reared in Sugarland, Texas. He earned his bachelor's degree from Sam Houston State University and his doctorate from Rice University. He taught at the University of Virginia and Northwestern University before returning to Texas and his current position as professor of political science at Texas A&M University. Professor Mladenka's principal scholarly interest is in the governing of cities.

Chapter 1

The Political Economy of Texas

Old images die hard. There are many who believe that Texas is still rural and agrarian, that government plays a small role in the affairs of the state, that oil continues to dominate, and that the economy is neither industrialized nor diversified. They would be wrong on all counts. Most Texans live in urban areas, and great numbers live in huge cities. Few Texans remain to farm the land and raise cattle. The wide-open spaces are still there, but the people have moved to the city. And though oil and agriculture are vital to the state's economy, other economic activities have assumed major significance. In fact, trade, manufacturing, and services such as finance, insurance, and transportation account for a majority of the economic activity in the state. Texas is now one of the most industrialized states in the country. In addition, the computer has emerged to challenge the cow and the oil well as one of the state's dominant economic symbols. The silicon chip, invented by an engineer employed by Texas Instruments, promises to revolutionize the economy of the nation as well as the state.

These economic changes have fundamentally transformed the state's governments. The great cities require a vast array of public services that are unnecessary in rural and small-town areas. The industrial economy, too, spawns a variety of new demands for governmental activity. Business regulation and promotion, the control of environmental pollution, and the provision of a host of public services necessary for industry and commerce are just a few examples of how government must respond to the modern economy. To meet those expectations, the size and scope of government have increased dramatically. As but one indicator of that expansion, Texas state and local governments employ more than a million workers today.

As the preceding examples suggest, the character of the economy has considerable influence on the political life of the state. In general, the nature and evolving fortunes of the principal industries of the state, the amount and distribution of wealth, and the general health and direction of the economy determine the level of resources available to government and the nature of many policy

2 *Chapter 1*

problems with which government must contend. The distribution of economic resources also profoundly affects the social and economic status of individual Texans, and it shapes their political attitudes and demands on government as a result.

The importance of these matters for politics has been long recognized. The study of such relations is often called the study of **political economy**. Because Texas is in a period of unusual economic change, the political economy of the state is closely linked to a number of topics to be raised in subsequent chapters of this book. Many Texans are at least somewhat aware of the connections between the economy and the political life of the state. Yet many of those people often base their opinions on outdated stereotypes about the character of the Texas economy— much like those listed at the beginning of this chapter. Those stereotypes, in other words, arise out of what the economy used to be rather than what it is today.

At the turn of the present century Texas had an economy based overwhelmingly on agriculture. Some 70 percent of the work force was employed in that sector. Employment in manufacturing, in trade, and in anything comparable to today's technical and professional fields was modest. Relatively early in the century, however, the oil and natural gas industries began to boom, leading to the development of the manufacturing sector. Many Texans probably assume that agriculture and the oil and gas industries are still the backbone of the state's economy. The traditional symbols of that economy have been cattle, cotton, and oil wells. Yet there has already been considerable movement toward a more diversified economic system. Such movement is still proceeding at a relatively rapid pace.

The Current Character of the Texas Economy

As we will explain in more detail shortly, the state's economy is in a period of dramatic change that will have a number of important political consequences. But some enduring characteristics of the economy deserve mention first. Texas has one of the largest, and therefore most important, economies of any of the fifty American states. The size of a state's economy is measured by its **gross state product**, the total monetary value of all the goods and services produced in the state in a given year. By that measure Texas has the third largest state economy in the United States, behind only California and New York (U.S. Bureau of the Census, 1991:439).

In addition, the economy of the state is now rather diversified, contrary to the stereotypes mentioned above. It is true that the state is still a leader in agriculture and in the oil and gas industries. As examples, Texas is second only to California in gross farm income, is first in the nation in the monetary value of cattle and calf production, and leads the nation in the value of crude oil production. (But we will shortly have more to say about the declining contribution of such industries to the overall state economy.) Other figures indicate the diversification of the economy. The character of the Texas work force, for example, has changed tremendously in the last half century (Table 1-1). Not only have agriculture, forestry, and fishing declined to a minuscule proportion of overall employment, but today aggregate employment is also well divided among a number of industrial categories. Many different forms of business contribute in significant magnitudes to the health of the economy. Of special note has been the growth of the manufacturing, finance, insurance, real estate, professional services, and government sectors.

Other data illustrate the relative importance of these growing economic sectors. Texas has the seventh largest state work force in manufacturing, and it has the second highest state volume of manufacturing shipments by dollar value (U.S. Bureau of the Census, 1991:746). In still another category—retail trade—Texas has the third largest dollar volume in the nation (U.S. Bureau of the Census, 1991:774). Finally, like all of the nation, Texas has been experiencing in the 1980s and 1990s an especially high rate of growth in employment in the various service industries.

The Declining Importance of the Oil and Gas Industries

Through a good portion of the twentieth century, crude oil and natural gas were remarkably important to the economy of Texas. Those natural resources influenced a host of specific industries, from the actual drilling and extraction operations to refining industries, transportation via pipelines and trucking, wholesale and retail

Table 1-1 | Composition of Texas employment by industry, 1940 and 1990

Industry	1940 (%)	1990 (%)
Agriculture, forestry, and fishing	30.4	1.3
Mining	2.9	2.6
Construction	5.3	4.9
Manufacturing	9.9	14.3
Transportation, communications, and utilities	6.6	5.8
Wholesale and retail trade	18.1	24.8
Finance, insurance, and real estate	2.7	6.0
Domestic and related services	14.1	1.4
Professional and other services	6.5	21.8
Government	2.4	17.0
Not reported	1.3	—

Sources: Office of the Governor (1982); Texas Employment Commission (1990).

4   *Chapter 1*

trade, and the construction industry, which produced facilities for all the preceding ones. Government was greatly affected as well. Representatives of the oil and gas industries had considerable political clout because of the importance of those industries to the state economy. And taxes on oil and gas production—along with the various sales and business taxes paid by the related industries noted above—amounted to a sizable proportion of all state and local government revenues.

Yet the sun is setting on those industries—or at least on their former importance—largely because of international forces beyond the control of the state or the industries. In 1985 the Organization of Petroleum Exporting Countries (OPEC) abandoned its production and price controls, and in response to the expanded production that followed, the market prices of crude oil and natural gas plummeted. The industries associated with oil and gas were thrown into recession, along with the entire state of Texas. Many exploration, refining, and marketing firms went out of business. The sharply lower market prices of oil and gas even made it economically infeasible to drill for or refine many known reservoirs of those resources.

To exacerbate matters, the state's reserves of oil and gas are inevitably being depleted. The number of barrels of crude oil produced in the state has been in decline for the last twenty years, and natural gas production has been declining since the early 1980s. Texas is simply running out of these natural resources, regardless of what price they might command in the market.

As a result of these trends the political clout of the oil and gas industries is also declining. State and local governments are forced to court other industries—like the high-tech ones discussed below—to replace the economic activity, jobs, and associated benefits that oil and gas once produced. Thus other kinds of firms and industries now enjoy considerable attention from government officials, and they compete on unusually favorable terms with oil and gas representatives to influence government policy.

An especially good indicator of the declining political importance of the oil and gas industries can be found in state tax revenue data (Table 1-2). The severance taxes imposed on oil and gas production are based on the market value of oil and

Table 1-2 | **State tax revenues from Texas oil and gas production, 1975–1990**

Oil and Gas Production Tax Revenues	1975	1980	1985	1990
Total (in millions)	$665	$1,215	$2,163	$1,084
As percentage of total indigenous state revenues[a]	16.0	15.1	15.8	6.2

[a]Excluding federal aid.

Sources: Comptroller of Public Accounts (1991a) and earlier volumes.

gas, so the total tax received declines when either the market price or the quantity of gas or oil produced declines. The tax data provide vivid evidence on the declining importance of the two industries. The dollar amount of state tax revenues from those sources has declined by more than half since 1985, as has the percentage of total revenues.

Local governments have lost equally significant tax revenues with the decline of these industries. The decline in the market value of oil and gas reserves reduces local property tax revenues levied on those reserves, and declining sales of refined oil and gas products reduce sales tax revenues to both state and local governments. Thus the data in Table 1-2 indicate the likely general percentage, but not the total dollar amount, of government revenues lost.

The Prominence of High-Tech Industries

Many business and government leaders in Texas have wished to lure high-technology industries to the state. Such businesses are thought to be attractive for a variety of reasons, and they are believed by many to be the wave of the future. Because of that prominence, it is important to consider the character of high-tech development in some detail.

One might ask initially just what is meant by the term **high tech**. A useful explanation is offered by Harry Hurt (1984:134–135):

> *The term usually refers to the vast array of businesses that all rely upon the same essential element: the silicon chip. Makers of semiconductors, micro-processors, and most forms of computer hardware and software obviously fall into this category. Other businesses termed high tech include producers of telecommunications devices, automatic bank tellers, fiber optics and character-recognition equipment, aerospace guidance systems, and certain types of medical instruments and industrial robots.*

But the term *high tech* also refers to various industries that are just beginning to emerge into prominence. Biotechnology, for example, holds extraordinary promise. Examples of biotechnological advances include the development of "biochips" that might be used to create computers with living organisms, the use of microscopic germs to clean up oil spills and detect toxic wastes, and the production of grains that can resist drought, insects, and disease as well as create their own fertilizer. San Antonio is already advertising itself as a major center for biotechnology research and development.

The commercial use of outer space is another emerging industry. Many of the conditions on earth that enormously complicate manufacturing processes—gravity, atmospheric pressure, vibration, convection currents—are absent in space.

6   *Chapter 1*

Consequently, traditional production techniques might derive enormous benefit from a space location. In addition, biotechnology firms anticipate that space might well provide an ideal environment for the development and testing of biochips, biosensors, and agricultural organisms. Houston hopes to capitalize on the Manned Spacecraft Center and emerge as a leader in the field of space business.

Despite these hopes, high-tech industries are still only a small part of the overall state economy, and they are heavily concentrated in select areas. Austin, Dallas, and Fort Worth in particular have experienced success in attracting such firms. Smaller but notable concentrations of high-tech companies also exist in Houston, San Antonio, and Bryan–College Station.

The Future of High Tech in Texas

One major development that bodes well for the high-tech future of the state was the decision of the Microelectronics and Computer Technology Corporation (MCC) to locate in Austin. MCC is a joint research firm controlled by eighteen microelectronics and computer companies, including Honeywell, Motorola, Control Data, Rockwell International, Lockheed, Eastman Kodak, and Martin-Marietta. The intent of MCC is to pool private resources to undertake major research programs in areas ranging from a new generation of computers to computer-assisted design and manufacturing. The corporation anticipates that it will eventually employ 400 scientists and engineers and spend $100 million per year. It is widely hoped that the selection of Texas as the site for this highly ambitious research venture will attract a large number of other high-tech firms to the state.

In part, these optimistic expectations have already been realized. In January 1988, Sematech, a consortium of fifteen of the country's major semiconductor firms, decided to locate in Austin. Semiconductors are essential components of most electronic products and systems. Sematech will undertake advanced semiconductor research and development projects and make the findings and results available to its member firms. The operation is expected to create about 11,000 new jobs in the area and will further enhance Austin's reputation as an emerging center for high-tech research and development.

The predictions for the state's long-term success in attracting high-tech industries are not all rosy, however. Several formidable problems stand in the way. First, the state must frequently compete with other states to persuade high-tech firms to locate in Texas. Referring to that competition, an advisory committee to the state Senate's Special Committee on Business, Technology, and Education recently observed, "We are playing amateur hour against people who are far more professional." Those professionals are from states like California and Massachusetts, whose high-tech economic sectors are the largest in the nation. Their state governments have been especially successful in working with high-tech firms, and their major universities have long held the lead in research related to high tech.

Of course, Texas is not competing only with other states to win high-tech business. Texas often has to compete additionally with Japan, Korea, Singapore, Mexico, and a host of other nations. Many of those nations offer high-tech firms attractive government-sponsored tax rebates and other financial inducements along with a surplus of low-wage workers. Regardless of whatever incentives Texas's government and business leaders can offer in international competition, many factors will be beyond their control. Texas public officials cannot manipulate the state's wage structure, the nation's trade laws, the value of the dollar vis-à-vis the Japanese yen, or numerous other variables that affect a firm's decision to locate abroad or in the United States.

So far, high-tech industries have depended heavily on the national defense spending of the U.S. federal government. Military contracts for electronics and communications equipment, missile and space equipment, and aircraft are typical examples of the contributions of defense to the state's economy in general and to its fledgling high-tech industry in particular. The breakup of the Soviet Union, however, and the apparent end of the Cold War are likely to signal considerable reductions in military research and development and in the actual construction of military hardware. Thus another international development beyond the control of the state—and one that should doubtless be applauded—may dampen the growth of high-tech industries in Texas.

Finally, a number of observers have argued that one of Texas's critical weaknesses in the high-tech race is its educational system. At the highest level, the state's best universities have been unable to match the research and grant-getting successes of such institutions as the Massachusetts Institute of Technology, Johns Hopkins, Stanford, and other major East and West Coast universities. At the lower levels, Texas's elementary and secondary schools are widely criticized as being seriously underfunded and considerably deficient in preparing students for the challenges of high-tech professions. The educational system is one resource that is controllable by public and private leaders in the state. To date, however, they have not invested sufficient resources for the educational system even to approach its potential. Such resources could be an investment in the future of the state.

High Tech—Famine or Fortune?

Despite the problems involved, high technology could still play an important role in the state's economic future. Yet even if it does, many current predictions may misapprehend the character of the high-tech age and its social and political implications. The more careful forecasters have pointed out, for example, that the number of jobs for true high-tech professionals may always be a rather small

8   *Chapter 1*

portion of total employment. Many of the jobs in high tech—such as in computer and electronics manufacturing plants—may not be remarkably high paying, nor are they likely to lead to interesting career opportunities.

Furthermore, the largest numbers of new jobs in the foreseeable future are now widely believed to be in the service industries instead of in glamorous high-tech professions. Bob Kuttner (1983:60) has observed:

> *As the economy shifts away from its traditional manufacturing base to high technology and service industries, the share of jobs providing a middle-class standard of living is shrinking. An industrial economy employs a large number of relatively well-paid production workers. A service economy, however, employs legions of key punchers, salesclerks, waiters, secretaries, and cashiers, and the wages for these jobs tend to be comparatively low.*

That forecast has been supported by other observers. The Texas Employment Commission (1989:6–7), for example, predicted that the fastest-growing occupations in the state through the mid-1990s would be for registered nurses, nursing aides and orderlies, cashiers, waiters and waitresses, elementary teachers, food preparers, and janitors and cleaners. The large number of Texans who will clean bedpans in the future will hardly be the beneficiaries of the high-tech age.

A high-tech economy, in other words, may produce one very small group of highly paid professionals and managers and one very large group of marginally rewarded clerks, secretaries, fast-food workers, and janitors. The former group will reap enormous benefits from the system; the latter group will suffer underemployment, low wages, and little opportunity for advancement. As Kuttner states, such a system results in the shrinking of the middle class. Former U.S. secretary of labor Ray Marshall (1984:11) has added:

> *While nobody knows for sure what kinds of jobs will be created and how much unemployment will result, my guess is that, in the absence of a comprehensive economic policy, the pessimists will be right: There will be widespread unemployment and a continued polarization of society between a few haves and many and growing numbers of have nots.*

Several negative trends can therefore be projected for an economy dominated by high-tech industries. Such class distinctions and differences in economic fortunes, should they arise, will surely have political consequences as well. Those with the most economic power and status will also have the most political power, just as the leaders of the agriculture and oil and gas industries once had such power in Texas. The polarization of social classes that some see in the future could also lead to considerable discontent and even political conflict arising from those at the bottom of the high-tech society. The people at the bottom, if their circumstances prove to be as poor as Marshall's pessimists suggest, may challenge the political power of the high-tech elite.

The Future of the Texas Economy

Many people believe that Texas, and indeed the entire United States, is on the threshold of an economic transformation. The industrial era, it is argued, is slowly coming to an end and will be replaced by what some have called the **postindustrial era**, for lack of a more precise name. The industrial era featured an economy whose central component was the manufacturing of equipment for heavy industry, hardware for national defense, and durable goods for business and family consumers. Other components of the economy—wholesale and retail trade, finance, construction, transportation, and so on—were largely dependent on and supportive of the industrial production at the core of the system.

The character of industrial production is now changing, however, as automated processes and robotics steadily reduce the number of jobs available in that sector. In addition, many manufacturing jobs in the United States have been lost to foreign nations, especially in such industries as steel, automobile, electronic, and clothing manufacturing. As we noted earlier, many such jobs in defense contracting firms may also disappear in the near future.

The question arises, then, What will replace these declining components of the economy? Most observers hope that high technology, finance, insurance, and various professional services will constitute the central elements of the postindustrial economy. The most important jobs in all of those sectors would require advanced professional education and would also be relatively high paying and attractive. Such jobs are the principal ones that Texas—and every other state—hopes to attract in large numbers in the future. At the same time, it has become apparent that low-tech and low-paying service industries will also be a major component of that future system.

A recent twenty-year forecast for the future of the Texas economy suggests that at least some of the hopes for the state will be realized (Comptroller of Public Accounts, 1991b). Some of the most notable predictions from that forecast for the year 2011 include the following:

> Oil and gas, once the cornerstone of the state's economy, will continue to diminish in importance.
>
> Some goods producers, including many manufacturers, will play a smaller role in the total economic mix than today.
>
> Job growth will be concentrated in a wide variety of service-producing industries.

Wholesale and retail trade will contribute a declining share of Texas' nonfarm jobs.

The forecast mentions high-technology industries as being especially important only in the future of selected metropolitan areas, including Dallas, Austin, and Fort Worth.

Conclusion

We have described a number of aspects of the economic past, present, and future of Texas. Of most importance to this book, however, are the effects that economic forces and events will have on the politics and government of the state. Many of those effects will be discussed in detail in later chapters. Our present goal is to lay the foundations and assumptions for those discussions to come. A brief sketch here will indicate the general conclusions that will be supported by those more detailed discussions.

One of the most important consequences of the economic changes occurring in the state is that economic growth and how to ensure it have become prominent concerns of public officials in Texas. The state and many local governments have developed vigorous policies to attract new businesses, encourage the expansion of existing ones, create diversified economies, and respond to the needs of new industries. Elected officials and candidates for office tout their particular strategies for economic development and criticize their opponents for having poor strategies.

Thus the governments of the state of Texas are now in the economic development business, whereas only a decade or so ago the state allowed the market to operate without a comparable degree of subsidy or intervention. This political change is remarkable in a state that prides itself on its conservative political ideology. Traditional conservative theory argues that government should allow the economy to operate without interference—that is, government should take the laissez-faire approach. Contrary to such theory, Texas now has active government intervention to promote growth. We will have a good deal more to say about this seeming change in political philosophy at a number of subsequent points in this book.

Adding economic development responsibilities to the agenda of government is a bit risky for elected officials. They have created a situation in which the public and the voters will judge them by the success of their economic policies. And as we noted earlier, those public officials face some formidable obstacles, some of which they cannot influence or control, in their economic development efforts.

Virtually every major public policy question has also somehow become linked to the concern for economic growth. As one example, the Texas Legislature has argued about the adequacy of the state's tax system in every recent legislative session. Some legislators have lobbied for a state income tax, some for a "reform" of existing taxes on business, and some for still other changes. Every proposed change has been critiqued with regard to its fairness as well as its potential to generate revenue. But every proposal has also been critiqued—often with conflicting conclusions—with regard to how it might aid or harm existing businesses and how it might work to attract or repel firms that might want to locate in the state.

Public education offers another excellent example of how other issues have become embroiled in this debate. As we noted earlier, the elementary, secondary, and university educational systems of the state have come under considerable criticism for their weaknesses relevant to present and future economic needs. Those criticisms are especially notable because of the widely held view that education is critical to the state's future. The Texas Chamber of Commerce, for example, has flatly observed, "The quality of a state's public education system may have more impact, especially in the long term, on the state's business climate than any other single factor."

With these arguments in mind, the state legislature has struggled throughout the 1980s and 1990s to reform elementary and secondary education and to fund education adequately at all levels. (The details of these policy debates and some additional reasons they have arisen are discussed at length in Chapter 12.) Yet even education experts disagree about which reforms are most desirable. Thus it is not surprising that legislators, business representatives, and members of the general public disagree as well. Furthermore, the high cost of many proposed reforms has intensified these debates considerably.

We could discuss additional examples of how policy issues have become embroiled in the debate over economic development. The general point, however, should be clear already. Economic development and growth in Texas have become dominant political concerns against which policy efforts in many other areas must be assessed.

Some other, quite different political consequences also arise from present-day economic circumstances. The long-term economic transformation the state is facing will have a number of social consequences of direct political relevance too. The decline of agriculture, mining, and the oil and gas industry will weaken the political power of rural areas in the state, which traditionally have dominated state government. The rise of manufacturing, services, and high-tech fields will strengthen the power of urban and suburban areas, which have been traditionally politically weak in Texas. New economic elites and new interest groups will emerge from this same process to challenge established groups centered in the old industries. There may even be a sharp decline in the size and economic power—and hence the political power—of the middle class in the state. These substantial social changes will fundamentally reshape political power in Texas.

12   *Chapter 1*

Some of these changes will also affect the political party system of the state. The long-dominant Democratic party has traditionally been tied to elites in agriculture, in oil and gas, and in the cattle industry. The rise of new elites and interest groups will mean more conflict within the Democratic party and the prospect, as well, for an increasingly stronger Republican party.

Many of these economic and social changes will undoubtedly lead to demands for more and better public services. Growing urban areas—the locales of most of the state's economic expansion—require increasing expenditures both for capital improvements and for routine services like police, fire, and public health protection. New industries often have new service needs as well, and the leaders of high-tech and other new industries are often powerful advocates of increased service levels. Indeed, some new firms may choose to locate in Texas only if they receive guarantees of certain public services or amenities. Thus economic transformation may well reshape the public policies of the state of Texas.

Inevitably, demands for more and better services will result in higher taxes. Some of the most difficult, and perhaps bitterly fought, decisions in the state in the next decades will revolve around the issues of whether to increase public services, which services should be increased, and which taxes—and hence which taxpayers—should bear the burdens of those increases. Those decisions will be made, moreover, during a time when the distribution of political power in the state will be undergoing a transformation itself.

There are, then, a variety of intimate connections between the Texas economy and the political life of the state. Although the outlines of the economy, the directions in which it is changing, and the character of some of those connections have been discussed here, the same issues constitute important themes that will appear in later chapters.

References

Comptroller of Public Accounts. 1991a. *Texas Comprehensive Annual Financial Report, 1990.* Austin.
———. 1991b. "Texas to 2011." *Fiscal Notes* 91 (October): 1–13. Austin.
Hurt, Harry, III. 1984. "Birth of a New Frontier." *Texas Monthly* (April): 130–135.
Kuttner, Bob. 1983. "The Declining Middle." *Atlantic Monthly* (July): 60–72.
Marshall, Ray. 1984. "High Tech and the Job Crunch." *Texas Observer* (April 6): 7–11.
Office of the Governor. 1982. *Texas Past and Future: A Survey.* Austin.
Texas Employment Commission. 1989. "The 20 'Hottest Jobs' in Texas." *Texas Business Today* (May): 6–7.
———. 1990. *Covered Employment and Wages by Industry and County.* Austin.
U.S. Bureau of the Census. 1991. *Statistical Abstract of the United States, 1991.* Washington, D.C.

Chapter 2

The Population of Texas

Just as a state's political life is closely tied to economic opportunities and problems, it is influenced by such population characteristics as citizens' ethnicity, education, wealth, and distribution throughout the state. This chapter will show how these features of the Texas population affect Texans' evaluation of, demands on, and participation in government. Moreover, these population characteristics reveal many of the most important policy problems facing the state of Texas.

The History of Population Growth in Texas

By 1990 Texas was estimated to have about 17 million citizens, ranking the state as the nation's third largest. The most notable division of those 17 million people is probably along ethnic lines. About 61 percent of Texans are Anglo-American, 26 percent are Mexican American or "Spanish-surnamed," and 12 percent are Afro-Americans. The remaining 1 percent of the population is a mixture of mostly Asians, Native Americans, and Middle Easterners.

Many of the social and cultural traits dealt with in this chapter could simply be elicited from the percentages just cited—as could many of the state's major political problems. The relationships among the state's ethnic groups and the particular political interests and needs of those groups have shaped much of Texas political life. Yet we cannot fully understand the influence of ethnic variations on Texas politics unless we consider at least briefly the history of population growth in the state. Of particular importance in that history are the migration and settlement patterns of the major ethnic groups noted above.

Historical population data are available for Texas's major ethnic groups since 1850, the date of the first complete census after Texas became a state (Table 2-1). Because of incomplete and changing census methods, however, some of the figures in Table 2-1 must be taken only as reasonable estimates. The figures on the Mexican American population of the state, for example, have always

15

16   *Chapter 2*

Table 2-1 | **Population growth in Texas, 1850–1990**

Year	Total Population	White	Black	Spanish-Surnamed
1850	213,000	154,000	59,000	11,000
1880	1,592,000	1,197,000	393,000	—
1900	3,049,000	2,427,000	621,000	165,000
1920	4,663,000	3,918,000	742,000	510,000
1940	6,415,000	5,488,000	924,000	—
1960	9,580,000	8,375,000	1,187,000	1,418,000
1980	14,228,000	11,198,000	1,710,000	2,986,000
1990	16,987,000	14,702,000	1,976,000	4,340,000

Note: All the numbers are rounded to thousands. Spanish-surnamed individuals have been included among those identified as white in Census Bureau tabulations, as well as being detailed in the Spanish-surnamed column.

Sources: Principally U.S. Census Bureau data supplemented—for the Spanish-surnamed estimates—by Barrera (1979:75).

been rough approximations—in part because the U.S. Census Bureau has used several different definitions for counting the Hispanic, or Spanish-surnamed, population and in part because of the difficulty of accurately counting illegal Mexican aliens. Nonetheless, the data in Table 2-1 reflect fair estimates of population trends, with one qualification: The 1980 and 1990 figures on Spanish-surnamed residents of the state probably underestimate the actual populations, perhaps by as much as a third.

A relatively continuous trend of growth is evident not only in the total population but also in each of the three main ethnic subgroups. Yet some qualifications to that overall trend are noteworthy. First, the relative positions of the state's two largest ethnic minorities have been reversed in the period covered in Table 2-1. In 1850 blacks accounted for almost 30 percent of the total population, whereas the Spanish-surnamed were only 5 percent of the total. By 1990 blacks were only 12 percent of the population, and the Mexican American minority constituted 26 percent of the population in official U.S. census data. If an accurate estimate of the number of illegal Mexican aliens were available, the percentage of Texas residents who are Spanish-surnamed would be even higher. A second qualification concerns the impression of continuous growth. Behind these figures are, in fact, some notable patterns of a much less continuous character. To understand those patterns, we must look into the history of migration of the state's major ethnic and national groups.

Anglo-American Migration

Anglo-American migrants have always constituted the largest source of the state's eventual citizens. Even as early as 1850 almost 60 percent of the state's residents were of Anglo-American descent, and 54 percent of the population had migrated from the southern United States (Jordan, 1969). Thus American migrants from a particular region and culture formed the backbone of early Texas society. Of those southern American migrants alone, about half were from the Lower South states of Alabama, Georgia, Louisiana, and Mississippi, where the economy relied heavily on the plantation system served by slave labor. The remaining half of the southern Americans were from the Upper South and border states of Arkansas, Kentucky, Missouri, and Tennessee, where small farms had been more the rule (Jordan, 1967).

The vast bulk of the Anglo-American migrants who arrived before the Civil War settled in the eastern half of Texas in patterns somewhat regionalized in terms of their states of origin. In other words, Upper South and Lower South migrants generally settled in different areas of Texas, as indicated in Figure 2-1. The immigrants also replicated as much as possible the agricultural systems of their home states. Thus migrants from the Lower South brought substantial numbers of black slaves and established a slave-labor system based primarily on cotton production. Upper South migrants relied predominantly on the production of wheat and small grains with relatively modest use of slave labor (Jordan, 1967).

Migration to Texas by all groups was interrupted by the Civil War and Reconstruction. But in the 1870s, migration on a large scale began again. The major

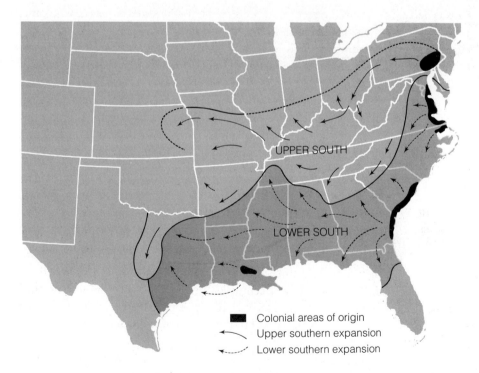

Figure 2-1 | Anglo-American migration to Texas, 1860
Source: Jordan (1967:668)

source of that migration was the southern United States. In that period, therefore, the cultural patterns of earlier migrants were largely reinforced by those of the newly arrived residents. And the numbers of new Texans were quite large. As D. W. Meinig (1969:64) notes of the last third of the nineteenth century, "In any one of those years well over half the population of Texas had been born outside the state."

Migrants from the southern United States have continued to be important through most of the twentieth century, as well. Yet two shifts in Anglo migration in this century are notable. First, around 1900 the Old South's contribution of new migrants to Texas began to decline. In the place of that group, the states bordering Texas furnished the largest number of migrants until around 1950. Second, and more important for the different cultural values they carried, a notable though smaller stream of migrants from the Northeast and the Midwest began to flow to Texas after 1900. Those two regions provided a steady number of new Texans through the first six decades of this century. Then, because of the dramatically shifting economic fortunes of certain regions of the United States in the 1970s, the number of such migrants swelled.

These "Yankees," as "native" Texans like to label them, have also been termed Sunbelt migrants. The 1970s and early 1980s witnessed a substantial in-migration of such people, joined by a large number of Californians and a modest continued flow of southerners. The number of such migrants declined after about 1982, when Texas's economy went into recession. Yet research on the kinds of people who came to Texas mostly in that period indicates they may have an influence on the state greater than their numbers might suggest. The migrants of that period—and even those coming as recently as 1987—were predominantly young, relatively well-educated, white-collar workers (Schwaller, 1983; Yuen, 1987). Additionally, many of these people brought social and political values to Texas that were quite different from the values of the state's traditional southern and southwestern culture. Thus, because of both their economic and professional positions and their cultural values, these new migrants may be a significant force for change in the social and political life of the state.

The Migration of Blacks

The vast majority of blacks in Texas in 1850 had been brought to the state as the slaves of Anglo-American migrants from the Lower South. Thus most black Texans at the time came from the same cultural and social background as did those Anglo-Americans. But the blacks occupied a different position in that original setting, just as they did in Texas. Another result of this dual migration was that black Texans in 1850 were regionalized in their areas of residence along with their Anglo masters.

The importation of slaves continued up until the Civil War, and the black population continued to increase faster than the total population until about 1870.

After 1870, however, the numbers of black Texans continued to grow, but at a much slower rate than the numbers of the other major ethnic groups. Like most of the Old South, Texas never attracted particularly large numbers of new black residents after Reconstruction. The state actually witnessed substantial out-migration of blacks in the decades 1900–1910, 1940–1950, and 1950–1960.

The Migration of Mexicans

Although Texas was part of Mexico until 1836, the area had not been heavily settled by Mexican nationals in the nineteenth century. Cary McWilliams (1949:52) estimates that as late as 1848 only about 5,000 Mexicans lived in what is now Texas. In the 1850 census the Spanish-surnamed population of the state amounted to only 11,212, or just over 5 percent of the total population. Of that group, about 40 percent had been born in Mexico.

The Mexican American population of Texas grew rapidly, however, during the latter half of the 1800s. Estimates of the number of Mexican-origin Texans in any year are subject to some error, but their numbers had grown substantially by the turn of the century (Table 2-1). The bulk of them worked as cowboys and herders on the cattle and sheep ranches of South Texas or as agricultural workers, particularly in cotton. Most of the original Mexican landowners had, by one means or another, been driven from their land by Anglos after the Texas Revolution. Although modest middle-class Mexican American contingents could be found in some of the towns of Central and South Texas, they suffered the same discrimination as all the others of their background. They typically worked only within Mexican American communities or were hired by Anglo business establishments to serve their Mexican American customers.

Around the turn of the century there began the first of three cycles of Mexican immigration to Texas that are not revealed by the aggregate figures in Table 2-1 (Fogel, 1979:9–18). The cycles were closely related to the shifting fortunes of the Texas economy; hence they constitute historical examples of political economy forces. From around 1900 to the beginning of the Great Depression in 1929, the demand grew for cheap Mexican labor to work in the cattle, cotton, railroad, and fruit and vegetable industries—all of which were expanding across Texas.

Moreover, throughout much of that period, Mexico experienced considerable social and political strife—leading up to and following the revolution of 1910 in that country. To make the prospects for immigration even more attractive, the U.S. government made virtually no effort to control Mexican immigration—legal or illegal—during that time. Thus both immigration and the Spanish-surnamed population of Texas swelled during those years.

The Great Depression, however, brought an entirely different set of circumstances that reversed the flow of migrants from Mexico. The demand for foreign laborers fell sharply. Domestic workers replaced foreign nationals in most of the

20   *Chapter 2*

available jobs. And a wave of antiforeign sentiment and vigorous government efforts to repatriate Mexican nationals ensued (Kiser and Silverman, 1979). As a result, the number of Mexican nationals in Texas fell by around 30 to 40 percent in the 1930s. Even some American citizens of Mexican descent (many of them children of Mexican nationals born in the United States and thus dual nationals) were repatriated to Mexico. Many others, both American and Mexican citizens, left voluntarily for Mexico because of the antiforeign sentiment of the time. This period of a significant return flow of people back to Mexico thus completed the first cycle of twentieth-century Mexican migration in Texas.

A second cycle of massive immigration from Mexico—also beginning with large numbers of immigrants and ending with a sharp outflow reinforced by U.S. government action—occurred in 1945–1965. Once again the major stimulus for the immigration came from the labor demands of agricultural and other industries in Texas and the relative attractiveness of employment in the United States as opposed to Mexico. A good portion of this second wave of immigration came under the auspices of the contract labor (or popularly termed bracero) programs agreed to between the United States and Mexican governments. But much of that migration was illegal, as well.

In the mid-1950s the U.S. government began an immense effort to stem the flow of illegal immigration. Most observers agree that, through aggressive Border Patrol and Immigration Service activities, the policy was a success for a time. The flow of illegals apparently fell off sharply between 1956 and 1965 and was, in part, replaced by greater numbers of contract laborers allowed into the United States each year. Yet the contract program, which had always been controversial, was terminated in 1965, a victim of the reformist mood of the U.S. Congress at the time (Hawley, 1979).

In the middle and late 1960s what looks like the third cycle of Mexican immigration to Texas began. This period of heavy illegal immigration has continued to the present. The relative attractiveness of even low-paying jobs in America, especially in light of the difficulties the Mexican economy has suffered, is once again the major stimulus for the flow. The tide of immigration has run high despite relatively vigorous U.S. government efforts to slow it.

In 1986 the U.S. government passed the Immigration Reform and Control Act to solve the problem of illegal immigration. Under the act, illegals who had lived continuously in the United States since January 1, 1982, were offered temporary legal residency and the chance to gain permanent residency and U.S. citizenship. Further, employers who hired illegal aliens could face stiff fines. Experts are divided on how successful this effort will be. In 1987 the number of new illegal migrants to Texas dropped dramatically. Arrests of illegals by the U.S. Border Patrol dropped 45 percent from the prior year, and the decline was attributed to knowledge by Mexican nationals that jobs for undocumented workers are far more difficult to find because of the new law. The number of illegal aliens arrested began to rise again in 1990, however, and was projected by 1992 to equal or surpass the 1986 record number. Most observers attribute this trend to the greater economic opportunities in the United States for many Mexican nationals.

One major difference between the present cycle and the former ones—and a change that can be explained in terms of the shifting Texas economy—is the much greater prevalence of illegal immigrants in unskilled, semiskilled, and service jobs in urban areas (Barrera, 1979:125–126). Several of Texas's major cities, particularly San Antonio, Houston, and Dallas, today harbor many such illegal aliens. Recent estimates place the number of illegal Mexican aliens in the entire state at around 1 million.

Before leaving the subject of Mexican immigration, a few words are necessary about the pattern of the illegal portion of that flow. Through most of the twentieth century the typical Mexican illegal immigrant has been a male, usually between the ages of 17 and 30, who comes to the United States for seasonal employment and then returns home to Mexico within a year (King and Rizo-Patron, 1978; Fogel, 1979:75–81). Most of these men save the bulk of their earnings to send home to the families they help support in Mexico. Although these men might make their round-trip many times, their immigration pattern is clearly distinct from the so-called European pattern of people seeking permanent residence in the United States. Obviously, as well, although the pattern of Mexican immigration creates social strains and public problems, those problems are somewhat different from the problems that would arise if all of the immigrants were seeking permanent residence in the United States. Thus, as long as the traditional pattern holds, the vast majority of the million or so illegal Mexican aliens in Texas do not intend to stay permanently but are seeking seasonal or short-term employment. Furthermore, if the dynamics of past cycles of immigration hold true, the illegal aliens are subject to the shifting labor market demands of the American and Mexican economies.

There are no firm estimates of how many illegals stay in the United States permanently, but certainly over the period of the entire twentieth century the cumulative numbers, even if small at any single time, have been crucial in the growth of the Mexican American population of Texas. Thus 80 percent or so of all the Spanish-surnamed residents of Texas are citizens of the United States, but many of their parents and grandparents emigrated from Mexico in this century.

Increasing evidence, however, suggests that many of the current illegal immigrants hope to stay permanently in this country and that the continuing economic and political problems of their home country will drive many more of them to the United States with the same intent. Mexico's economic troubles also appear to be changing the traditional pattern of migration—today whole families are seeking to enter the United States illegally and to remain permanently. In fact, political conflict in several Central American nations has led to the same result. Yet the current cycle of Mexican and Central American immigration, like the cycles

22 *Chapter 2*

of the past, will depend above all on the job possibilities and other incentives arising from the American economy and on the success of U.S. immigration policies.

European Migration

By 1850 Texas already had a notable number of European-born migrants, largely from Germany and the Germanic regions of Austria and Switzerland. In fact, there were more German-origin than Spanish-surnamed residents in Texas at the time (Jordan, 1969). Constituting just over 5 percent of the total population, the Germans settled in a belt from Galveston westward to the general San Antonio area. The largest German settlements were at New Braunfels and Fredericksburg. In fact, Texas gained more European immigrants during the period around 1850 than any other southern American state. As late as 1900 the number of central European immigrants living in Texas rivaled that of Texans born in Mexico.

Especially the Germans, but also some of the other European immigrant groups, lived in relatively exclusive communities, maintaining their native culture and language to a considerable degree. Beginning in the 1920s the numbers of new arrivals fell off substantially, and, without reinforcement, the cultural separatism of the European groups began to decline (Meinig, 1969:85). A few aspects of the old exclusivity and some of the regional distinctiveness of these groups remain, but these cultural traits are far weaker today than they were even a generation ago.

A Pattern of Cultural Diversity

This review of the settlement of Texas and subsequent population trends indicates why the state's core cultural values are derived from those of the southern United States. The South provided the bulk of Texas's early settlers and has continued to provide a notable number of new migrants to the present day. At the same time, Texas's society is considerably more cosmopolitan than that of perhaps any other southern state. The state's southern immigrants represented two distinct cultural subgroups, and both European and Mexican influences were also important even before Texas became a state. Indeed, Texas has been culturally diverse since the earliest years of Anglo settlement. As an inscription on the base of the San Jacinto Monument reminds us about the soldiers who fought at the battle of San Jacinto (1836):

> *Citizens of Texas and immigrant soldiers in the Army of Texas at San Jacinto were natives of Alabama, Arkansas, Connecticut, Georgia, Illinois, Indiana, Kentucky, Louisiana, Maine, Maryland, Massachusetts, Michigan, Mississippi, Missouri, New Hampshire, New York, North Carolina, Ohio, Pennsylvania, Rhode Island, South Carolina, Tennessee, Texas, Vermont, Virginia, Austria, Canada, England, France, Germany, Ireland, Italy, Mexico, Poland, Portugal, and Scotland.*

In recent years the state's cultural variety has been enriched by large numbers of Mexican and Central American immigrants, Sunbelt migrants from other regions of the United States, and Asians and Middle Easterners from several nations.

For most of the state's history, however, little interchange took place among cultural groups. The rigid regionalization of settlement patterns precluded much contact. Data from the 1880 census indicate the extent to which those patterns separated the different cultures of the state. (See Figure 2-2; in each county, the group indicated is the largest one in the population, excluding people born in Texas.) The only regions where different ethnic groups lived in any notable proximity in the 1800s were where blacks and Lower South Anglos shared portions of East and Southeast Texas. But strong ethnic prejudice against blacks militated against any social or cultural exchange between the two groups.

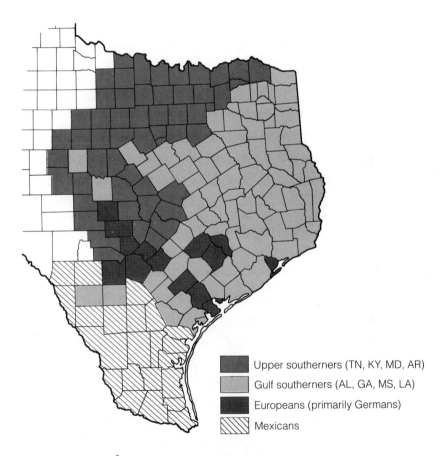

Figure 2-2 | **Origins of the immigrant population of Texas, 1880**
Source: Jordan (1967:671)

The Future of Population Growth in Texas

As we observed above, the population of Texas grew rapidly in the 1960s and 1970s, and then the rate of increase declined in the 1980s. Nonetheless, a number of forecasts anticipate a growth rate in the state considerably higher than the national average and a total population of at least 20 million by the year 2000, or a 30 percent increase since 1980.

Such rapid growth will pose major problems for both state and local political leaders. Increasing demands for public services; the accelerated wear and tear on public facilities like roads, schools, and parks; the impact on the quality of life in the state—these will be major issues for public action in the years ahead. The rapid growth of past decades, despite the recent slowdown, has already brought a number of these issues to the public agenda. Compared with states that are losing population, Texas is in an enviable position. But the challenges inherent in that position may be difficult.

Population experts also observe that a significant shift in the ethnic composition of the state is now under way. The Anglo population has long been the overwhelming majority, even as long ago as 1850 (Table 2-1). Yet the state's minority groups—especially Hispanics—are now growing so rapidly, because of the large number of new immigrants and a high birth rate, that together they will displace the Anglo majority early in the next century. One projection is that by the year 2015 Mexican Americans will constitute 39 percent of the state's population, blacks 11 percent, Asians and other minorities 6 percent, and Anglos only 44 percent.

If these predictions are realized, they will have far-reaching consequences for Texas politics. For example, the ethnic composition of the voting public will be reshaped. The demands this new electorate will press on government may be radically different, too, from those of today. The new majority in 2015 may still harbor resentment for being mistreated as a minority in times past. As we will show later in this chapter, the low income, educational, and occupational status of blacks and Mexican Americans today can be expected to continue well into the future. Thus the political interests of the new majority in 2015 will be shaped by those social and economic circumstances.

Major Demographic Characteristics

Beyond the variations in population size and ethnicity described above, several other characteristics of Texas's population influence the state's political affairs in one way or another. The most important of these features concern patterns of settlement and residence of the population across the state, levels of education and income, and the occupational makeup of the state's work force. In the remainder of this chapter we will examine these characteristics in some detail, relying particularly on information from the 1980 census. That census makes it possible to separate the Anglo, black, and Spanish-surnamed citizens of the state and to describe the distinctive social and economic positions of these ethnic groups. As we will see, the social and economic position of the state's minority ethnic groups is strikingly divergent from that of the Anglo majority.

Urbanization

One of the most dramatic changes in the state in the twentieth century has been the transformation of a heavily rural and small-town population to one that is predominantly urban. In the nineteenth century the overwhelming majority of Texans lived in rural areas. In the 1850 census, for example, only 4 percent of the state's population was classified as urban, and an "urban" area was any place with a population larger than 1,000. Beginning early in this century, however, the "urban" population of the state began to grow quite rapidly. During the 1940s the number of urbanites first exceeded the number of people living in rural areas. By the 1980 census about 80 percent of the state's residents were classified by the Census Bureau as urban dwellers. Another indication of this radical shift in the residential status of the population is that in 1980 only 2 percent of Texans lived on farms. Not only do most contemporary Texans live in urban instead of rural areas, but the very concept of what constitutes an urban place has undergone considerable transformation.

More than half the state's population in 1980, for example, lived in the Census Bureau–designated Standard Metropolitan Statistical Areas (SMSAs) of Houston, Dallas–Fort Worth, San Antonio, and Austin—all metropolitan areas with populations greater than 500,000. Thus Texas has experienced more than rapid urbanization. It has experienced the growth of huge urban areas with all the attendant social and political problems. No longer can Texans dismiss big-city problems as those of the East Coast and West Coast. Today the majority of Texans face the same problems themselves. In this sense "urban" life means something far different today from what it meant even a generation ago. And these big-city problems will probably become even more important in the years ahead.

Along with the appearance of large cities has come another development: the growth of large suburban communities as a portion of those cities. There is no precise definition of what constitutes a suburb; nor is there an ideal way to estimate the number of people who live in such places. Population researchers generally equate the suburban population with the number of people who live in SMSAs but are outside the central city portion thereof (Haar, 1974:27; Muller, 1981:5).

For a compelling demonstration of the importance of suburbia in Texas, we can examine data on the growth of suburbs for some of Texas's largest SMSAs

26   Chapter 2

between 1970 and 1990 (Table 2-2). In all of these SMSAs the suburbs grew at a higher rate than did the central city.

This pattern of rapid suburban growth characterizes virtually all the metropolitan areas of the state. It also means, of course, that the physical size of the suburban areas has grown, encompassing land that was once essentially rural and distant from the central city. The territorial spread of suburbia can be so vast that it even makes comparisons with prior population figures difficult. Houston is excluded from Table 2-2, for example, because its suburban area today extends across several counties and includes a number of small towns and the periphery of a number of other cities such as Galveston whose population would have been counted entirely separately in earlier census reports. Thus Houston has experienced such rapid suburban growth that it is difficult to portray the magnitude of that growth in simple population figures.

Suburban areas create distinctive political demands and public service needs. Although a significant portion of Texas residents already live in suburbs, the number of suburbanites will surely climb substantially over the next few decades. And in the years ahead their distinctive political interests and demands are certain to become more prominent in the state's politics.

Another development coincident with urbanization has been the dispersion of population across the state, at least in comparison with the situation in the 1800s. The western half of Texas remains much less densely settled, just as it was in the last century, but a significant movement of people to that region has occurred in recent decades (Figure 2-3). Each of the SMSAs of El Paso, Amarillo, Lubbock, Midland, Odessa, Abilene, San Angelo, and Laredo is home to more than 100,000 people today. Some of these metro areas have been among the fastest-growing cities in the state in recent years. The growth of these cities is breaking down the distinctiveness of West and Central Texas, and it is bringing to those regions the same problems that large urban governments face elsewhere in the state.

Table 2-2 | Growth of suburbs in major Texas cities, 1970–1990

| City and Area | Increase in Population (%) | |
	Central City	Suburbs
Austin	184	669
Corpus Christi	125	437
Dallas–Fort Worth	118	341
El Paso	160	1,600
San Antonio	143	556

Sources: U.S. Census Bureau data from various years.

The Population of Texas 27

Another component of the urbanization trend concerns the patterns of residence of the state's two largest ethnic minorities. In the 1800s both blacks and Mexican Americans lived in rigidly defined and mostly rural areas. Blacks were heavily concentrated in rural East Texas, the area to which they were originally brought as slaves. Similarly, Mexican Americans were mostly concentrated along the Texas–Mexico border, an obvious result of their own migration pattern and the availability of the agricultural and cattle ranching jobs they mostly assumed.

Those regional patterns of ethnic location are still important today. The vast majority of black Texans still live in the eastern half of the state, and it is not uncommon for blacks to make up 20 to 35 percent of the population of many rural East Texas counties. Likewise, in rural counties along the Mexican border, Spanish-surnamed Texans typically constitute 70 to 90 percent of the population. Yet focusing only on those places where ethnics compose high percentages of the residents would obscure a second aspect of current ethnic distribution in the state. For these two groups are also heavily urbanized today, even more so than are the state's Anglo residents.

In 1980 in Texas some 86 percent of Mexican Americans, 88 percent of blacks, and only 76 percent of Anglos lived in urban places. The largest numbers of Mexican Americans inhabit, in order, San Antonio, Houston, El Paso, and Dallas, and the Mexican American residents of those metropolitan areas constitute almost half the state's total. Similarly, more than half of all black Texans live in the Houston and Dallas–Fort Worth metro areas alone, and other large groups of blacks reside in the Golden Triangle of Beaumont–Port Arthur–Orange and in San Antonio.

Income and Poverty Levels

The levels of personal income and wealth in the state are also of obvious importance to political life. Taken all together, Texas levels compare modestly well with the national averages. In 1989, the most recent year for which data are available at this time, per capita personal income in the state was estimated to be $15,702, whereas the national average per capita income was $17,596. The statewide average is misleading, however, because of the great variations, especially on the basis of ethnicity, that it obscures. More-detailed figures, which are collected only in the decennial U.S. census, are necessary to illustrate those variations.

In each census year, people are asked about their individual and family incomes in the prior year. Data on family incomes from the 1980 census, the most recent information on this matter now available, are presented in Table 2-3 for each of Texas's major ethnic groups. (Below, we will discuss the information that is available on subsequent trends in family income, education, and occupation by ethnic group.) The percentages of each group whose family incomes fell below the federal government's poverty threshold are also given in Table 2-3. The poverty

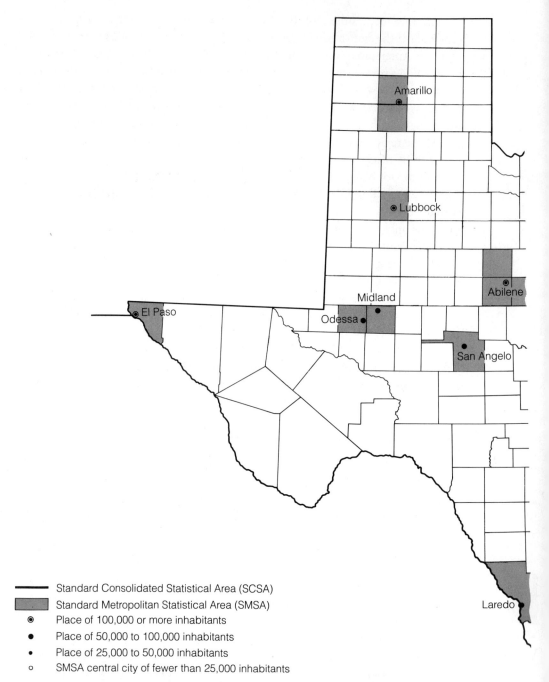

Figure 2-3 | **Standard Consolidated Statistical Area (SCSA) and Standard Metropolitan Statistical Areas (SMSAs) in Texas, 1981**
Source: U.S. Bureau of the Census, 1981

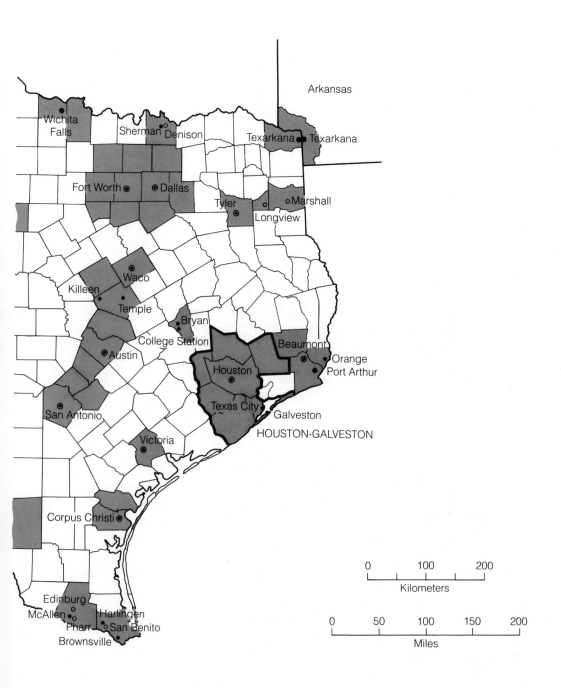

30   *Chapter 2*

Table 2-3 | Income and poverty among Texas's major ethnic groups, 1979

Data	Anglo	Black	Spanish-Surnamed	State Total
Family Income				
0–$4,999	5%	18%	15%	8%
$5,000–$9,999	11%	21%	21%	14%
$10,000–$14,999	13%	17%	20%	15%
$15,000–$24,999	29%	25%	27%	28%
$25,000–$49,999	35%	18%	15%	29%
$50,000 and above	8%	1%	2%	6%
Median Family Income	$22,162	$13,064	$13,293	$19,618
Families with Incomes Below Poverty Line	6%	24%	25%	11%

Source: U.S. Bureau of the Census, 1983.

threshold is based on the federal government's estimate of how much annual income families of different sizes must earn to be living "above the poverty line." Many observers argue, we should add, that the poverty threshold is too low and underestimates the numbers of people actually living in poverty.

Relatively poor and wealthy Texans exist in all three groups, but the two minority groups are heavily skewed toward the poor end of the income continuum. For example, almost 40 percent of black and Spanish-surnamed families earned less than $10,000 in 1979, but only 15 percent of Anglo families earned that little. Another comparison is of median family incomes. In 1980 the minority groups' median incomes were only about 60 percent of the median income for Anglo families. In addition, the ratio of each minority group's income to the Anglo group's actually declined slightly since the previous census in 1970.

The estimates of families living in poverty sharpen the contrast between the Anglo and the minority groups. Both ethnic minority groups have about four times as large a proportion in poverty as do their Anglo counterparts. If one believes, as many do, that the poverty threshold does not really measure the number of people who are truly poor, then many more Texans would have to be included in that group. In fact, the federal government itself now implicitly concedes this criticism of its poverty threshold index and reports, as a second poverty estimate, the percentages of the population living below 125 percent of the standard poverty threshold. Using the latter figures, 33 percent of Spanish-surnamed families, 32 percent of black families, and 9 percent of Anglo families in Texas were living in poverty in 1980.

Education Levels

It is generally expected that in any large grouping of people there will be a substantial correlation between the income level and the education level of its members. Such is the case in Texas, particularly if we examine the levels of formal education within the three principal ethnic groups (Table 2-4).

In Table 2-4 the two minority groups are skewed toward the low-education end of the continuum. The Anglo population, on the other hand, is skewed toward high education. Notable in the table are the large percentages of blacks and especially Mexican Americans with an elementary education or less and the relatively small percentages of the same groups with college educations. Certainly the lower education levels of the two minority groups are, in part, the product of the limited educational opportunities available to older members of those groups when they were of school age. Yet even in the current school-age population, particularly at the late high school and college levels, there is a significant gap between school enrollments of Anglos and those of the two minority groups. A recent study, for example, found that the dropout rates for Texas high school students over 1982–1986 were 27 percent for Anglos, 34 percent for blacks, and 45 percent for Hispanics.

Occupational Categories

As we discussed in Chapter 1, the Texas economy has been moving in recent decades toward a diversified manufacturing, service, and high-tech character, and the occupational structure of the state has been shifting in the same direction. Because of their differing education levels and general social positions, however, the state's ethnic groups do not all have the same opportunity to adapt with changes in the economy. Traditionally, members of the two largest minority groups were relegated to the lesser occupations in the economy, and that situation is still true for many ethnics today. Employment figures for the state and the three major ethnic groups illustrate the current occupational structure of the state (Table 2-5).

Table 2-4 | **Formal schooling for the Texas population 25 years old and older, 1980**

Schooling	Anglo (%)	Black (%)	Spanish-Surnamed (%)	State Total (%)
Elementary or less	13	25	51	21
Some high school	17	22	13	17
Four years of high school	31	29	20	29
Some college	19	15	10	17
Four years or more of college	20	9	6	16

Source: U.S. Bureau of the Census, 1983.

Table 2-5 | **Occupational categories among Texas's major ethnic groups, 1980**

Occupation	Anglo (%)	Black (%)	Spanish-Surnamed (%)	State Total (%)
Managerial and professional	26	12	11	22
Technical, sales, and administrative support	34	24	25	31
Service	8	25	16	12
Farming, forestry, and fishing	3	2	4	3
Precision production and craft	15	11	17	15
Operators, fabricators, and laborers	13	27	27	17

Source: U.S. Bureau of the Census, 1983.

The categories of occupations in Table 2-5 are broad, but they still reveal some strong contrasts among the three main ethnic groups. Of particular note are the differences between the Anglo and the minority groups at the highest occupational levels (professional, managerial, and technical employment) and at the lowest level for those whose jobs depend largely on strong backs and hands (operators, fabricators, and laborers). Anglo Texans are concentrated as disproportionately in the higher jobs as ethnic-minority Texans are in the lower ones. These occupational differences are not surprising in light of the educational and income differences that separate these groups.

Recent Trends in Income, Education, and Occupation

The preceding information from the 1980 census illustrates sharp contrasts in the demographic circumstances of the state's three major ethnic groups. One might wonder, of course, how the three groups have fared subsequently. Systematic information on that question, as would come from the 1990 census when its results are ultimately released, is not now available. Yet other, more fragmentary information suggests that the differences among these three groups have probably not improved and may have worsened since 1980.

During the 1980s and early 1990s, for example, the percentage of Americans living in poverty increased nationwide. The rate of increase was especially high, however, for ethnic minorities and Hispanics in particular. In Texas the statewide poverty rate rose from 11 percent of all families in 1980 to 14 percent in 1990. Although the rates for separate ethnic groups in the state are not yet available, we suspect that they followed the national trend—that is, higher increases in poverty occurred among minorities.

The information presented above on secondary school dropout rates in Texas is also relevant to this discussion. Much higher percentages of blacks and Hispanics, as opposed to whites, leave school before earning a high school diploma. Because of that fact, and for other reasons such as the relative poverty of their families, many fewer minorities go on to college, as well. Thus much higher percentages of minorities will be unemployed or will be employed in low-wage occupations. And that is just as likely to be true for young blacks and Hispanics as it is for their parents—again because of their high dropout rates. In sum, the available information indicates that the same general demographic differences that separated whites, blacks, and Hispanics in the early 1980s still exist today.

| Conclusion |

This chapter has shown how Texas's original population and settlement patterns—based on rural and small-town settlements regionalized by ethnicity—have been substantially reshaped in recent decades. What has emerged in their place is a rapidly growing, highly urbanized, increasingly big-city and suburbanized population with considerable representation of all three of the state's ethnic groups in the major urban centers. This shift means that the state's political problems are increasingly those of growing big cities. The remainder of this book will be concerned, therefore, with the efforts of Texas state and local governments in grappling with those problems.

The breakdown of the old cultural regions, the emerging ethnic diversity of the state's urban areas, and the rapidly increasing minority population also mean that Texas will be forced more and more to confront the differing interests and political demands of its various ethnic groups. Simple proximity, along with the heightened political activity of blacks and Mexican Americans of recent years, will force such confrontations. One could also argue that this new situation offers an opportunity for cultural interchange and the sharing of cultural values in ways that might benefit the entire state—socially, economically, and politically. Yet this chapter has also described how the state's major ethnic minority groups occupy positions in Texas society far different from those of the Anglo majority. In the minority groups, education levels are lower and occupational opportunities are thus considerably more limited. As a result, the income and wealth of blacks and Mexican Americans in Texas are also lower, and the levels of poverty are much higher than among Anglos. These circumstances are considerable obstacles the state will have to overcome if it is to profit from the cultural diversity within its boundaries.

References

Barrera, Mario. 1979. *Race and Class in the Southwest*. South Bend, Ind.: University of Notre Dame Press.

Benjamin, Gilbert G. 1908. "Germans in Texas." *German American Annals* 10 (January–February): 325–340.

————. 1909. "Germans in Texas, Continued." *German American Annals* 11 (January–February): 103–113.

Fogel, Walter. 1979. *Mexican Illegal Workers in the United States*. Los Angeles: Institute of Industrial Relations, University of California.

Haar, Charles M. 1974. *The President's Task Force on Suburban Problems*. Cambridge, Mass.: Ballinger.

Hawley, Ellis W. 1979. "The Politics of the Mexican Labor Issue, 1950–1965." In George C. Kiser and Martha Woody Kiser (eds.), *Mexican Workers in the United States*. Albuquerque: University of New Mexico Press.

Jordan, Terry G. 1967. "The Imprint of the Upper and Lower South on Mid-Nineteenth-Century Texas." *Annals of the Association of American Geographers* 57 (December): 667–690.

————. 1969. "Population Origins in Texas, 1850." *Geographical Review* 59 (January): 83–103.

King, Allan G., and Rizo-Patron, Jorge. 1978. "Counting Illegal Mexican Aliens: Myths and Misperceptions." *Texas Business Review* 52 (June): 101–105.

Kiser, George C., and Silverman, David. 1979. "Mexican Repatriation During the Great Depression." In George C. Kiser and Martha Woody Kiser (eds.), *Mexican Workers in the United States*. Albuquerque: University of New Mexico Press.

McWilliams, Cary. 1949. *North from Mexico: The Spanish-Speaking People of the United States*. Philadelphia: J. B. Lippincott.

Meinig, D. W. 1969. *Imperial Texas: An Interpretive Essay in Cultural Geography*. Austin: University of Texas Press.

Muller, Peter O. 1981. *Contemporary Suburban America*. Englewood Cliffs, N.J.: Prentice-Hall.

Schwaller, Bob. 1983. "Here's Johnny-Come-Lately." *Texas Business* 7 (March): 24–29.

U.S. Bureau of the Census. 1981. *1980 Census of Population, Supplementary Report: Standard Metropolitan Statistical Areas and Standard Consolidated Statistical Areas*. 1981. Washington, D.C.

————. 1983. *1980 Census of Population, General Social and Economic Characteristics: Texas*. Washington, D.C.

Yuen, Mike. 1987. "New Arrivals in Texas a Rarity." *Houston Post* (December 6): 1B.

Chapter 3

The Political Cultures of Texas

This chapter will examine in some detail the attitudes of Texans toward their state and local government and the sources of their views. These attitudes have considerable relevance for several aspects of political life in the state—such as the goals Texans want their state to pursue through its policies and the extent to which individual citizens wish to participate in government. Because of the many ties between these political attitudes and other aspects of state government, in later chapters we will occasionally refer back to the material presented here. At the same time, some of the most important sources of these political attitudes are the cultural and social roots of the groups whose migrations to Texas were chronicled in the last chapter.

Popular literature and journalism have for many years indulged in a caricature of the culture of the typical Texan. Anyone who has lived for even a short period in the state has surely been exposed to such literature. In fact, the portrait of the typical Texan that arises in such writings is probably well known across the United States. D. W. Meinig (1969:89) has aptly summarized this portrait:

> *The Texan emerges from these investigations as one who is strongly individualistic and egalitarian, optimistic and utilitarian, volatile and chauvinistic, ethnocentric and provincial, as one still very much under the influence of older rural and moral traditions. Such a person regards government as no more than a necessary evil, distrusts even informal social action as a threat to his independence, and accepts violence as an appropriate solution to certain kinds of personal and group problems. Material wealth is much admired for its own sake but industriousness has no particular value. . . . There is an easy acceptance of equality among one's own kind but a rigid sense of superiority over other local peoples, and a deep suspicion of outsiders as threats to the social order. The narrow moral strictures of Protestant fundamentalism are accepted as an ideal moral code but certain covert violations are routinely tolerated (such as the use of hard liquor).*

38 *Chapter 3*

No doubt some elements of this portrait are accurate for some Texans. But like all stereotypes, this superficial portrait glosses over some important aspects of Texans' social and political attitudes. Above all, this stereotype obscures the existence of several distinct attitudes toward government that are held by different groups of Texans. To offer a more sophisticated rendering of political attitudes in the state and to take account of these different outlooks, we must turn to scholarship in political science on the subject of political culture.

The Concept of Political Culture

Political culture refers generally to people's attitudes toward and evaluations of their government. But political culture has several specific components, as well.[1] Citizens' attitudes under this broad heading, for example, can be divided into concerns about three main issues:

1. The appropriate role of government in society—in other words, what should and should not be the responsibilities of government?

2. The appropriate role for the individual citizen in relation to government—in other words, what constitutes a citizen's duty, what level of participation in politics is to be expected of the average citizen, and what individual goals as opposed to community goals should the citizen pursue by means of that participation?

3. Evaluations of existing government institutions and officeholders—in other words, to what extent are these institutions and officials seen as legitimate expressions of the public will, to what extent are they held in esteem or mistrust, and to what extent are the policies enacted by these institutions thought to be satisfactory responses to citizens' desires?

At this point one might ask whether Texans do not simply hold the same political culture attitudes—under the three subheadings listed above—in which all American citizens are presumably instructed as a normal course of their civic education. In other words, do they not hold the attitudes presented in civics-text discussions of such matters? There are several problems with such an assumption, but there is an element of truth in it, as well. Both the strength and the difficulty of this assumption can be illustrated by reference to the actual content of some typical civic education materials.

One civics textbook that has been widely used in Texas's secondary schools is *American Civics*, by William H. Hartley and William S. Vincent. Hartley and Vincent (1970:38) offer an excellent example of typical civics-text instruction in political culture values:

The Political Cultures of Texas

American citizens have many responsibilities as citizens of our great nation. These responsibilities are the "shoulds" of citizenship. That is, American citizens are not required by law to carry out these actions. However, most Americans accept these responsibilities and carry them out because they are so important to the success of our government. These are the most important responsibilities of American citizens:

1. *American citizens should vote in all elections.*
2. *American citizens should be interested in their government and study the activities of their government.*
3. *American citizens should tell their representatives what they think about the problems facing their government.*
4. *American citizens should be willing to support the work of their government either as members of a political party or as independent voters.*

All Americans have probably been exposed to instruction like this at one time or another in their elementary and secondary education. Indeed, such teaching is one source from which Americans derive their political attitudes. Nevertheless, the actual political attitudes and behavior of many citizens deviate considerably from the standards posed for the "good citizen." Many Americans at times question whether their individual participation will in fact influence the government, and therefore they may come to question the importance of participation at all. At times some Americans may also doubt that the public interest is being served by this or that government official, agency, or policy. Such doubts can lead to disillusionment with politics and with individual participation. Clearly, not all citizens use their opportunities to participate in government—even by exercising the simple right to vote.

These observations should remind us of many instances in which our own political attitudes or those of our friends have differed sharply from the models established in civics texts. Yet these differences should not be surprising, for there are many sources from which one might learn such attitudes. The principal source is, of course, the family. At a young age children learn from their parents trust or cynicism or indifference toward government. Moreover, parents offer models for their children in their participation as well as their attitudes. Whether they vote regularly, participate actively in a political party or nonpartisan political organization, or otherwise involve themselves in political affairs will be a cue for their children's eventual political behavior.

As a person matures, his or her own political experiences and evaluations also become important. Personal experiences may reinforce what was learned from one's parents, or they may lead a person to question the value of that learning.

40 *Chapter 3*

Even the political environment in which a person lives will provide many subtle, or even not so subtle, influences that shape attitudes and behavior. The organizational climate of politics, particularly that managed by political parties, may offer strong encouragement or discouragement for citizen participation. In other words, the political party system of a state—whether it is a one-party or two-party state, whether parties encourage public participation, and so on—will influence individual attitudes and behavior.

Even such mundane matters as the voter registration system and the election calendar may influence citizen participation in politics. State laws regulating voter registration can depress voter turnout. (Chapter 5 discusses several ways in which that was precisely the case in Texas as recently as the 1970s.) The timing of elections can affect voter turnout too. If, for example, state and local elections are held simultaneously with national elections, such as for the presidency and congressional seats, voter turnout will be high. If state elections are held at odd, separate times, turnout will be considerably lower.

Finally, elected public officials can shape public attitudes and participation in government by controlling political party activities, setting particular voting requirements and election calendars, and simply encouraging and promoting democratic procedures. Public officials can set examples for individual involvement with government, and they can carry out their public duties in such a way as to inspire public trust and high esteem for government.

It should now be clear that political culture is shaped by many forces. Thus individuals may differ in their specific values because of their unique family socialization and personal political experiences. At the same time, large numbers of citizens share many general political values. Indeed, we should expect to discover many such shared values because different people and their families share common social and cultural experiences and live in the same political environment.

We have seen, then, what political culture is and why both shared and differing political culture values might coexist in the same state. Yet the importance of this topic—not only for the study of Texas government but also for the study of any other level of government—has not been directly addressed. Before we turn to the specifics of political culture in Texas, one might ask why anyone should care about this subject in the first place. Is it merely an arcane topic of interest only to scholarly political scientists? Or does it have some broader significance? A strong case can be made for the latter position by using two examples.

One aspect of political culture involves citizen preferences about the role of government in society. That phrase may sound vague, but it actually addresses quite down-to-earth matters. What Texan has not heard (or even participated in) arguments about whether the state is sufficiently generous—or, conversely, is too generous—toward the poor in its welfare programs? Likewise, arguments about such diverse subjects as capital punishment (whether the state is justified in taking human life as punishment for crime), the state's commitment to secondary and higher education, whether the state should outlaw abortions, and whether the state should have an equal rights amendment for women's rights—to name a few recent controversies—all revolve around different citizens' evaluations of the appropriate roles for government in society. This dimension of political culture is directly relevant to many deeply felt concerns of Texans about their government.

Similarly, another aspect of political culture involves citizen evaluations of what their personal role in politics should be. Presumably, once we know about the political culture of a state, we will understand how active the citizens as a collectivity are likely to be in political affairs. More specifically, we might hope that a knowledge of political culture would help explain why only 46 percent of voting-age Texans voted in the 1988 presidential election while many other states had turnouts of 60 to 66 percent. The civics-text explanation for democratic politics regards citizen participation as vital to the healthy operation of the nation's government. Although we may doubt whether the majority of citizens in any state fulfill the dictates of civics-text democracy, surely a low-participation state like Texas is fundamentally different from high-participation states where 60 percent or more of the citizens regularly turn out to vote.

Political culture actually concerns many important everyday matters of politics and government. Research on this topic, it should also be noted, has uncovered a variety of other connections among state political cultures, the behavior of citizens, and the public policies of their states (Kincaid, 1982). To understand how these connections arise, we must consider, first, the origin and dispersion of political cultures in the United States and, second, the specific political cultures of Texas. The plural *cultures* is used quite explicitly with regard to Texas, as well, for several distinct political cultures are found in the state.

The Patterning of America's Political Cultures

One of the most compelling explanations for the patterning of American political cultures is that developed by Daniel Elazar in a book entitled *American Federalism: A View from the States* (1984). To explain the relevance of Elazar's view for Texas, it is necessary first to recapitulate his general thesis. Elazar argues that three political subcultures have been of primary importance in the historical development of the United States. Each of these three subcultures was rooted in a particular social and geographic setting early in the history of the nation, and each has spread westward across the entire United States in a distinct pattern. Thus today each state is dominated by one or a particular combination of these subcultures. Evidence about the character of the dominant subculture can be found in several aspects of each state's politics.

Elazar calls the first of these subcultures *moralistic*. According to this perspective, government is one means to attaining the good society for all citizens.

As Elazar (1984:117) writes of this subculture: "Good government, then, is measured by the degree to which it promotes the public good and in terms of the honesty, selflessness, and commitment of those who govern." Politics is seen here as a concern of all citizens; thus public participation in politics is strongly encouraged.

Moralists hold that government service is public service, and it is expected that public officeholders will not derive special personal benefit from their positions. Political parties, though they might be seen as useful organizational devices, also are viewed distinctively here. Parties are merely means to larger and more important ends, such as the public good. Party loyalty, therefore, is less important than are those larger, more important ends.

Elazar traces the roots of the moralistic culture to the Puritans, who, in settling New England, attempted to establish as religiously pure a society as possible. And government played an integral part in that effort. The descendants of the Puritans, coupled with groups of later-arriving Scandinavian immigrants with similar religious attitudes, pushed this cultural variant into the Great Lakes region of the Midwest and on into Minnesota, Iowa, Oregon, and Washington. Other carriers of this culture settled in smaller numbers in several other midwestern and western states.

The second subculture Elazar calls *individualistic*. In this culture citizens desire only a government with limited functions and goals. This culture is the laissez-faire concept of government: government should perform only limited and essential functions so that individuals can pursue their private (mostly economic) interests unfettered by governmental constraints. At the same time, government is itself thought to be closely intertwined with this orientation toward individual economic opportunity. As Elazar (1984:115) expresses it:

> *The individualistic culture holds politics to be just another means by which individuals may improve themselves socially and economically. In this sense politics is a "business" like any other that competes for talent and offers rewards to those who take it up as a career. Those individuals who choose political careers may rise by providing the governmental services demanded of them and, in return, may expect to be adequately compensated for their efforts.*

In this subculture, holding political office becomes a profession that is best left to specialists. Thus, in a sense, mass participation is not strongly encouraged. Yet on certain occasions participation and partisan loyalty are highly encouraged. Commensurate with this businesslike character of politics, political parties become instruments of the "business." In the fashion most commonly associated with machine politics, government officeholders depend upon well-organized parties to maintain their positions and the rewards derived there-

The Political Cultures of Texas
43

from. There are those at every echelon in the party who are kept loyal by a flow of material rewards.

The individualistic subculture arose principally from the Germanic and non-Puritanical English settlers of the Middle Atlantic states. Among these groups the pursuit of individual opportunity was placed ahead of communal goals. The descendants of these settlers eventually moved westward in relatively distinct patterns just as those of the original moralistic Americans did. Elazar traces the movement of these people into a number of midwestern and western states, more or less within the middle third of the nation.

The final subculture in this scheme is *traditionalistic*. In the original version of this culture, government was just one element of an elitist, precommercial social order. Government's principal function was to preserve that social order and the relative positions of different classes in it. Not surprisingly, then, politics is dominated by representatives of the social elite. In fact, Elazar argues that participation by non-elites is actually discouraged. It should also be obvious that the elite will benefit directly from politics as long as their position at the top of the social order is maintained. It is this class basis for the distribution of government benefits that distinguishes this system from the individualistic one.

As a final point of comparison, political parties are held to be of much less importance in this traditionalistic culture than in either of the first two. The principal reason is that parties are by their design intended to strengthen ties between the mass of citizens and their leaders. But those ties can come to imply that leaders should respond to grass-roots party members as well as to the elite. Equally unfortunate from the perspective of traditionalistic elites is that political parties customarily encourage certain forms of mass political participation. Thus the development of parties is discouraged in this culture by the solidarity of the elite's interests and by the elite's fear of mass participation.

The traditionalistic culture originated, as one might have guessed by now, in the plantation-based agricultural system of the Old South. The plantation system created a social and political elite that was already well formed by the time of the American Revolution (and which in fact furnished many of the distinguished leaders of that revolution). Elazar asserts that although this culture was most fully developed in Virginia and South Carolina, other southern states were important homes for it, as well. Migration from those states carried this traditionalistic culture across all of the southern states that eventually formed the Confederacy and into a few other midwestern and southwestern areas.

The effects of migration patterns on the dispersion of these subcultures across the country are illustrated in Elazar's geographic representation of the locales of settlement of major streams of migrants (Figure 3-1). The principal regional homes of each of the three subcultures and a general sense of their separate streams of westward movement are indicated. In Texas both the traditionalistic and the individualistic cultures are represented. Elazar argues that the state's overall culture

44

Figure 3-1 | **Regional distribution of political cultures within the states**
Source: Elazar (1984:124–125)

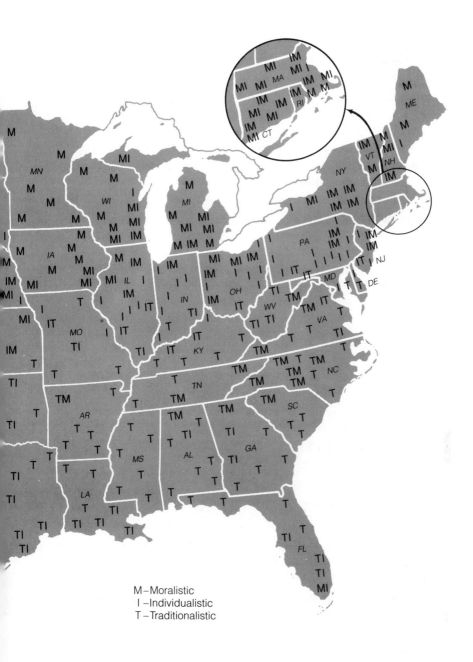

M–Moralistic
I –Individualistic
T –Traditionalistic

is a mixture of these two with the traditionalistic element predominating. This conclusion should not be surprising, for the last chapter showed that the major source of migrants to Texas was the southern United States, home of the traditionalistic culture.

Elazar recognizes that these subcultural values will be subject to some modification over time. One of the most important forces for such change has been continued migration among the various states. Certainly migration has been responsible for some mixing of cultures, and Texas, as we will see, has been particularly influenced in this fashion in recent decades. Another force for change has been internal evolution within certain subcultures. Of relevance to Texas is the assertion by Elazar (1984:133) that the traditionalistic culture has "tended to adopt individualistic elements as its traditional social bases have eroded." This kind of change may have reversed the relative importance of these two subcultural variants in the state.

Political Subcultures in Texas

With a general notion of political culture in mind, it is now possible to explore the specific political cultures of Texas in more detail. We will begin by focusing on the subcultures of the several groups of migrants that have come together to form the current residents of the state. First we will examine the original cultural pattern of each group; then we will consider what forces might be changing the composition of that original set of values.

Southern Anglo-Americans

Elazar argues that many of the southern Americans who migrated to Texas brought with them the traditionalistic culture. Thus they would have upheld a preponderant role in political life for elite citizens, a modest role for the average citizen, and the maintenance of the social status quo (running from the elite at the top to slaves at the bottom) as principal objectives of government. The fact that Texas followed the rest of the South into the Confederacy is important evidence for that conclusion. Likewise, one can find other evidence (particularly relevant to the idea that government should preserve the social status quo) both in the political role that landed elites played later and in the state's post-Reconstruction efforts to keep blacks in an inferior social and political position despite their emancipation.

Yet a more detailed study of southern migration to Texas suggests that the individualistic culture may have been of near-equal importance from the earliest days of Anglo settlement. Chapter 2 discussed Jordan's research on the Upper South and Lower South origins of early Texans. (Recall that in 1850 those two regions had provided almost equal numbers of Texans.) According to Elazar's scheme, the Lower South migrants came from areas dominated by the plantation system and sustained by a traditionalistic culture. Much of the Upper South, on the other hand, had been settled by individualistic groups of Germans, Scotch-Irish, and non-Puritanical English (Jordan, 1967:667–668), many of whom had come from Pennsylvania, a core individualistic state in Elazar's model.

The large numbers of Upper South immigrants in Texas surely gave prominence to individualistic values. Few of those people owned slaves, their support for secession in 1860 was mixed, and hence their commitment to a rigid social order must have been weaker than that of their fellow Texans from the Lower South. Thus an important strain of the individualistic culture has long been present in the state.

One might question the primacy of the traditionalistic culture in Texas for other reasons, as well. Certainly the plantation system, and hence the landed social and political elite that was based on it, was ill-developed in Texas relative to the system in the Lower South, where it had originated (Kousser, 1974:196). As Seymour V. Connor (1971:182–185) has written about 1860, "There were very few actual plantations in Texas and very few large slaveholders." Although slaveholders might have been disproportionately influential in both social and political life, there had simply not been sufficient time for the traditionalistic elite to become as entrenched in Texas as elsewhere in the Lower South.

Also moderating the influence of the traditionalistic culture were the frontier spirit associated with the settling of much of the state and the individualistic ethic in the early years of the cattle and oil and gas industries in Texas (Meinig, 1969:86–89). These developments helped create new elites with social and political values somewhat different from the more rigid ones of the traditionalistic Lower South group. Surely these newer elites were the prototypes for much of the myth of the typical Texan.

In summary, one could argue that the political culture of Anglo Texans has from the first been a mixture of traditionalism and individualism. At the same time, there are several reasons for believing that the individualistic culture has been growing in influence over the history of the state, perhaps becoming the more important of the two. Yet one component of the traditional culture was accepted by the majority of all Anglo Texans well into the mid-twentieth century: the belief that those at the bottom of the social order—blacks and Mexican Americans—should be kept at the bottom. As we will see, that belief had important consequences for the political cultures of these minority groups.

Mexican Americans

What was the original political culture of Texans of Mexican origin? That culture, we must conclude, was a version of traditionalism. Mexican society in the early 1800s—whether in central Mexico or in the region that is now part of Texas—was a preindustrial one dominated by a landed elite and characterized by several

48   *Chapter 3*

features similar to those of the traditionalistic culture of the Lower South. (Mexico, however, did not tolerate a slave system among its indigenous people.)

Elements of this traditionalistic Mexican culture have remained vital well into the late twentieth century—both in Mexico (Almond and Verba, 1963:414–428; Needler, 1982:54–56) and in the United States among Mexican Americans (Vigil, 1977:75; Cortes, 1980:714–715). A great respect for the extended family is one of those elements. A rigid role structure for family members, such as husbands and wives, is a second element. Adherence to the Catholic faith is a third. Indeed, some scholars have argued that Mexican culture still places considerably more emphasis on family and religious values than on individual achievement (Vigil, 1977:75–76).

There is evidence for the evolution and, at times, erosion of all these original values (Moore and Pachon, 1976:137–138; Cortes, 1980:715); yet they remain key cultural guideposts for many Mexican Americans. These values are traditionalistic in Elazar's terms. To the extent they remain important in the Mexican American community, so does the traditionalistic political culture, even if to a lesser degree than in past generations. Indeed, some argue that these values are regularly strengthened by the steady influx of illegal immigrants from Mexico, many of whom hold these values with particular tenacity (Cortes, 1980:715).

We must not, however, fall into the intellectual trap that ensnared many early students of Mexican American culture—the conclusion that indigenous values alone kept Mexican Americans in a traditionalistic or "backward" role in American society (Garcia and de la Garza, 1977:34–39). Undoubtedly, traditionalistic elements exist in traditional Mexican American culture. Yet the political and social culture of this group has been shaped, in part, by experiences with Anglo society—and the characteristic features of those experiences have surely been Anglo discrimination, segregation, and exploitation of ethnic minorities.

From their earliest encounters, the relations between Anglos and Mexicans were characterized by such features (DeLeon, 1983). Revolution against Mexico, the takeover of Mexican-owned lands by Anglos, and a variety of discriminatory public laws and private practices institutionalized the subordinate social position of Mexican-origin Texans well before the turn of the twentieth century. The demand for agricultural and other low-skilled workers throughout this century also reinforced a lower-class character and purely instrumental value for the Mexican people in the minds of many Anglos.

Thus Mexican Americans in Texas came to be locked into the lowest level of society. They were physically encapsulated in rural or urban barrios separated from the areas where Anglos lived. They were denied equal educational opportunities, which, along with Anglo prejudice, ensured they would remain in the lowest occupational positions in the society. In many cases they were co-opted into migratory work patterns and forced to follow the sequence of agricultural harvests from place to place or even state to state.

The Political Cultures of Texas   49

In light of these circumstances, one might conclude along with many students of Mexican American culture that continued reliance on the extended family, maintenance of the Spanish language, and several other traditionalistic cultural features are defensive reactions to Anglo prejudice and discrimination (Moore and Pachon, 1976:135–136). Thus it can be argued that the character of ethnic relations is responsible for some portion of Mexican American social and political values.

Blacks

The original culture of Texas blacks was traditionalistic, as well. Moreover, it was the culture of those who were enslaved at the bottom of a traditional society. Blacks were members by force, in other words, of the traditionalistic society of Lower South Anglo immigrants to Texas. In pre-Reconstruction Texas, blacks had no political role and no reason to hope that they might rise from their slavery.

The Civil War and Reconstruction eradicated for a time the bonds of law and slavery that kept blacks in that subordinate role. But the end of Reconstruction and the return of state government to the hands of the Anglo majority eventually resulted in a reinstitution of many legal barriers to black social and political freedom. By means of the poll tax, the white primary (see Chapter 5), and violence and intimidation, black Texans were effectively precluded from political participation by about 1910 (Key, 1949:535). Further, the "Jim Crow" laws passed between 1870 and 1910 established racial segregation in schools, public transportation, and virtually all other public and private settings (Rice, 1971:140–150; Kousser, 1974:196–209; Woodward, 1974). These sanctions were only a few of the many discriminatory barriers erected by Anglo society against blacks. Many of these practices, one must remember, remained in force well into the 1960s.

The intent of these post-Reconstruction laws and practices was to keep blacks, like Mexican Americans, at the bottom of Texas society. Slavery had been abolished, but in many practical ways the black's role was unchanged. In terms of social and economic advancement the result—as Chapter 2 explained in detail—has been the severe restriction of educational, occupational, and material opportunities of black Texans. In political terms the result was to teach blacks that they could have no active role in the governing of the state—that they could be, at best, mere subjects of the system and would never be able to influence its leaders or policies by their own participation (Almond and Verba, 1963:214–229; Meier and Rudnick, 1966:171–172).

In short, while the Anglo society was evolving around them, blacks as well as Mexican Americans were for many years kept in a social and political position much like that of their original, traditionalistic culture of pre–Civil War days. Their exposure to individualistic values was limited because most avenues of opportunity were closed to them. And moralistic political notions must have been foreign to

50 Chapter 3

a people who could see the immorality of the way they were treated—even by government itself—simply because of the color of their skin.

As a result of their inferior social position, blacks came to adopt some of the same defensive cultural responses of Mexican Americans. Similarly, some old traditionalistic values remained vital because of the limited opportunities for cultural evolution. Religion and the church played a particularly important role in the black community (Smallwood, 1981:96–108). To some extent, religion served a compensatory function, helping blacks suffer the burdens of the present world because of what they could expect, as good Christians, in the next one (Sernett, 1975:165–167; Raboteau, 1978:305–314). In many black communities distinctive language dialects developed—in part because of the limited social interactions allowed outside the community and in part as a defense against a hostile outside world (Baugh, 1983).

For most blacks as well as Mexican Americans, therefore, the traditionalistic political culture endured well into the mid-twentieth century. But much of that culture was a product of the inferior and constricted social roles forced on both minority groups.

Germans

Although the cultural distinctiveness of German Texans has declined considerably, a few remarks about the original political culture of that group are instructive for comparative purposes. The German immigrants to Texas in the nineteenth century had many of the characteristics Elazar identified with the individualistic culture. Their motivations to immigrate in the first instance centered around the search for individual opportunity in America (Geue and Geue, 1966:1–18; Jordan, 1966:38–59). Like many other individualistic groups, the Germans might best have been called ambivalent toward the issues of slavery and secession in the 1860s. The fact that few Germans owned slaves has been interpreted by some historians as a moral indictment of the institution on their part. Terry G. Jordan (1966:106–111), however, makes a good case that a lack of sufficient capital accounted for the limited slave holdings of the Germans, as it did for the Upper South Anglo immigrants.

Secession was itself controversial among German Texans. Some German areas voted heavily against it in the public referenda on the subject, whereas others voted in favor. Apparently a number of motives, some having nothing to do with slavery or states' rights, account for these differences (Jordan, 1966:182–185). Yet the Germans were labeled by many Anglos as abolitionists, and the resultant anti-German sentiment, along with the distinctiveness of German political views on some other issues, resulted in relatively high support for the Republican party among the Germans well into the mid-twentieth century (Key, 1949:275–276). With the decline of the group's cultural distinctiveness, however, their political distinctiveness has faded as well. Today the traditionally German regions of the state are no longer notable for their Republicanism, and one must suppose that other aspects of this once-distinctive political culture are also vanishing.

Conclusion

This chapter has demonstrated how the political culture of Texas is in some senses a mixed one, much as Chapter 2 showed the diversity of the population itself. In spite of that diversity, however, key elements in the political culture of the state have long existed. At least from the time of the Republic of Texas, the culture of the state has been dominated by a mix of traditionalistic and individualistic values originating primarily in the two subregions of the American South. In that period and well into the middle of the twentieth century the political cultures of the state's two largest ethnic minority groups were also traditionalistic. These two cultures integrated relatively smoothly, therefore, with the dominant Anglo culture.

The primary elements of this cultural mix were such that most Texans expected traditionalistic and individualistic elites to benefit personally from politics. Because both elite groups were politically conservative in most ways, government was expected to play a limited role in social and economic life. These limitations on government can still be seen today in the relatively modest state regulatory structure, in the wide latitude given private business to pursue individualistic goals, and in the state's low taxes. These aspects of contemporary state government—all derived in part from the original political culture of the state—will be the subjects of extended discussion in later chapters.

In other areas, however, both the traditionalistic and individualistic elite groups expected government to be quite active—largely where such action might be necessary to preserve the power of the elites. In Chapter 5 we will see, as examples, how a number of political party activities and public laws were developed to restrict popular participation in Texas government. Similarly, some government agencies have worked diligently to serve the interests of elite-dominated sectors of the economy.

Moralistic elements, as Elazar defined them, have from the first been rare in Texas's political culture. Instead, the goals of government were framed in terms of traditionalistic or individualistic objectives. And corruption, just like legal opportunities to derive personal benefit from government service, was easily tolerated and even, at times, envied.

Along with Elazar, we must recognize, however, that powerful, though slowly acting, forces are changing Texas's political culture. Industrialization and postindustrial development as described in Chapter 1 are two of those forces. Moreover, urbanization has been a related agent of cultural change. Together, industrialization and urbanization have brought diversity to Texas while creating new social

52 *Chapter 3*

and economic elites at the same time. In the process they have eroded the power base of the rural and traditionalistic elite.

A second force for change has been the steady in-migration of nonsouthern Americans throughout the 1900s but particularly in the era of Sunbelt migration. Many of these immigrants came from moralistic states or from places where individualism was not associated with ethnic prejudice as has been the case in Texas. Surely these migrants will experience some degree of assimilation to Texas values. But—recalling from Chapter 2 the relatively well-educated, career-oriented, and professional character of most of these people—they may also be articulate and capable advocates of values new to Texas. One might speculate that, just as industrialization and urbanization did, these new migrants will weaken the remnants of traditionalistic culture, will strengthen the individualistic culture, and will be at least a modest force for the inclusion of moralistic values in the state.

Finally, significant changes are under way within the state's ethnic minority cultures. The eradication of all the legal obstacles and many of the social barriers to their participation in society at large—which will be explained in detail in Chapter 5—has created a sense of opportunity among blacks and Mexican Americans. Not only may they now participate in political life, but the political consciousness of both groups has also been stirred to seize this new opportunity. One of the resultant cultural changes within these groups has been the adoption of certain individualistic values, now that social and economic opportunities have been opened to them. Another change has been the adoption of certain moralistic values, at least in the sense that blacks and Mexican Americans have come to demand government action to redress inequities against their people. Thus progress among Texas's ethnic minorities will undoubtedly erode the traditionalistic culture even further, expand the individualistic culture, and emphasize certain moralistic concerns.

Political culture helps determine the structure of government, the character of government policies, and the nature of public participation in government. Although this chapter has indicated some of the ways Texas government is linked with the state's political culture, many details of that linkage must await the extended discussions of later chapters. The principal conclusions of this chapter, however, constitute underlying themes we will encounter again throughout the book.

Note

1. The political science literature offers several distinct though interrelated approaches for the study of political culture. Representative discussions of this subject are provided in Almond and Verba (1963), Devine (1972), Kincaid (1982), and Elazar (1984). The empirical research on America's political cultures and their relation to other aspects of political life is reviewed in Savage (1981) and Kincaid (1982).

References

Almond, Gabriel, and Verba, Sidney. 1963. *The Civic Culture*. Princeton: Princeton University Press.

Baugh, John. 1983. *Black Street Speech*. Austin: University of Texas Press.

Connor, Seymour V. 1971. *Texas: A History*. New York: Thomas Y. Crowell.

Cortes, Carlos E. 1980. "Mexicans." In *Harvard Encyclopedia of American Ethnic Groups*. Cambridge: Belknap Press of Harvard University.

DeLeon, Arnoldo. 1983. *They Called Them Greasers: Anglo Attitudes Toward Mexicans in Texas, 1821–1900*. Austin: University of Texas Press.

Devine, Donald J. 1972. *The Political Culture of the United States*. Boston: Little, Brown.

Elazar, Daniel J. 1984. *American Federalism: A View from the States*. 3rd ed. New York: Harper & Row.

Garcia, F. Chris, and de la Garza, Rudolph O. 1977. *The Chicano Political Experience*. North Scituate, Mass.: Duxbury.

Geue, Chester William, and Geue, Ethel Handel. 1966. *A New Land Beckoned: German Immigrants to Texas, 1844–1847*. Waco: Texian Press.

Hartley, William H., and Vincent, William S. 1970. *American Civics*. Rev. ed. New York: Harcourt Brace Jovanovich.

Jordan, Terry G. 1966. *German Seed in Texas Soil: Immigrant Farmers in Nineteenth-Century Texas*. Austin: University of Texas Press.

———. 1967. "The Imprint of the Upper and Lower South on Mid-Nineteenth-Century Texas." *Annals of the Association of American Geographers* 57 (December): 667–690.

Key, V. O. 1949. *Southern Politics in State and Nation*. New York: Vintage Books.

Kincaid, John. 1982. "Introduction." In John Kincaid (ed.), *Political Culture, Public Policy, and the American States*. Philadelphia: Institute for the Study of Human Issues.

Kousser, J. Morgan. 1974. *The Shaping of Southern Politics: Suffrage Restriction and the Establishment of the One-Party South, 1880–1910*. New Haven: Yale University Press.

Meier, August, and Rudnick, Elliott M. 1966. *From Plantation to Ghetto*. New York: Hill & Wang.

Meinig, D. W. 1969. *Imperial Texas: An Interpretive Essay in Cultural Geography*. Austin: University of Texas Press.

Moore, Joan W., and Pachon, Harry. 1976. *Mexican Americans*. 2nd ed. Englewood Cliffs, N.J.: Prentice-Hall.

Needler, Martin C. 1982. *Mexican Politics*. New York: Praeger.

Raboteau, Albert J. 1978. *Slave Religion*. New York: Oxford University Press.

Rice, Lawrence D. 1971. *The Negro in Texas, 1874–1900*. Baton Rouge: Louisiana State University Press.

Savage, Robert L. 1981. "Looking for Political Subcultures: A Critique of the Rummage-Sale Approach." *Western Political Quarterly* 34 (June): 331–336.

Sernett, Milton C. 1975. *Black Religion and American Evangelicalism*. Metuchen, N.J.: Scarecrow Press.

Smallwood, James M. 1981. *Time of Hope, Time of Despair: Black Texans During Reconstruction*. Port Washington, N.Y.: Kennikat Press.

Vigil, Maurilio. 1977. *Chicano Politics*. Washington, D.C.: University Press of America.

Woodward, C. Vann. 1974. *The Strange Career of Jim Crow*. 3rd ed. London: Oxford University Press.

Chapter 4

The Texas Constitution

Because the Texas Constitution was written in 1875 and ratified by the voters in 1876, its history is intimately connected with some of the other nineteenth-century events discussed in earlier chapters. Of particular relevance is the development of the political culture of the state. The constitution was heavily influenced by some of the same forces that shaped the political culture. In consequence, the material in this chapter builds upon themes developed in previous ones.

At the same time, this chapter looks forward to the remainder of the book. Certainly the constitution has significantly influenced the character of Texas's contemporary political institutions and policies. One might think of the constitution as an architectural blueprint for the state government. Yet it is not simply the organizational form and arrangement of these structures that are prefigured in the constitution. The constitution is also the source of several strong points and an even larger number of weaknesses inherent in the current governmental system.

The Functions of State Constitutions

State constitutions are the fundamental laws of states. That is, they define the powers of the state government, how those powers will be exercised, and how they will be limited—subject only to the constraints on state governments imposed by the United States Constitution, the supreme law of the nation. The U.S. Constitution allots to the states what powers will be theirs—the so-called residual powers left to the states after the enumeration of the federal government's own responsibilities, largely in Article I of the federal document. Moreover, amendments to the U.S. Constitution have often defined more clearly or limited more narrowly the powers of the states. The Fifteenth Amendment, for example, made unconstitutional any state government actions that discriminate on the basis of race.

Decisions of the U.S. Supreme Court in the twentieth century have often served both to extend and to limit the powers of state governments, regardless of their

56   *Chapter 4*

own original constitutional provisions. Extensions of state power have arisen particularly from Supreme Court acceptance of new state regulatory powers. Limitations on state power have arisen most typically through Court decisions on individual rights. An example of the latter kind of decision, discussed at length in Chapter 5, was the Supreme Court decision in 1966 outlawing poll taxes as a requirement for voting in state or local elections. Such examples illustrate that state constitutions exist within a larger legal environment delimited by the U.S. Constitution and that this environment and the limitations it imposes are dynamic, not static.

The principal manner in which state constitutions go about detailing the powers of the state government and how they will be exercised is by describing the various institutions of that government. Like the U.S. Constitution, state constitutions divide governmental power among executive, legislative, and judicial branches. The major institutions within each branch are described at least in outline, and the powers and limitations of each branch, along with the checks and balances among the branches, are typically listed. Furthermore, state constitutions list the qualifications for serving in elected and certain appointed offices of government.

State constitutions also describe the political rights of their citizens. Most of those rights are set forth within a bill of rights much like the Bill of Rights embodied in the first ten amendments to the U.S. Constitution. State bills of rights were necessary at one time because the individual rights guarantees of the federal document originally limited only the federal government itself. Several decisions of the U.S. Supreme Court, particularly in the twentieth century, have extended the provisions of the federal Bill of Rights and all of the U.S. Constitution to the states. Yet in recent years state bills of rights have taken on new significance because they sometimes have provided individual rights guarantees that are more extensive than those in the U.S. Constitution. For example, Texas voters approved in 1972 an amendment to the state constitution that ensures one's civil rights regardless of "sex, race, color, creed, or national origin." The federal constitution, on the other hand, still has no so-called Equal Rights Amendment (ERA) with reference to sex.

Another important component of every constitution is its provision for an amendment process. The principal means of amending the Texas Constitution is through ratification by the state's voters of proposals initiated in the state legislature, as was the case with the Texas ERA noted above. Some of the constitution's shortcomings to be described have made the amendment process—along with its own limitations—of considerable importance to Texas government.

One other typical characteristic of state constitutions is believed by many critics to be a significant shortcoming. Most state constitutions include a large number of details about how state and local governments should operate, how specific government policies should be executed, and what limits are to be imposed on the government. In short, one might say that most state constitutions contain a considerable amount of ordinary instead of constitutional law—that is, they contain many provisions that should be in statutory law passed by the state legislature.

Including ordinary law in the constitution might not seem a bad idea at the time constitutions are written, because such provisions might accord well with public preferences and the political needs of the time. Yet 50 or 100 years later, when public preferences and political needs may have changed dramatically, such detailed provisions may impose unfortunate limitations on government. Such has surely come to be the case in Texas.

One can get a vivid indication of just how common and extensive are the ordinary-law provisions of state constitutions by comparing their length with that of the U.S. Constitution. The latter document contains about 8,700 words. The average state constitution is today about 26,000 words long, even though in recent decades some of the longest ones have been revised and shortened considerably. The Texas Constitution is, at 62,000 words, the fourth longest in the nation. Even before examining the text of the Texas Constitution, we can be sure we will find in it many detailed, ordinary-law provisions simply because of its length.

More than ordinary-law provisions account for the length of the Texas Constitution, however. The constitution also contains a great deal of unnecessary language. An illustration of the wordy, duplicative, obsolete language of the constitution can be drawn from any of the several proposed revisions of that document that have rewritten it into a simplified, reorganized, and nonredundant form—without any change in its substantive meaning. One such effort, prepared for the Constitutional Convention of 1974, reduced the then 52,000-word constitution to only 17,000 words (Searcy, 1973).

Another sign of the character of the Texas document is that it is not reprinted in the back of this book. Almost every text on the American national government routinely includes the U.S. Constitution as an appendix. That custom is practical because of the document's brevity. But it is also academically sensible because virtually every line of the U.S. Constitution is meaningful and profitable for study or discussion. Such is hardly the case with the Texas Constitution. Not only is it exceedingly long, but it is also boring and extraordinarily tedious to read because of the amount of detail it includes. A brief perusal of the Texas Constitution would satisfy any reader that printing the full text of the document could be of little profit either to the student of Texas government or to a publisher. (The most convenient source for the complete text of the state constitution is probably any biennial edition of the *Texas Almanac*, which is usually available in the reference section of public and university libraries.)

The History of the Texas Constitution

Having outlined the principal purposes of state constitutions and having, as well, begun to hint at the character of the Texas Constitution, we will now consider the latter document in some detail. First we will discuss the architects who drew up this blueprint for state government, the forces influencing their decisions, and the goals they envisioned for the government they were designing.

The present constitution of Texas is the fifth one under which the government has operated since the admission of Texas to the United States in 1845. The first of these constitutions was adopted in 1845 with statehood; the second was the 1861 Confederacy constitution; the third took force in 1866 when Texas reentered the Union; the fourth was adopted in 1869 under the relatively stringent Reconstruction criteria imposed on the state by the Radical Republicans in the U.S. Congress. The present document was written by a constitutional convention in 1875 and ratified by the voters in 1876 at the end of the Reconstruction era. The political and social circumstances of those times are clearly evident in the instrument.

The Intent of the 1875 Convention

The authors of the present state constitution were influenced by three principal forces arising out of the social, political, and economic circumstances of the times. These separate forces all worked to influence the constitutional convention toward the same general architectural design for state government.

Ending Reconstruction Government The first of the three forces was a passionate desire to rid the state of all traces of the Reconstruction-era government. The white majority had found the entire period of Reconstruction a hardship, but the time between 1867 and 1874 had been especially unfortunate in the minds of most Texans. In the latter years the U.S. Congress imposed explicit and, to most southerners, harsh conditions for an eventual unqualified return to the full rights of statehood and the end of Reconstruction. Texas was occupied and its government controlled by the Union army for much of that period. Blacks were enfranchised and given new social privileges. Many of the state's military officers and government officials from the Confederacy were initially imprisoned and then later, after they were freed, barred from holding public office or even voting.

To make matters worse, the civilian government of the state was run during the Radical Reconstruction period by a coalition of carpetbaggers, blacks, and longtime Union sympathizers. They had reshaped the government—by means of the constitution of 1869 and by the so-called Obnoxious Acts passed in 1870 and 1871 by the state legislature—to ensure that they could dominate the political life of the state. The 1869 constitution created a strong, central state government. The governor was given broad appointive and policy supervision powers. Local government was closely controlled by the central state authorities. Elections were carefully monitored and, some said, manipulated by the Republican regime. And taxes were considered by the white majority to be onerously high.

Moreover, certain policies of the Republican government received strong criticism. Much of the tax money went to support an extensive system of public elementary and secondary education that many Texans thought was unnecessary and far too expensive. To promote the construction of a railroad system in the state, the Republicans had subsidized the rail companies—first with state bonds and later, when the bonds were declared unconstitutional by the state supreme court, with large gifts of state land based on mileage of rail lines completed. As a consequence of these and other expansive public policies, both the tax rate and the indebtedness of the state ballooned under Radical Republican rule.

Although historical scholarship is divided on the validity of some of the criticisms of the Republican regime, those complaints were strongly felt by many Texans at the time (Connor, 1971:221–223). One might say, in the language of political culture, that the majority of Texans believed that many of the Republican activities fell outside the appropriate role of government in society. Additionally, of course, they believed that the government was controlled by people who did not represent the popular will. To use another political culture idea, the regime was seen as illegitimate.

For most Texans the low point of the Reconstruction era was the administration of Governor E. J. Davis in 1870–1874. Davis was the only Republican governor to serve under the 1869 constitution, and most Texans at the time would probably have said he used it to the fullest. Along with his Republican state legislature, Davis passed what his Democratic critics called the Obnoxious Acts, giving more executive powers to the governor along with control of a state militia to back them up. Davis used those powers vigorously, even going so far as to declare martial law at four different times in various counties in the state. The state militia itself was widely criticized as being more lawless than law-enforcing. The spending proclivities of the Republican regime were also highly criticized. Davis's administration was responsible for much of the public debt incurred during Reconstruction, a point that is well illustrated by a single comparison (Miller, 1910:107): The 1866 constitution had limited the public debt to $100,000, but under the 1869 constitution and in the years of Davis's governorship alone, the public debt of the state grew by more than $2,100,000.

The control of government by Davis and the Republicans was short-lived. They would have been opposed by most Texans regardless of their policies, but the policies they did pursue brought a fierce public reaction. In 1872, at the first election after Davis had assumed office, the Democratic party regained control of the state legislature. The new legislature quickly set about repealing the Obnoxious Acts and as much else of the Republican program as they could. Then, in the 1874 election, the Democrats won control of the governorship. The consolidated Dem-

60 *Chapter 4*

ocratic government, after struggling with the task of rewriting the constitution itself, called for a constitutional convention to do the job. Thus the first and most forceful motivation for a new constitution was to eradicate the Radical Republican blueprint from state government.

Responding to Farmers' Demands A second factor in the 1875 convention was the political agenda of the Patrons of Husbandry, better known as the Grange. The Grange was a society intended to further the interests of farmers and the rural population. Members of the Grange made up almost half of the constitutional convention, and they had some well-developed ideas about how state government should be structured and how it should be limited. The Grangers wanted to create an economical government that could exist on a modest tax structure. At the same time, they wanted the government to limit the powers of the banks and the railroads, the two private-sector institutions that most affected the livelihood of farmers. The Grange amounted to a second force at the convention that was pressing for a reduction in the power and expense of state government. Furthermore, just as the typical convention delegate wanted to eradicate the power of outside political forces over Texas government, the Grangers wanted to weaken the power of outside economic forces over their lives.

Responding to the Panic of 1873 The third force influencing the convention was the state of the economy. Texas, like the rest of the nation, was still in the midst of the Panic of 1873, an economic depression that began in the fall of 1873 and lasted well into 1878. In many respects the depression was just as severe as the Great Depression of the 1930s. The similarities extended beyond economics to political life. Joseph Schumpeter (1939:337) has described the similarity between these two depressions: "The political complement was also similar—Granger movement, agitation for inflation, strikes, and riots being, if we take account of differences in social and political structure and attitude, more than fair counterparts of corresponding phenomena in the recent instance." The economic hardships brought on by the 1870s depression constituted, then, a third force encouraging thrift in government.

The New Blueprint for Government

When the convention met in 1875, the motivations of the Democrats and the farmers, as well as the state of the economy, were foremost in the minds of the delegates, and the delegates themselves were representative of those interests. Some ninety delegates (three from each state Senate district) had been chosen to attend the convention by public election. Of them, seventy-five were Democrats who broadly represented the anti-Reconstruction majority of the population. Almost half the delegates were also members of the Grange, and thus more farmers were present than members of any other occupation.

It is not difficult, then, to imagine the kind of government that the 1875 convention designed. A principal motivation was for thrift in government. To achieve that aim, the convention authored a host of changes from the existing system, including reducing the salaries of state officials and legislators (with a 20 percent reduction in the governor's salary), stipulating biennial instead of annual legislative sessions, reducing the government's tax revenues and spending commitments for big-ticket items like public education, and fixing a constitutional limit of $200,000 on the state's debt.

One of the major changes was in public education. The 1869 constitution had provided for a free public school system, with a compulsory attendance law and sufficient taxes to support the system. But public education was opposed by the Grangers, and the new constitution provided for a quite limited and ill-funded school system with no compulsory attendance. These changes were controversial even at the time. Indeed, a Galveston newspaper commented that "the convention, after decreeing universal suffrage, had now also decreed universal ignorance" (McKay, 1942:105).

A second motivation was to weaken the central state government—in part as a reaction to Davis's autocratic governorship and in part to return more control to the public at large and to local officials. To achieve that aim, several state agencies were disbanded, and control of their functions was returned to local officials. The governor was stripped of most appointive powers, and most of the offices the governor had previously filled by appointment were made elective. Terms of office were also shortened to keep elected officials "closer to the people."

Finally, to ensure that their objectives would be met, the delegates went into considerable detail in the text of the constitution to lay out explicitly their ideas for a limited government. Thus the great length of the document is in good part a product of their zealous effort to weaken the government and to make their intentions clear and unalterable.

Some of that explicitness served to fulfill the positive functions desired by the convention. The constitution writers ensured, for example, that the state would have the power to regulate banks, railroads, and private corporations (in accordance with Granger fears about those institutions). Similarly, a prohibition against usurious interest was included along with one to prevent the forced sale of a homestead for nonpayment of debts. The latter provisions also came from the Granger agenda.

Ratification of the New Constitution

When the draft of the new constitution was submitted to the voters in early 1876, it was approved by more than a 2-to-1 margin (136,606 votes for and 56,652

62   *Chapter 4*

against). That the document would be accepted by the voters was surely to be expected. There was too much hatred for the Radical Republican government on too many different issues for the outcome to have been otherwise. Nevertheless, not all parts of the state favored the new document. Voter support was highest in the rural and small-town areas, and the proposed constitution was actually defeated in several of the bigger cities. Its rejection in urban areas was in some sense prophetic, because the limitations of the new constitution have probably come to affect urban areas most particularly. It is in the cities, after all, that nineteenth-century agrarian strictures against big government are felt most acutely by twentieth-century Texans.

Revising the Constitution

Agitation to revise all or part of the Texas Constitution began virtually from its initial ratification. At three different times that agitation has produced proposals from the state legislature for constitutional conventions to rewrite the document completely. The first proposal in 1917 died because of the opposition of Governor "Farmer Jim" Ferguson. A second in 1919 was defeated by the voters. The third, providing for a constitutional convention made up of state legislators to meet in the summer of 1974, was accepted by the voters in 1972.

The 1974 convention proved, however, to be at least a partial failure. Its committees produced a draft constitution, but full agreement on the draft could not be reached before the term of the session ended. Perhaps out of some embarrassment over the failure, the legislature took up the draft when it met in regular session the succeeding year. With a few modifications, the draft constitution was presented to the voters as a set of eight amendments that would have completely revised the 1876 document.

The proposed new constitution drew considerable support from key groups in the state. As one observer has put it:

> *The document drew the support of the deans of all eight Texas law schools, over 200 professors of government at 31 colleges and universities throughout the state, most of the state's major newspapers, respected authorities on constitutions, and a number of civic and political groups, among which were the Texas Municipal League (for the local government article), the Texas State Bar (for the judiciary article), the Junior Bar (for all the proposals), the AFL-CIO (for six of the eight proposals), the National Farmers Union, Common Cause, the League of Women Voters, the Texas Association of College Teachers, the American Association of University Women, and the American Association of Retired Persons. Barbara Jordan, Leon Jaworski, and Robert Strauss were among the well-known Texans in favor of the document. (May, 1977:66)*

The Texas Constitution

In spite of the impressive support, all eight amendments were soundly defeated by the voters in 1975. Postelection analyses suggested that the revision effort failed for three major reasons:

1. Lack of vigorous political leadership in support of the new document
2. Outright opposition of the governor to some of the provisions
3. Poor organization of the pro-ratification election campaign

The constitution also provides for a process of item-by-item amendment of its separate provisions, and this second route has been used quite often since 1876. The amendment process requires that proposed amendments must be initiated in the Texas Legislature and must be approved by two-thirds of the full membership of each house. Once so approved, a proposed amendment must be accepted in a general or special election by a majority of those voting. (The legislature decides which upcoming election ballot will present a given amendment.)

The use of the amendment process gives testimony to the extent to which the constitution gets further out of date with the passage of time. Over the life of the constitution, more and more amendments have been both proposed and adopted (Table 4-1). In recent years Texas voters have been confronted with an election on proposed amendments almost annually, and it has not been uncommon for eight to a dozen amendments to appear on a given year's ballot.

Table 4-1 | **Texas constitutional amendments proposed and adopted, 1880–1991**

	Number Proposed by Legislature	Number Adopted by Election
1880s	13	5
1890s	16	11
1900s	20	10
1910s	32	9
1920s	25	12
1930s	46	34
1940s	39	25
1950s	39	33
1960s	81	55
1970s	74	40
1980s	117	91
1990–91	14	12
Total	**516**	**337**

Sources: Marburger (1956:52–54); May (1972:21); *Texas Almanac* (various years).

64   *Chapter 4*

Another perspective from which to consider the frequency of constitutional amendment in Texas is to compare the Texas and U.S. constitutions. The latter document, ratified in 1789, is almost twice as old as the Texas Constitution. But the U.S. Constitution has only 26 amendments, whereas more than 300 have been added to the Texas Constitution. Moreover, the first 10 amendments to the U.S. Constitution (the Bill of Rights) were added together virtually as part of the process of original ratification. Thus one could fairly argue that the U.S. Constitution has been amended only 16 times.

Voter Turnout for Constitutional Amendments

Proposed constitutional amendments generate little voter interest. When such proposals have been presented in **special elections** (elections in which no races for public office are on the ballot), they have typically drawn less than 20 percent of the registered voters (and much less of the voting-age population) to the polls. Turnout is higher in nonpresidential and particularly presidential **general-election** years but only because of the pull of the races on the ballot. (See Table 4-2, which is based on the most comprehensive study of amendment voting available.)

Recent elections provide good illustrations of the low interest that constitutional amendments stimulate. In November 1988, Texas voters were presented eight constitutional amendments on a ballot headed by the U.S. presidential election. About 5.4 million Texans, or 46 percent of the voting-age population, voted in the presidential race. Yet only slightly more than 4 million of those same voters, or about 35 percent of the voting-age population, were interested enough or persistent enough to vote even on the constitutional amendment that got the most votes. Further evidence of voters' low interest in constitutional amendments is provided by the voting on the 1991 special election ballot, which included thirteen constitutional amendments. One of those proposals—to create a state lottery—had generated remarkable public interest, debate, and media coverage. Further, a number of municipalities were holding their local elections for mayor and council posts at the same time, providing additional inducements for voter

Table 4-2 | **Voter turnout for Texas Constitutional Amendments, 1951–1972**

Elections	Registered Voters Voting (%)
Special (only constitutional amendments on the ballot)	16
Off-year general	39
General, in presidential election years	51

Source: May (1972:20).

turnout. Despite those circumstances, only about 1.9 million Texans, or about 15 percent of the voting-age public, voted on the lottery amendment, which received the most votes on any item on the ballot.

Regardless of the kind of election, one must admit that voter interest in state constitutional amendments is not impressive. Furthermore, in low-turnout elections, those who do vote are unrepresentative of the population at large. Those who go to the polls on such occasions are, on average, of much higher education, income, and social status, and they are much more likely to be Anglos. Thus an untypical sample of Texans makes the decisions about most constitutional amendments.

Results of the Amendment Process

The most obvious result of the process outlined above is that it allows only piecemeal revision of a constitution that most observers would agree is in need of a comprehensive reworking. The passage of time has supplied evidence to support that conclusion, given the increasing frequency with which the legislature must turn to the amendment process. But other factors exacerbate the problems with the constitution and even encourage more amendments, which in turn make it a worse legal instrument.

One problem is that the original detail in the constitution breeds more detail. The constitution's conservative authors went to great lengths to ensure that the government would be constrained in its powers. The result has been that succeeding generations of state leaders—largely a conservative lot, as well—have had to go back time and again to revise first this passage, then another, and yet another in an attempt to keep a highly specific legal instrument relevant to the governmental needs of a changing society.

Nor is detail the only problem. From the first, the constitution has provided a way to secure special economic or political interests. Farmers and local business people in competition with out-of-state interests had their special concerns guaranteed in the constitution as it was first written. Yet those groups only served as examples to others who desired the same security. If one's position could be safeguarded by the constitution, instead of by mere statutory law subject to change by any session of the legislature, it would be far more likely to remain secure. Even a casual examination of the constitution reveals a multitude of such provisions. How else can we explain the presence in the document of the outlines of the state employee retirement system, the Veterans Land Board, the Veterans Land Fund, the state medical education fund to pay scholarships for medical students who promise to practice medicine in rural areas, or the section empowering the legislature to provide financial assistance to the survivors of law enforcement officers killed on duty? How else, as well, might we explain the special tax treatment in the constitution given to agricultural property, including livestock and poultry,

66 *Chapter 4*

and to solar and wind-powered energy devices? Regardless of how worthy such provisions might be, their presence in the constitution instead of in statutory law must be attributed to efforts by special interest groups to seek maximum security for state policies that favor their economic or social positions.

Another way we can evaluate the results of the amendment process is to ask what kinds of proposals have been more and less likely to receive majority voter support at elections. An analysis of this question for amendments voted on in 1951–1972 concluded that voters were mostly negative toward changes in the basic structure of the state government, toward state finance proposals, and toward tax exemptions for special groups. On the other hand, amendments in the fields of education, welfare, and health care and for revising the judicial branch were more likely to be successful (May, 1972:24–25). The fate of more recently proposed amendments appears to have been generally similar—with one qualification.

A strong argument can be made that the amendment process amounts to nothing more than a toss of a coin for the average voter. That is, the true intent of any given amendment is often hidden from the voter. Some of the time, but not all of the time, the special interest proposals are obvious. Some of the time, but again not all of the time, the proposals that relate to serious governmental problems are obvious. Rarely in any case is the significance of the amendment made clear to the average voter.

This problem certainly arises, in part, because most voters do little to acquaint themselves with proposed constitutional amendments. After all, recall how little interest such amendments stimulate among voters. In part the problem also arises because these issues typically receive little media coverage. Unlike races for elected office, elections for constitutional amendments have no human candidate to make speeches, kiss babies, and otherwise communicate directly with voters. Instead, voters must confront ideas in constitutional amendments—and that, for many people, is a far more difficult task.

The state government itself does a poor job of educating the voter with regard to constitutional amendments. Proposed amendments must be published before the election in major newspapers in the state, along with a brief explanatory statement of the intent of the proposed change. The amendment and the explanation for it must also be posted in each county courthouse thirty days prior to the election. The legislature even publishes pro-and-con pamphlets analyzing upcoming amendments. But none of these three advertising methods reaches many voters. Surely many voters give detailed attention to proposed amendments only when they first encounter them on an election ballot.

But consider what a voter will see on such a ballot. The proposed amendments appear last on the ballot and then only in simplified form. As examples of this procedure, the eight amendments presented to the voters in the 1984 election are reproduced in Figure 4-1 exactly as they appeared on the ballot. Although the average voter might fairly surmise that abolishing the office of county treasurer

PROPOSITION NO. 1 — PROPOSICION NÚM. 1

"The constitutional amendment to provide state banks the same rights and privileges as national banks."

(La enmienda a la constitución para darles a los bancos estatales los mismos derechos y privilegios que tienen los bancos nacionales.)

FOR (A FAVOR DE)	239 ▶
AGAINST (EN CONTRA DE)	240 ▶

PROPOSITION NO. 2 — PROPOSICION NÚM. 2

"The constitutional amendment to create from general revenue a special higher education assistance fund for construction and related activities, to restructure the permanent university fund, and to increase the number of institutions eligible to benefit from the permanent university fund."

(La enmienda a la constitución para establecer de ingresos generales un fondo especial de apoyo para la instrucción superior, para propósitos de construcción y otras actividades respecto a eso, para reorganizar el fondo de universidad permanente, y para aumentar el número de instituciones elegibles para aprovecharse del fondo de universidad permanente.)

FOR (A FAVOR DE)	249 ▶
AGAINST (EN CONTRA DE)	250 ▶

PROPOSITION NO. 3 — PROPOSICION NÚM. 3

"The constitutional amendment authorizing the legislature to provide for payment of assistance to the surviving dependent parents, brothers, and sisters of certain public servants killed while on duty."

(La enmienda a la constitución autorizando a la legislatura para suministrar un pago para asistir a los sobreviviente padres, hermanos, y hermanas que dependen de ciertos empleados públicos que hayan muerto durante el cumplimiento de sus obligaciones oficiales.)

FOR (A FAVOR DE)	258 ▶
AGAINST (EN CONTRA DE)	259 ▶

PROPOSITION NO. 4 — PROPOSICION NÚM. 4

"The constitutional amendment to abolish the office of county treasurer in Bexar and Collin counties."

(La enmienda a la constitución para eliminar el puesto oficial de tesorero del condado en los condados de Bexar y Collin.)

FOR (A FAVOR DE)	265 ▶
AGAINST (EN CONTRA DE)	266 ▶

PROPOSITION NO. 5 — PROPOSICION NÚM. 5

"The constitutional amendment authorizing the state senate to fill a vacancy in the office of lieutenant governor."

(La enmienda a la constitución autorizando al senado del estado para llenar una vacancia en el puesto oficial de vicegobernador.)

FOR (A FAVOR DE)	272 ▶
AGAINST (EN CONTRA DE)	273 ▶

PROPOSITION NO. 6 — PROPOSICION NÚM. 6

"The constitutional amendment to permit use of public funds and credit for payment of premiums on certain insurance contracts of mutual insurance companies authorized to do business in Texas."

(La enmienda a la constitución para permitir el uso de fondos y crédito público para pagar las primas sobre ciertos contratos de seguro perteneciendo a compañías de seguros mutuales autorizadas para manejar negocios en Texas.)

FOR (A FAVOR DE)	280 ▶
AGAINST (EN CONTRA DE)	281 ▶

PROPOSITION NO. 7 — PROPOSICION NÚM. 7

"The constitutional amendment relating to the membership of the State Commission on Judicial Conduct and the authority and procedure to discipline active judges, certain retired and former judges, and certain masters and magistrates of the courts."

(La enmienda a la constitución perteneciendo a los miembros de la Comisión Estatal Sobre Conducta Judicial y a la autoridad y procedimiento de castigar a jueces activos, a ciertos jueces retirados y a los que fueron jueces, y a ciertos asesores del juez y magistrados de las cortes.)

FOR (A FAVOR DE)	294 ▶
AGAINST (EN CONTRA DE)	295 ▶

PROPOSITION NO. 8 — PROPOSICION NÚM. 8

"The constitutional amendment to provide a per diem for members of the legislature equal to the maximum daily amount allowed by federal laws as a deduction for ordinary and necessary business expenses incurred by a state legislator."

(La enmienda a la constitución para disponer una asignación por día para miembros de la legislatura igual a la cantidad máxima que se permite diariamente por ley federal como un descuento de los gastos de negocio ordinarios y necesarios incurridos por un legislador del estado.)

FOR (A FAVOR DE)	303 ▶
AGAINST (EN CONTRA DE)	304 ▶

Figure 4-1 | Texas constitutional amendments on election ballot, 1984

68 *Chapter 4*

in Bexar and Collin counties is a minor change of no great significance to state government at large, that voter would have no clue to the importance of the other seven amendments from what appears on the ballot alone. Thus voting on such amendments often becomes a toss of a coin for the average voter.

The problem is not simply the difficulty of separating the trivial from the consequential in the amendment process. Under a constitution like the present one in Texas, the process is inevitably cluttered with both trivial and highly detailed proposed amendments. Special interest proposals will continue to appear from time to time. A highly detailed—and outdated, to boot—constitution that has traditionally been seen as a haven for special interests breeds just such a process. Some proposed amendments appear trivial because they are intended to revise trivial-looking but often quite important elements of the constitution. Others, perhaps the majority, appear highly narrow in their application, again because they are intended to alter specific provisions.

On the last point, one might once again profitably compare the Texas and U.S. constitutions. Because the U.S. Constitution is written in broad rather than specific language, it invites amendments of considerable breadth. The implications of such amendments, though they still can be controversial, are more obvious and of more obvious importance than those that are typically put forward to revise a constitution like that of Texas. Recall, as just one example, the recent and long-running national debate engendered by the proposed Equal Rights Amendment to the U.S. Constitution. Both supporters and opponents of the proposal agree that it would have considerable importance if adopted (although they disagree on what all its consequences would be). Because people recognized how important the proposal was, it received considerable public debate and comment. We should not be surprised, in contrast, to see how little public attention is given to proposed amendments to the Texas Constitution. Nor should we be surprised to see that, in consequence, truly important amendments and even the general importance of the amendment process itself get little public recognition in Texas.

Impacts of the 1876 Constitution

The 1876 constitution affects the present structure and operations of government in Texas in several ways. To summarize the most important of those effects, we can draw upon an excellent series of monographs on the topic, prepared by the Institute of Urban Studies at the University of Houston during the early 1970s—the period of the last effort at comprehensive constitutional reform in the state. By summarizing the institute's conclusions with regard to the major institutional divisions of state government, we can demonstrate the contemporary impact of the 1876 constitution.

Impact on the Chief Executive

Because of significant constitutional limitations on the governor's powers in all the separate areas of traditional executive responsibility (management of the executive branch, control of policy implementation, and recommendation of new policies and programs, to name only a few), the Texas governor is one of the weakest governors in the nation. The Texas governor's power is constrained in several ways: by a **plural executive** at the highest level of state government, in which the governor is only one of several officeholders elected separately by the people; by an executive system that relies heavily on agencies run by multimember boards or commissions that are independent of gubernatorial control; and by limited power vis-à-vis the legislature, thus greatly restricting the governor from fulfilling the role of chief legislator that has been assumed by many other state governors. Fred Gantt (1973:7) has summarized the situation, with a little assistance from someone who knew the office firsthand: "Because of the governor's largely ceremonial role, in which genuine authority is held to a minimum and in which his discretionary powers are carefully limited, former Governor Allan Shivers commented, 'The governor of Texas is something of a paper tiger.'"

Impact on the Executive Branch

Apart from its effect of weakening the governor's power, the plural executive diffuses responsibility for the operation of government in such a way that it is difficult for the public to know who or what agency is responsible for different government functions. Moreover, the plural executive leads to an inflexible executive structure (because it is established in the constitution and not in statutory law) that is difficult to change in response to shifting demands on government (Redford, 1973:73).

The use of the board and commission structure has similar effects. According to Redford (1973:88): "[The structure] fragments administration and insulates it from the influence of the governor in coordination, planning, and budgeting. The constitutional status of boards, either by their creation or by reference to their duties or structure, reduces the ability of the legislature to reorganize the administrative structure of the state." The management of the state's financial matters—whether in budget planning or implementation, in financial reporting, or in the procurement of goods and services—is similarly diffused among a large number of agencies and officials, once again making coordination, control, and even timely implementation difficult (Redford, 1973:97–113).

Impact on the Legislature

The consequences that the present constitutional system has for the legislative branch are aptly summarized in the following passage:

70   *Chapter 4*

Burdened by restrictions from another century, the legislature has been unable fully to rise to the challenges of the present age. Instead of a strong legislature performing its intended tasks of representation, problem resolution, and oversight of state administration, the present legislature is a weakened body constrained by limited biennial sessions, by its inability to review vetoed bills after adjournment, or to call itself into special sessions. These limitations together with constitutionally prescribed salaries, a senate presided over by an executive branch official (i.e., the lieutenant governor), and a multitude of constitutional legislation . . . restrict the legislature's power to act effectively. (Citizens Conference on State Legislatures, 1973:55)

Impact on the Judiciary

Like the other branches of government, the court system suffers from having too much of its structure specified in the constitution, making it difficult to adapt with changing demands on the system. The arrangement of Texas courts—with many different kinds and levels of courts, often with overlapping jurisdiction—is also unnecessarily inflexible, complicated, and confusing (Smith, 1973).

| Conclusion |

This chapter has surveyed the origin of the Texas Constitution and the consequences of that document for contemporary state government. Based on the foregoing survey, it would be fair to say that in some senses the authors of the constitution were highly successful. Their desire to create a low-cost, weak, highly fragmented governmental system has certainly stood the test of time, for such is the kind of government Texas still has today. But that original conception of what government should do and how it should be organized was a product of an entirely different social and political era. Texas was then a predominantly agrarian state with none of the social and economic problems of a large population, high urbanization, and extensive industrialization.

The constitution's authors could not foresee the serious problems that confront Texans today. Nor could they have anticipated that Americans in the twentieth century would radically shift their thinking about government's responsibility for such problems. In the mid-nineteenth century most Americans still held a laissez-faire conception of the appropriate role of government in society (to recall a phrase from the vocabulary of political culture). That is, Americans wanted government to be responsible only for a limited set of social, economic, and security matters.

Yet in the twentieth century, Americans have developed a desire for a quite different sort of government. Political scientists refer to this second type of government as the **positive state**—a government that has substantial responsibility for social and economic welfare. Even the majority of political conservatives today agree that government should have a major role in alleviating poverty in the nation, in guiding the economy to minimize recessions and prevent depressions, in promoting long-term economic growth, in reducing some of the most dangerous hazards of modern life like substantial crime and pollution, and in meeting the special needs of large urban areas in such matters as transportation, education, housing, and health care. Liberals and conservatives may disagree about exactly how big the government's responsibility is in these areas, and they may disagree about the practical policies that ought to be pursued to achieve specific goals; but they agree that government has a role in such matters, a role that exists because the American public has demanded it.

What should now be clear, however, is that the Texas Constitution weakens the state's ability to respond to this new role of positive government. The authors of the constitution produced a document well suited to their interests and their times but difficult to revise as public interests change. It is the citizens of the state who suffer most in this situation, which leaves state government ill-equipped to do what Texans expect of it. Elected officials are hampered in meeting public demands or even in carrying out some of their own too-ambitious campaign promises. Texas government is forced to practice a false economy in which simple cheapness is substituted for efficiency and effectiveness.

For these reasons the state of Texas is in dire need of a complete constitutional overhaul. Yet the state's elected officials at present express no serious interest in such change—and their leadership is certainly crucial as the 1972–1975 revision effort demonstrated. On the other hand, strong public demand for such a change is unlikely because the average Texan seriously misunderstands the character and impact of the state's constitution.

Many of the state's traditional elite groups—in other words, those groups whose interests were long ago provided for in the constitution and who therefore fear any change in the status quo—have promulgated the myth that changing the constitution would destroy the conservative and low-cost character of state government. There is no reason, however, why the state cannot have a modern, though still conservative, governmental system that is capable of addressing the state's problems both energetically and efficiently. In a state with a predominantly conservative citizenry, such as Texas, it is hard to imagine the public's accepting anything but a relatively conservative government.

The average Texan has apparently accepted the myth that constitutional change will bring higher taxes, governmental waste, and too-liberal policies. So far, no public official has come forward to explain the inaccuracy in that myth or the real implications of the current constitution as opposed to alternative arrangements. Thus Texans may have to live with their present constitution quite a bit longer, getting, as a result, far less and far worse government than they expect or deserve.

References

Citizens Conference on State Legislatures. 1973. *The Impact of the Texas Constitution on the Legislature.* Houston: Institute for Urban Studies, University of Houston.

Connor, Seymour V. 1971. *Texas: A History.* New York: Thomas Y. Crowell.

Gantt, Fred, Jr. 1973. *The Impact of the Texas Constitution on the Executive.* Houston: Institute for Urban Studies, University of Houston.

Marburger, Harold J. 1956. *Amendments to the Texas Constitution of 1876.* Austin: Legislative Reference Division, Texas State Library.

May, Janice C. 1972. *Amending the Texas Constitution, 1951–1972.* Austin: Texas Advisory Commission on Intergovernmental Relations.

————. 1977. "Texas Constitutional Revision: Lessons and Laments." *National Civic Review* 66 (February): 64–69.

McKay, Seth Shepard. 1942. *Seven Decades of the Texas Constitution of 1876.* Lubbock: Texas Technological College.

Miller, E. T. 1910. "State Finances of Texas During Reconstruction." *Quarterly of the Texas State Historical Association* 14 (October): 87–112.

Redford, Emmette S. 1973. *The Texas Constitution: Its Impact on the Administration.* Houston: Institute for Urban Studies, University of Houston.

Schumpeter, Joseph A. 1939. *Business Cycles.* Vol. 1. New York: McGraw-Hill.

Searcy, Seth S. 1973. *The Texas Constitution: A Reorganization and Simplification Without Substantive Change.* Austin: Texas Advisory Commission on Intergovernmental Relations.

Smith, Allen E. 1973. *The Impact of the Texas Constitution on the Judiciary.* Houston: Institute for Urban Studies, University of Houston.

Texas Almanac. Various years. Dallas: Dallas Morning News.

Chapter 5

Elections in Texas

Political Parties, Public Participation, and Interest Groups

Elections in democratic societies are intended to be occasions when citizens choose their public leaders and endorse the policies of a set of candidates. Public participation in the election system—and the extent of the opportunities for participation—is therefore an important concern of this chapter. Political parties and interest groups, on the other hand, play a major role in shaping the opportunities for public participation, but the influence of political parties and the system of parties may not be well understood by the average citizen. Most Texans, for example, are well aware of the Democratic party's historical dominance of state politics. Probably few citizens, however, are aware of the consequences of the one-party system for public participation and democracy in Texas.

To understand those consequences, we must first consider the role that political parties are supposed to play in a democratic society. Then, to assess the roles of elections and parties in Texas politics, we will review the origin of the one-party system in Texas and discover how that system has shaped opportunities for public participation in politics.

Interest groups, too, are centrally involved in the election process, and their involvement is shaped by the character of the political party system as well. It is useful to look at the role and importance of interest groups in conjunction with the election system, but interest groups also work to achieve their goals at several other points in the political process. To understand their role at those other points, we will consider interest group activities again in the chapters on the legislature, the executive branch, and metropolitan politics (Chapters 6, 8, and 10).

Political Parties in a Democratic Polity

To understand the place of political parties in a democratic nation, we might begin with a definition of what a political party is. In the words of a leading scholar on the subject, a political party in a democratic nation is "a group that competes for political power by contesting elections, mobilizing social interests, and advocating ideological positions, thus linking citizens to the political system" (Eldersveld, 1982:11). Beyond that simple definition there are, as Eldersveld points out, some notable aspects to the role of political parties. One of those aspects concerns the importance of parties in representing citizen preferences for government policy. The large size of modern nations like the United States precludes the operation of so-called direct democracy—all Americans cannot, for example, sit down together in the same room and take a majority vote on issues of government policy. But political parties make possible the indirect public control of government.

Parties help maintain public control because, first, it is expected that competing parties will form to represent at least the major political interests among all the interests that inevitably arise in a large, diverse society such as that of the United States (or the state of Texas). These different parties will then develop proposed government policies intended to satisfy the interests of their followers. Second, parties actually ensure public control, according to this argument, because the leaders of rival parties must vie for majority public support in elections to be able to control the government and transform their proposals into actuality. Periodically, as well, the leaders of the party in power must stand for reelection, when their efforts at policy making can be reevaluated by the voters (and attacked by the leaders of the out party or parties).

Parties perform many specific political functions in the process of carrying out the general ones just mentioned. They help recruit candidates for office. They assist candidates in organizing and paying for their campaigns. They run much of the apparatus of public elections. They attempt to negotiate with a variety of groups in society to create majority coalitions around mutual political objectives. Once a party controls a major part of the government (by controlling either the White House, the Congress, the governor's office, the state legislature, or the like), its elected leaders work together to shape public policy. But the two most critical functions of parties, and the ones that lie behind all their day-to-day political activities, are to represent the major political interests in the society and to provide a means for public control of at least the principal features of government policy.

Formation of the One-Party System in Texas

The Democratic party's dominance of Texas politics, still evident in the state today, was a product of the last twenty-five years of the nineteenth century, a period of intense political controversy and party competition. It is true that the Democrats had come to dominate the state shortly before the Civil War, coalescing out of a virtual no-party system early in the life of the state. Yet the Civil War and Reconstruction interrupted normal politics, with northern military rule and even Republican party dominance existing for a time during the latter period. The

Elections in Texas 77

termination of military occupation in 1870, however, foreshadowed the end of Reconstruction, when the control of government would be turned back to the white majority of the state. In 1874 the Democratic party regained control of the state's elective offices and began to eradicate many of the traces of Reconstruction government, as we discussed in Chapter 4. But several sources of competition for political dominance remained.

First, considerable numbers of blacks along with some Unionist sympathizers and carpetbaggers had formed the base of support for the Republican party. In the immediate post-Reconstruction period the Republican party could rally between a quarter and a third of the state's voters behind its candidates for governor, and in the so-called Black Belt areas, blacks dominated local politics because of their majority position in the population (Rice, 1971:86–112). Yet white Texans, like the white majority in all the former Confederate states, were not willing to allow blacks the political rights supposedly assured them by the Fourteenth and Fifteenth Amendments to the U.S. Constitution. By a variety of methods— including violence, intimidation, and ballot box fraud—whites quickly began to curtail the political rights of blacks (Barr, 1971:193–208; Rice, 1971:112–150). The final stroke in this process of disenfranchisement, as we will see, did not come until after the turn of the century.

A second threat to Democratic dominance also emerged in the latter part of the nineteenth century. This threat came from the various agrarian protest movements that culminated in the Populist movement in the 1890s. As early as 1875, similar interests had a telling impact on state government when members of the Grange, an early militant farmers' organization, played an important role in the state constitutional convention, as was described in Chapter 4. Later in the century several protest political parties vied for the support of poor whites and dissident poor farmers against the more elitist Democratic party. Thus the Greenback, the Farmers Alliance, and the Populist parties all fielded strong candidates for governor between 1880 and 1900. Moreover, the threat posed by these groups was heightened when the Republican party either ran a coalition candidate together with one of the latter parties or simply gave its official endorsement to one of their candidates and did not run a separate one.

The high tide of these second- and third-party movements peaked in the 1890s. In neither of the gubernatorial elections of 1892 or 1894 did the Democrats win even a majority of the votes cast. Indeed, their candidates won the office only because of the division of the remaining votes among the opposition parties. Furthermore, voter turnout was at an all-time high during this period, in large measure because of the popularity of the causes espoused by these third parties. The threat posed by these parties convinced Democratic party leaders of the necessity for action.

The course of the Democratic party's action in Texas was the same as that followed in every other southern state, all of which were experiencing the same

78 *Chapter 5*

surge of black and poor-white political support for second and third parties. The Democratic party's response took a form that one scholar has called the Bourbon Coup d'État, meaning a subversion of the electoral process by the dominant economic elites to ensure their own control of politics and to minimize the roles of poor dissident groups whether black or white. Although scholars differ on some of the details of how this coup came about, they are in agreement about its general consequences and its role in the formation of the succeeding one-party system (Key, 1949:533–643; Woodward, 1951; Kousser, 1974; Bartley and Graham, 1975:1–11).

The Bourbon Coup employed three tactics. First, the state Democratic party, just like the national Democratic party, co-opted certain policies of the Populist and then the Progressive parties to lure away some of their supporters. Beginning in the late 1880s, the Democrats created a number of state laws—in particular, laws regulating more closely the activities of the railroads, the insurance companies, and various out-of-state corporations operating in Texas—to mollify Populist party voters. Many historians, however, have argued that these and similar reforms actually benefited only the middle and upper classes at best or only the established and wealthy elites at worst (Woodward, 1951:369–395; Kousser, 1974:229–231). Certainly the reforms were, as C. Vann Woodward has put it, "for whites only." Moreover, they were for local whites only. Out-of-state corporate interests—railroads, insurance companies, oil companies—were principal targets of such reforms.

A second Bourbon tactic was to encourage (or simply ignore) the general white backlash against black political participation. Even though blacks constituted a smaller portion of Texas's population than they did in many Deep South states, they still could pose a serious political threat to Texas Democrats. Blacks were concentrated in a few geographic areas, as Chapter 2 indicated, and thus they could wield some power in those areas. Further, blacks provided the core of support for the Republican party in the state and, in coalition with other small parties, could pose a quite serious threat to Democratic control of state government, as they did several times in the 1890s. Thus the white elite stood to benefit directly from the general antiblack sentiment among the Anglo population. By means of violence, ballot box fraud, and collaboration with the state government, local white political leaders had largely disenfranchised most Texas blacks by the turn of the present century.

The third Bourbon tactic was simply to change the rules of the political game—that is, to alter the laws regulating the right to vote in order to minimize participation of the poor and weaken the opportunities of minority parties. One such legal change came about when the poll tax was adopted as a requirement for voting by a constitutional amendment in 1902. Another important change in the rules came in the form of the white primary, under which blacks were denied, by one means or another, the right to vote in Democratic party primaries. Beginning at least in the 1890s, this change was achieved by force and intimidation in a number of Texas counties. Eventually the whites-only feature of these elections was written not only into Democratic party rules but also into state law. Certainly those blacks who paid their poll taxes and weathered white intimidation, or worse, could vote in the general election. After all, the U.S. Constitution guaranteed that right. But in the era of one-party Democratic dominance the real election was the Democratic primary, for that was the only point at which any significant competition existed among candidates. Thus, effective participation in elections was denied blacks by the white primary.

The final rules changes came about when the state adopted the so-called Terrell Election Laws of 1903 and 1905. These changes put into statutory law the poll tax requirement, restructured the party nomination system, and imposed new organizational requirements on all parties. The new requirements were especially onerous for small, ill-developed parties—in other words, all parties except the majority Democrats (Weeks, 1972:205–211; Kousser, 1974:208–209).

Consequences of the One-Party System

The one-party Democratic system that arose from these developments reshaped Texas political life. The most drastic of its consequences was a reduction in public participation in politics (Table 5-1). From a high point of almost 90 percent turnout of voting-age citizens in 1896, for example, participation in gubernatorial elections fell sharply to about one-third of the voting-age population in 1908. Voter participation was slightly higher, but not dramatically so, in the Democratic party primary that preceded each such election. That fact should not be surprising, however, for the primary was the only point at which any real competition occurred in gubernatorial contests. The drop in turnout in presidential elections was equally dramatic, and only rarely did as many as a third of voting-age Texans vote in the presidential contests between 1904 and 1952.

The voter turnout declines in Table 5-1 reflect the shift in political participation that occurred for all three of the state's major ethnic groups, especially the

Table 5-1 | Voter turnout in gubernatorial and presidential elections in Texas, 1880–1908

	Voting-Age Population Voting (%)							
Election	1880	1884	1888	1892	1896	1900	1904	1908
Gubernatorial	69	80	69	76	86	65	36	34
Presidential	69	80	78	79	88	61	30	34

Sources: Kousser (1974:199); U.S. Bureau of the Census (1975:1071–1072); authors' calculations.

ethnic minorities. It has been estimated, for example, that as late as 1940 only 9 percent of black Texans were even registered to vote (Matthews and Prothro, 1966:148). Although comparable estimates are not available for Mexican Americans in Texas, research by V. O. Key (1949:271–274) indicates that they were also often disenfranchised by the rules of the game under the one-party system. Moreover, the bulk of those Mexican Americans who did vote in Texas did so under the orders of a local boss, or *jefe*, who paid their poll tax and told them how to vote in exchange for a job or small favors. The boss himself received political favors from those he helped elect to office (Weeks, 1930).

Such voter disenfranchisement was not unique to Texas but occurred throughout the South. In some of the other southern states the decline in turnout was even more striking than in Texas. In Alabama, Georgia, and Mississippi, as examples, turnout in U.S. presidential elections under the one-party system often was in the range of only 10 to 20 percent of the voting-age population. Another perspective on this aspect of the Bourbon Coup and the beginning of the period of disenfranchisement is gained by comparing the trends in voter turnout in presidential elections for Texas alone, for all the ex-Confederacy states averaged together, and for five moralistic states averaged together (Figure 5-1). The South as a whole and Texas in particular compared favorably with the moralistic states in the late 1880s and early 1890s, but as the Bourbon Coup commenced, turnout plummeted in the South. Turnout declined in the moralistic states as well, as the high tide of

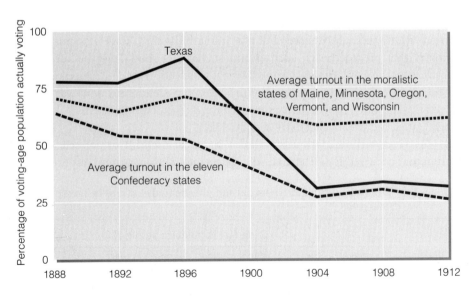

Figure 5-1 | **Voter turnout in presidential elections, 1888–1912**
Source: U.S. Bureau of the Census (1975:1071–1072)

populism receded, but those states continued to have double the turnout of the South through all its years of Democratic one-party control.

The second major consequence of the shift to a one-party system was the elimination of second and third parties as effective competitors in the state. After their peak in the 1890s, the agrarian and other protest parties were able to attract only tiny percentages of voters. Within two decades, most of those parties had vanished from the political scene. The Republican party continued to exist, but it lapsed into a minor, largely ceremonial role. In gubernatorial elections, for example, the GOP would go through the motions of running a candidate, but that candidate would typically garner only 15 to 20 percent of the vote. The outcome was never in doubt; the election was at best a formality. At the party's point of lowest political fortune during the midst of the New Deal and World War II, GOP candidates for governor sometimes polled only 2 to 5 percent of the total vote. Some scholars have argued, in fact, that the sole reason for even the ceremonial existence of the party during this period was to allow its state leaders to dispense whatever federal patronage might come to Texas when a Republican president was in office.

Finally, and most important, political life in the state was controlled during this period by the Democratic party alone. On the surface, the party often gave the appearance of at least some internal competition among its rival leaders, and that competition appeared to give voters some voice in party affairs. After all, they could choose among those leaders in primary elections. The appearance of competition was, however, misleading. Voter participation was quite low, as has already been indicated, because of the Bourbon Coup. Thus the extent of public control even in primaries was limited. In addition, the apparent competition within the party was only a surface phenomenon.

There were often controversial and passionately fought primary election contests between rival Democratic leaders. But rarely did such contests have anything to do with public policy. That is, candidates seldom offered different policy positions among which voters could choose. Instead, candidates often based their campaigns on personality differences, on moral issues like Prohibition, or on symbolic appeals to religious, family, or agrarian values. Thus the governor's office housed such figures as the controversial "Farmer Jim" (or "Pa") Ferguson, a folksy demagogue who rallied rural voters with attacks on the educated and the "city slickers." But once in office, he did little for his rural constituents. Ferguson was impeached in 1917 for misuse of public funds and a number of other charges. He then twice successfully ran his wife, Miriam "Ma" Ferguson, for governor and directed her tenure in office from behind the scenes.

Another governor cut from a similar mold was W. Lee "Pappy" O'Daniel, who first became popular as a radio country singer pumping the sales of his flour company's products with his band, the Light Crust Doughboys. O'Daniel suc-

82   *Chapter 5*

cessfully ran for governor in 1938 and 1940 on a platform advocating the Ten
Commandments and the Golden Rule. O'Daniel's appeal was, as well, to the
country vote, as typified in the campaign song he wrote himself, "Them Hillbillies
Are Politicians Now" (Gantt, 1964:290–291):

Been hangin' round the mountains all these years
Singin' songs about the train-wrecked engineers.
They've been pavin' all the cities
With their pretty corn-fed ditties,
And they've got the politicians all in tears.
They come to town with their guitars
And now they're smokin' big cigars—
Them Hillbillies are politicians now.

Beyond the flamboyant governors were the colorless and the incompetent
ones. Among them surely was Ma Ferguson. Charles Culberson, governor in
1895–1899, perhaps should be best remembered for calling a special session of the
state legislature to pass a law banning prizefights in the state. Joseph D. Sayers and
S. W. T. Lanham, the last governors who had served in the Confederate army, held
office in 1899–1907. They are best remembered (or perhaps remembered only) for
the air of Old South gentility they brought to the governor's mansion. Even in very
recent times the one-party system has produced several lackluster and do-nothing
governors.

The political competition on superficial and symbolic matters obscured the
policy aims that united the Democratic party. Those aims included keeping
government in the hands of a small, traditionalistic, and individualistic elite;
maintaining a state governmental system that was favorable to the economic
interests of such elites; and blocking the participation of groups who might
challenge the favored position of those elites—such as the poor blacks and whites
who had challenged that system in the 1890s. Clearly the Democratic party's
operations under this system differed sharply from the ideal functions of parties
in a democratic society.

Weakening of the One-Party System

The Democratic party still dominates many aspects of Texas politics, but in recent
decades several cracks have appeared in its formerly solid foundation. Although
the one-party system operated virtually undisturbed from the turn of the present
century to perhaps the early 1940s, several forces have been operating to weaken
the party and promote a competitive two-party system.

Socioeconomic Change

One of the major forces acting on the party system has been the socioeconomic change experienced in Texas during this century and discussed previously in Chapters 1 and 2. Most relevant to the party system have been the in-migration of many nonsoutherners to the state, the out-migration of blacks, the decline in the proportion of blacks in the total state population, the urbanization of the state, and the rise of the industrial economy.

A major consequence of these socioeconomic changes has been the formation of a new economic elite—primarily an urban and industrial elite—who have competed at times with the established rural, small-town, and agrarian leaders who traditionally controlled the Democratic party. The party has mostly been able to incorporate the new elite groups, in part because of its solid control of both the state government and elections for seats in the U.S. Congress. Yet in the process of co-opting the new groups, the party has become more diverse, more internally combative, and less able to maintain a united front on major policy issues.

At the same time, some of the new elite and some of the nonsouthern migrants have provided new sources of support for the Republican party. Many of the new elite have found the ideology and membership of the national GOP more suited to their own political interests. Many nonsouthern migrants have, as well, brought Republican party allegiance with them to Texas or have come from states where the party was well accepted and regularly competitive in state politics.

Among all the southern states, Texas has found the economic issues arising from the foregoing changes to be particularly important, because Texas has experienced more rapid socioeconomic change in this century than has the typical southern state. The rapid change, coupled with the relatively small proportion of the Texas population that remained black by the 1940s (in comparison with the typical Deep South state) meant that, first, the racial issue that could unite all whites under one party banner was relatively weaker in Texas and, second, new political issues arising out of economic transformation were relatively stronger.

The Impact of the New Deal

A second force also divided the Democratic party internally—the New Deal revolution in American national politics. Ironically, the nationwide political majority that President Franklin Roosevelt was able to create for the Democratic party carried with it the seeds for the eventual breakdown of the party in the South. That breakdown came about because of the economic and civil rights liberalism of the New Deal.

Texas remained solidly in the fold of the national Democratic party until about the 1940 presidential election. By that time the liberalism of the Roosevelt administration was clear, and many southern political leaders were beginning to support rival presidential candidates vigorously. Southern Democrats in Congress even moved as early as 1937 into an informal liaison with Republicans (known as the Conservative Coalition) to vote in opposition to many of Roosevelt's policy proposals. One of the most Republican-leaning of Democratic legislators was Pappy O'Daniel, who left the Texas governor's office to run successfully for the U.S. Senate in 1941 (Key, 1949:361–362).

In 1944 the Texas Democratic party split sharply over whether to support Roosevelt's reelection, and in 1948 a major break with the national party came in the form of the Dixiecrat party as a southern splinter group. By 1952 the leader of the state Democratic party, Governor Allan Shivers, was campaigning openly for the Republican presidential candidate, Dwight Eisenhower, under the banner of the Shivercrat faction. Shivers even ran for governor in 1952 as the candidate of both the Democratic and Republican parties. His campaign, like O'Daniel's Republican sympathies in the 1940s, was symbolic of the ideological upheaval of the times and demonstrated its influence on party politics in the state.

What had also transpired in Texas by the mid-1940s was the creation of a liberal wing of the Democratic party that endorsed the New Deal policies of the Roosevelt and Truman administrations and attempted to compete with the larger, traditionally conservative elements of the state party. The liberal wing, led at various times by such people as Lyndon Johnson, Ralph Yarborough, and Frances "Sissy" Farenthold, has remained a permanent if minority element of the party to the present day. It has scored occasional election victories, but it has never been able to wrest control of the party from the conservative element.

It was not just among the party leaders that the New Deal had a significant impact on Texas party politics. The liberalism of the New Deal proved too extreme for many of the party's rank-and-file followers, as well. Every Republican presidential candidate since Thomas Dewey in 1948 has received strong electoral support from Texas voters. More important, Republican candidates Eisenhower, Nixon, and Reagan carried the state in 1952, 1956, 1972, 1980, and 1984. Thus many Democrats in the state became what has been called Presidential Republicans—voters who remained Democratic in statewide elections but who were quite willing to vote for a Republican in the presidential race.

The Rise of the Republican Party

A third force in the weakening of the one-party system has been the slow but steady increase in the power of the Republican party in state politics. The most notable events in that process have been Republican victories in elections for major state and national offices. The party's candidates have been successful in Texas in more than half of the U.S. presidential elections since World War II. Other notable victories have been the election of John Tower to the U.S. Senate in 1961, Phil

Gramm to the Senate when Tower retired, and Bill Clements to the governorship in 1978 and 1986. But the total number of local and statewide offices held by Republicans has risen more slowly than these big victories might suggest. As recently as 1970, Republicans held only 10 of 181 seats in the state legislature. By the late 1980s they held a third of the seats in the Texas House of Representatives and about a quarter of those in the State Senate—still far too few to challenge Democratic control of the legislature. They have won only occasional, though still growing numbers of, elections for other statewide offices besides the governorship. Republican strength in local government races has grown slowly, too. The party is especially strong in large metropolitan areas like Dallas and Houston, but it has been less successful elsewhere. In the late 1980s, for example, Republicans held only about 14 percent of all of the state's locally elected positions (Stanley, 1987).

Of more promise for the party is the fact that as many Texans claim to identify with the Republican party today as do with the Democrats. Approximately 30 percent of the voting-age public claims to identify with each of the two major parties, and an equivalent percentage claims to be independents. The Republican party also has an advantage in the preferences of young Texans, which may be a good sign for its future. Whether Texas is a two-party state is debatable and depends on which of the various preceding statistics one thinks best represents the Republican party's size. Yet there is no question that the party plays an important role in Texas politics today. It enjoys sizable representation in the U.S. Congress and the state legislature, its candidates for statewide office run respectable and often successful races, and it is making inroads in local races, especially in metropolitan areas.

Federal Government Intervention

A fourth force operating on the party system has been federal intervention in the election rules. Beginning in the 1940s, a long series of federal court rulings and new legislation from Congress forced a transformation in the election system in Texas and every other southern state. Most of those actions were motivated by the discriminatory aspects of the former election rules—aspects that worked to the disadvantage of ethnic minorities. Yet those changes have also struck down features of the old rules that limited the voting participation of whites as well. In effect, the federal government has eradicated the old electoral system established by the Bourbon Coup, whose purpose was to restrict mass participation in government regardless of race. Thus Texas has moved from a system that discriminated against all ethnic groups to one that should discriminate against none.

The first of these legal changes came about in 1944 when the U.S. Supreme Court struck down the all-white primary. In the case of *Smith* v. *Allwright*, which specifically challenged the Texas all-white primary, the Court ruled that the system violated the Fifteenth Amendment constitutional rights of blacks. As was noted

Chapter 5

above, the all-white primary had appeared as early as the 1890s in some Texas counties, and in 1923 it was established in state law. An earlier Supreme Court ruling in 1927 had declared that such a primary system could not be a feature of state law, but in response the Democratic party had simply made the system a part of its rules and claimed the privilege to do so because it was a private and not a governmental organization. In 1944 the Supreme Court rejected that argument, deciding instead that a political party was "an agency of the state" because it was so closely regulated by state statutes in carrying out its electoral functions. Based on that interpretation, parties were subject to the provisions of the Fifteenth Amendment, which precludes denial of the right to vote on the basis of race by any state or federal government action.

The second major federal action came again from the Supreme Court but not until 1962. In that year and in 1964 the Court ruled in a series of cases (beginning with *Baker* v. *Carr* in 1962 and then with *Reynolds* v. *Sims* in 1964) that both houses of state legislatures should be regularly reapportioned so that each representative or senator would represent virtually the same number of constituents as every other representative or senator. In effect, the Supreme Court called for what has been termed "one man, one vote" apportionment—that is, a system in which each person's vote has the same weight in every election district.

These Court rulings were extremely important because in almost every state in the nation apportionment systems had, over a number of decades, become highly unequal and therefore discriminatory because of inequities in the number of citizens living in different districts. A study of the Texas Legislature in 1963, immediately after it had been reapportioned on the basis of the 1960 census, for example, showed that serious population inequalities remained among districts (Davis, 1965). Some 42 percent of the population could elect a majority of the members of the House of Representatives, and only 30 percent could elect a majority of the Senate. And it was the large, rapidly growing urban areas that were underrepresented by this system.

As a result of this older system of apportionment, rural and small-town areas of the state had greater representation in the Texas Legislature than did urban and rapidly growing areas. That is, rural Texans were able to elect a proportion of state legislators that was far greater than their own percentage of the state's population. Because rural and small-town areas were the heartland of the traditional Democratic party elite, as well, the system gave that elite disproportionate political power over political leaders from the growing urban and industrial centers. The situation was one major means, therefore, by which the traditional elites were able to retain control of both the party and state government even after their own role in the economy and society of the state had been considerably eroded.

The next round of federal intervention in the election system also began in 1964 when the Twenty-fourth Amendment to the U.S. Constitution was ratified, barring the poll tax as a requirement for voting in federal elections. Then, in 1966, the Supreme Court ruled that poll taxes violated the Equal Protection Clause of the Fourteenth Amendment and were, therefore, unconstitutional even in state elections. Texas, like the three other southern states that still employed that requirement for voting, was forced to drop it.

Perhaps the most extensive federal involvement in state election rules was initiated by the Voting Rights Act of 1965. Recognizing the low overall voter turnout in the South, the especially low voting of blacks, and the discriminatory state and local laws that were the probable explanation for the situation, the U.S. Congress passed this act to eradicate such discrimination. The act effectively eliminated all remaining discriminatory requirements like poll taxes and literacy tests, barred any other election laws or procedures that might restrict unfairly the right to vote, and subjected any change in voting or election procedures in the southern states to prior federal government approval to ensure that such changes would not dilute minority voting strength. The act went so far as to provide for federal examiners and election observers to oversee voter registration procedures and elections. The Voting Rights Act was extended for five years without change in 1970. Then, when the act was extended the second time in 1975, Hispanics and several other language groups were also given protection under its coverage. Finally, the act was extended in 1982 for another twenty-five years. The results of the Voting Rights Act in Texas were to place all Texas election procedures under federal government scrutiny, to ensure that all remaining restrictive election laws and practices were eliminated, and to encourage energetic voter registration efforts aimed at minority citizens of the state.

Finally, in 1971 a lower federal court found the system of voter registration in Texas in violation of the Equal Protection Clause of the Fourteenth Amendment. The culprits in this instance were the requirement for annual reregistration and the early deadline for registration (effectively, nine months before the customary November general election date). These requirements were found by the court to have discriminatory impacts on the registration of ethnic minorities. In response to this ruling the state has developed a system of virtually permanent voter registration with a far more lenient maximum waiting period of only thirty days between initial registration and ability to vote.

Changes in Public Participation

One result of the preceding changes in election and suffrage laws is that public involvement in Texas politics has expanded significantly since the 1940s (Table 5-2). Texans of all ethnic groups have benefited from these changes. Although comparable estimates for Mexican Americans are not available, the data for blacks and whites in Table 5-2 support this contention. Black voter registration jumped almost fourfold between the Supreme Court's decision in *Smith* v. *Allwright* (1944) and 1960. White voter registration did not change in that period, but white voters

88 Chapter 5

Table 5-2 | **Texas voter registration and turnout in presidential elections, 1940–1984**

Involvement	1940 (%)	1960 (%)	1980 (%)	1984 (%)
Voting-age white Texans registered	42	43	75	82
Voting-age black Texans registered	9	35	56	72
Total Texas voting-age population voting in presidential election	30	42	45	47

Sources: Matthews and Prothro (1966:148); U.S. Bureau of the Census (1975:1071–1072; 1983:261, 264; 1987:244, 245; authors' calculations.

were not affected by *Smith* v. *Allwright* and had not suffered unique discrimination in terms of access to the primary election as had blacks. After 1960, however, and with the banning of the poll tax and other restrictive aspects of the registration system, the registration of both groups increased dramatically.

In presidential elections the voting turnout of Texans has increased by about half since 1940. That is a considerable improvement, but the state still lags behind the national average. In the 1988 presidential election, for example, 46 percent of voting-age Texans voted, whereas the nationwide turnout was 50 percent and some moralistic states had turnouts in the range of 60 to 66 percent. Although the turnout in Texas has been moving closer to the national average, the nationwide voter turnout in presidential elections has itself been slowly declining since a peak of 63 percent in 1960. That decline has made Texas's relative performance look better.

Reasons for Low Voter Turnout in Texas

Several explanations have been advanced to account for the continued low involvement of Texans in politics (in comparison with national averages). One of those explanations concerns the historical legacy of the traditionalistic political culture. For decades traditionalistic values framed Texans' thinking about politics. Public participation was not highly encouraged. Reliance on the wisdom of political elites, rather than the dependence of those elites on the public, was emphasized. And as we have seen, political elites created a system of suffrage and elections that reinforced the values taught in the traditionalistic culture. Public involvement in politics was sharply limited. What participation was allowed was largely ritualistic: the party of the ultimately successful candidate was never in doubt, and no public policy matters of great consequence were to be settled by elections.

In the past the absence of two-party competition contributed to low public participation—as the limited extent of such competition does today. States with meaningful two-party competition consistently evidence greater public involvement in politics than do one-party states. Texas itself provides evidence for that conclusion, given that public involvement was quite high in the state in the 1880s and 1890s when second and third parties were strong. As we noted earlier, a competitive second party helps mobilize opposition against the in party. It serves as the constant critic of the in group, as well, keeping its failures in the public eye. And second parties can appeal to those in society whose interests are being ignored by the dominant party. Thus the continued weakness of Texas's second party contributes to the low level of public involvement.

The potentially beneficial effects of two-party competition in Texas are limited, however, because both the Democratic and Republican parties wish to appeal primarily to conservative voters. Both parties have traditionally offered little in the way of specific proposals to aid the liberals, the poor, or the minorities in the state. Hence what might generally be called the liberal interests in Texas have been given little attention as both parties play to the middle-of-the-road and conservative elements.

One final element discourages public participation in politics in Texas: the demographics of the state's population. Research on political participation in the contemporary United States has demonstrated that certain kinds of people are more likely than others to vote and engage in political activities. For example, Americans nationwide who are white, older, wealthier, and better educated tended to vote in greater numbers in the 1988 presidential election (Table 5-3).

It is generally argued that persons of higher education, wealth, and so on have been better socialized into moralistic and participatory values, regardless of the dominant political culture of the state where they reside. Similarly, such people show greater interest in politics and higher levels of what is called **political efficacy**, the belief that one's personal involvement can directly influence political outcomes. Such people typically have a set of political beliefs—a product of their socialization and life experiences—that supports the value of democratic political participation. In contrast, the poor, the less well educated, the ethnic minorities, and even relatively young voters typically have less interest in politics and much weaker political efficacy. Thus the lower voting turnout of these groups can be explained in the same terms.

As was demonstrated in Chapter 2, the population of Texas has significant percentages of some of these low-participation groups. More than a third of the population is composed of ethnic minorities. The low participation of blacks and Mexican Americans is explainable partly by the political role they were socialized to accept during the era of one-party government and partly by the fact that so many of them are relatively poor and poorly educated. Texas also has a notable number of poor and poorly educated whites who contribute to the low public participation in the state.

Table 5-3 | **Participation of national electorate in 1988 presidential election**

Demographic Characteristic	Percentage Reporting Having Voted
Age	
18–20	33
21–24	38
25–34	48
35–44	61
45–54	67
55–64	69
65–74	73
75 and over	62
Years of Schooling	
8 or fewer	48
9–11	53
12	65
More than 12	78
Ethnicity	
Black	52
Spanish-surnamed	29
White	59

Source: U.S. Bureau of the Census (1989).

These demographic factors help explain the current levels of public involvement of Texans in politics, but one should not make too much of these factors or generalize them out of their context. They refer only to the character of participation in the contemporary United States. In Texas in the 1890s, as in most of the nation at that time, participation was high among all groups, including the poor, the poorly educated, and the recently enfranchised blacks. The high participation in that earlier era was a product of a dramatic set of political issues, but it was also the result of a competitive party system and liberal suffrage laws. Thus demographic factors may be important today, but they are themselves influenced by the party system, the electoral system, and the nature of the political times.

| Obstacles to Two-Party Competition |

Public participation in Texas elections has been transformed in the last thirty years. Competition between rival factions has increased in the Democratic party, and the Republicans have made significant inroads. Indeed, Texas could be fairly described as a two-party state, at least in presidential elections. Why, then, one might ask, has the progress toward a two-party system been so much slower in state elections? The answers to this question provide additional perspectives on the evolution of election and party systems.

One principal difficulty for the Republican party in all of the South has been the traditional conservatism of the local Democratic party. Although the national Democratic party—both in Congress and as represented in many of the party's presidential nominees—has been considerably more liberal since the New Deal, southern Democrats have on the whole remained highly conservative on the issues of major interest to southern voters. Thus the Democratic party in the South has occupied the ideological ground that the Republicans themselves would typically hold. Democratic leaders in the South have even made explicit their dissatisfaction with the liberal wing of their party, going so far at times as to openly support Republican nominees for the presidency.

The conservatism of the typical southern Democrat makes Republican electoral strategy far more problematic. Republicans must make more sophisticated distinctions between themselves and the Democrats. They must present themselves as different kinds of conservatives or as more honest or more capable leaders. Clearly such arguments are difficult to substantiate and therefore may not prove convincing to many voters. It would be much easier for the Republicans if they were able simply to write off their opponents with a single verbal stroke as "liberals" and then to occupy the conservative territory alone.

The longtime dominance of the Democratic party and the traditional view that its primary constituted the real election for most state and local offices have also worked to the disadvantage of the Republicans. Many voters who might otherwise prefer to vote Republican probably feel that to have any influence on the outcome of state elections they must vote in the Democratic primary. Thus the GOP primary attracts fewer voters and less attention than it otherwise would. The Republican voter's best strategy at this point is also uncertain. Should Republicans vote for the most conservative candidate in the Democratic primary to help ensure, at the least, that a conservative will win the general election? Or should they vote for the more liberal Democratic candidate in the primary and then vote for the Republican in the general election, hoping that the general election will be between the liberal Democrat and a Republican more suited to the conservative temperament of the state? Or should the Republican voter ignore the Democratic primary to participate in the GOP contest, knowing that a conservative Democrat will probably face a conservative Republican in the general election? The potential force of Republican voters is probably dissipated in many elections because some choose the first alternative, some the second, and some the third.

Yet another factor has limited the growth of the Republican party in Texas: the use of the **long ballot** in state and local elections. The term *long ballot* refers to a system whereby voters elect a large number of executive officers rather than a single chief executive who then appoints his or her principal subordinates. The most notable example of the long ballot is that for state executive officers. Texans elect, in separate races, not only the governor but also the lieutenant governor, the attorney general, the state treasurer, the comptroller of public accounts, the commissioner of the General Land Office, the commissioner of agriculture, and the board members who head the Railroad Commission and the State Board of Education. One might contrast this system with that of the federal government, in which voters choose only among tickets of candidates for the presidency and the vice presidency to head the entire executive branch. Once elected, a president then appoints all the cabinet officers and a large number of other high-level executive branch officials, creating in the process an entire administration devoted to the pursuit of the president's policy goals.

The long ballot is particularly disadvantageous for small second parties attempting to compete with a large, well-established party such as the Democrats in Texas. The smaller party has a difficult time finding a sufficient number of attractive, experienced, or well-known candidates to run for all the positions on the long ballot. It often has difficulties, as well, in attracting the funds to pay for a large number of such campaigns. Thus when the occasional Republican scores a major campaign victory, he or she may stand virtually alone in a forest of Democrats elected to other posts. In effect, executive power is highly dispersed in such a system, and winning a single election places only a small portion of such power in the control of the second party.

An excellent example of the effects of the long ballot came about in 1978 when Bill Clements was first elected to the governorship. Republicans were jubilant, but all the other state executive offices and 85 percent of the seats in the state legislature were held by Democrats. Clements had almost no one even to talk to in Austin from his own political party. A strong argument can be made that in the succeeding four years Texans learned nothing about what a Republican administration could really have accomplished. Clements had so little control over the executive branch of the state, despite occupying its highest office, that his power was severely limited. When he was reelected to the governorship in 1986, Clements found himself in much the same situation. (A number of other important consequences of the long ballot, beyond their impact on party politics, are considered in detail in Chapter 7.)

Some changes in the party system have likely been held back, too, through tinkering with the election calendar. Before the 1974 election, the governor and other chief state executive officers served two-year terms and ran for election in November of even-numbered years—on the same election day when the U.S. presidential race was held every four years and, in the intervening even-numbered years, when U.S. congressional elections were always held. That pre-1974 system led to a particularly high voter turnout in every other state election—in those years when the high-stimulus presidential election headed the ballot. In the intervening election years, when only congressional and senatorial races would be on the ballot along with those for state offices, voter turnout would average about 20 to 25 percentage points lower. Coincident gubernatorial and presidential elections also meant that the state office candidates running under the same party banner as a popular presidential candidate might ride into office on the latter's coattails. Thus state political races might get caught up in national political movements.

In 1971, however, the Democrat-controlled state legislature approved for submission to the voters what appeared to be an unrelated reform proposal: to give the governor a four-year instead of a two-year term of office. That proposal was primarily justified by the argument that the four-year term would give the governor more time to develop a program while having to spend less time running for reelection. That argument and related ones addressed the legitimate concern that the two-year term unnecessarily restricted a governor's ability to meet the demands of the office. But the proposed amendment also stipulated that gubernatorial elections would be held in off years, or nonpresidential election years. This schedule was justified by the argument—proposed by the Texas Legislative Council, a research arm of the legislature—that it would generate greater interest in state politics (Texas Legislative Council, 1972:26).

The proposed amendment was approved by the voters in the 1972 general elections and took effect with the 1974 state elections. But contrary to the argument of the Texas Legislative Council, the result of the reform was that voter turnout in gubernatorial elections remained at the traditionally lower level of off-year contests (Table 5-4). Although turnouts in these elections have gradually increased, they are still considerably lower than those in presidential years.

Table 5-4 | **Voter participation in Texas gubernatorial elections, 1972–1990**

Year	Percentage of Voting-Age Population Who Voted
1972	44
1974	20
1978	26
1982	30
1986	29
1990	32

Sources: U.S. Bureau of the Census, *Statistical Abstract of the United States* (various years).

94   *Chapter 5*

The precise motivations of those who proposed the reform are not known, but the net result was clearly twofold. The altered election calendar reduced the electoral role of poor and minority voters—the people shown by research on voter turnout to be the least likely to participate in low-stimulus, off-year elections. In effect, the change eliminated some of the expansion of popular participation in elections that had been achieved largely under federal pressure since the 1940s. It thus helped the traditional leaders of the Democratic party regain some of the control over party affairs that had been threatened in the last several decades. At the same time, the change meant that highly popular Republican presidential candidates could not induce Presidential Republicans in the state to become full-fledged Republicans on election day. Hence the prospects for continued Democratic control of state government were clearly enhanced.

Interest Groups in a Democratic Polity

Interest groups are formal, private organizations that attempt to influence government decision making by involving themselves in election campaigns and by lobbying government officials directly. Like political parties, interest groups can play an important and positive role in the working of a democratic government. They can facilitate the communication between citizens and government by making known the political views of particular groups. In Texas the interests of such diverse groups as accountants, farmers, oil companies, environmentalists, and Mothers Against Drunk Drivers (MADD) are introduced into political debates.

To represent the views of their members and sympathizers, interest groups do many things that political parties also do. They help recruit candidates for public office (who must, of course, become the nominees of parties). They contribute and encourage campaign funds for candidates. They also advertise their views on prominent political issues to the general public, in the hope of encouraging widespread support for those views. What an interest group does uniquely, however, is to lobby government officials to convince them of the wisdom of the group's position. Thus nearly all elected officials and executives and even heads of executive branch agencies are routinely lobbied by such groups.

Lobbying also has promulgated a negative image for interest groups. At times they seemingly try to persuade government officials to ignore the general public interest and adopt the special interests of a particular, narrow group. At times lobbying also has the appearance of buying political favors with campaign contributions and other benefits for public officials. Lobbyists sometimes seem to have easy access to sympathetic government officials even when members of the general public find that those officials are distant and difficult to influence.

Thus, determined, well-organized interest groups of all kinds have at least the possibility of getting some response from government. A large membership, a high level of professional expertise, or good organization can offset limited financial resources. Of course the larger, the more prestigious, and the better-funded the group, the more likely it will enjoy such political good fortune. But even small or ill-funded interest groups can be politically successful.

The negative image that interest groups endure is sometimes well-deserved. Yet these groups can, as we observed earlier, assist the democratic process. In large diverse societies, many social, cultural, and economic interests may be affected by government. As government grows in its power and responsibility, its influence on those interests becomes more prominent. For that reason many Texans might wish to have a voice in the making of government policy. At the same time, most people will not take the time personally to carry through on that wish. Government is too distant and sometimes too complex for citizens to know how to make their views known effectively. And the time, expense, and energy necessary to do so prevent many citizens from making any effort.

Many Texans are surely happy, then, that interest groups exist that share their political preferences and that regularly press those views on government. Those employed in the oil business, those concerned about environmental matters, and those favoring pari-mutuel betting—to name but a few of many possibilities—have been recent beneficiaries of such organized efforts. Thus most people would readily agree that their own interest groups are good and legitimate in their efforts to influence government and that it is only those other groups that are the bad ones and deserve the negative image.

Checks on Interest Group Power

The contradiction in the preceding conclusion about attitudes toward interest groups is readily apparent, but it also attests to the two-sided role interest groups can play in our government. They can be highly beneficial to the democratic process, but they can also be highly detrimental to it if the broad public interest is subverted by their efforts. To ensure that such groups perform in only a beneficial way, checks must be placed on their unique powers of organization, financial capability, and access to government officials. Those checks can arise out of the number and diversity of (and hence competition among) interest groups, out of the political culture, out of the political party system, or out of the activities of government institutions.

Socioeconomic Structure

One of the strongest influences on interest group power is the character of the socioeconomic structure of the state. States with relatively homogeneous economies have fewer but more powerful interest groups than do states with more diverse, complex, and developed economies (Zeigler, 1965).

Advanced economic development creates diversity in the economy and accords significant economic power to a broad range of economic sectors and interests. Homogeneity, on the other hand, typified by a state with an economic system highly dependent on only a few key industries, means that the leaders of those key industries have by far the highest economic and, hence, political status in the state. Homogeneity also means that few alternative centers of private power exist to compete against the primary ones in efforts to influence state politics.

We have noted that throughout most of this century the Texas economy has relied on agriculture and on the extraction of natural resources like oil and gas. That period was one of economic homogeneity that ensured the political power of interest groups from agriculture and the oil and gas businesses. We have seen, too, that recent social and economic changes like advanced industrialization, high-tech development, and urbanization have begun to diversify the economy and society of Texas. These changes mean that new centers of economic power are developing to compete with the old ones and with each other. Over time this process should mean the weakening of older interest groups and, perhaps, of all groups collectively.

Political Culture

A second check on the power of interest groups can arise out of the political culture of the state. The viewpoints of the three basic political cultures with regard to the advancing of private interests through politics were explained in Chapter 3.

Under individualism, advancing one's private interests through political activity is culturally acceptable. That culture, in fact, has a particularly open and sympathetic attitude toward such efforts. The traditionalistic culture has a similar but slightly restrictive attitude toward self-advancement. Under traditionalism, only the social elites are expected to advance their private interests through the political arena. Such private action is justified as the prerogative of the elite, or it is rationalized as actually being in the interests of the entire state. In a moralistic society, finally, cultural norms discourage private gains through political action. Political activity in such a society is supposed to serve the broad public interest.

Texas, we recall, has a mixed individualistic and traditionalistic culture with just a few strands of moralism. Thus interest group power arising from political culture has few of the restraints that are present in more moralistic states. Indeed, we must conclude that the political culture of Texas actually encourages interest group activity in the pursuit of narrow private interests.

Political Party System

A third characteristic of states that has been linked to the strength of interest groups is the nature of the political party system. States whose governments are regularly controlled by only one political party typically also have especially powerful interest groups (Zeigler, 1965). As we noted in our earlier discussion of the political party system in Texas, one-party dominance of state politics has inevitably meant that not all legitimate interests will be well represented in politics. The existence of two competing parties broadens the range of interests represented and creates competition among different points of view for influence over political decisions. A two-party system does not inevitably weaken the power of interest groups, but at the least it fosters greater competition among the most influential groups and less likelihood that one or a small number of groups will dominate the state.

Another consequence of a one-party system lies in the possible influence of small interest groups in addition to that of the biggest and best-known organizations. In a one-party state, like Texas, a small and little-known group representing narrow interests can be quite influential simply by gaining the support of the leaders of the one major party. Such groups as the Texas Automobile Dealers Association, the Texas Brewers Association, and the Texas Association of Realtors, to name a few examples, can have considerable impact on certain aspects of government and policy. In a two-party system, by contrast, the power of small interest groups will at times be limited because the members of one of the two parties oppose a particular group's policy demands. For especially big and powerful organizations, the situation is somewhat different. Acknowledged powerful interest groups will typically get at least a hearing from both parties.

Thus in a state like Texas a variety of interest groups can at times be quite influential with respect to government policy that concerns their members. Naturally, the longtime dominance of Texas politics by the Democratic party has meant that Texas has not enjoyed the benefit of the two-party check on interest group power.

Character of the State Legislature

We observed earlier that checks on interest groups can arise out of the activities of governmental institutions. Such checks can take several forms, but a particularly important one for Texas concerns the level of professionalism of the state legislature. In general, the lower the level of legislative professionalism, the greater the likelihood that interest groups can sway the decision making of that governmental body. Unprofessional legislatures have members who are relatively ill-qualified for their positions, have a high turnover of members, pay their members low salaries, and provide only limited technical and staff resources for legislative decision making. In Chapter 6, we will explain in more detail both why lobbyists more easily influence unprofessional legislatures and what methods lobbyists use to exercise their influence.

Unfortunately, Texas has one of the least professional state legislatures in the nation. Again, the details explaining that phenomenon are presented in Chapter 6. We can conclude here, however, that legislative professionalism is one other

98   *Chapter 5*

possible check on interest group power from which Texans derive no benefit. In fact, Texans are significantly disadvantaged because of the character of their legislature.

Interest Group Power in Texas

All of the conditions cited above actually strengthen rather than check the power of interest groups in Texas. Indeed, throughout its history, Texas has been an excellent example of how interest groups can be especially powerful. One of the best early illustrations of that power comes from the Constitutional Convention of 1875, which wrote the state's present constitution. As we explained in Chapter 4, that convention was dominated by the political interests of the Grange, a powerful farmers' organization. The content of the new constitution, and thus the character of Texas government and public policy, was shaped to conform to the interests of the Grange. Agrarian interests remained important in Texas for many years, but the development in the twentieth century of the oil and gas industries produced powerful new rivals for the control of state government. Those groups became so important that in the 1940s the chairman of the Democratic party's State Executive Committee admitted, "It may not be a wholesome thing to say, but the oil industry today is in complete control of state politics and state government" (Stilwell, 1949:315).

Economic homogeneity, Democratic party domination, restricted public participation in elections, and the character of the state's political culture also meant that particular kinds of interest groups would be most powerful. Established business interests and professional groups linked to the dominant economic sectors—and favoring conservative, status quo–oriented policies—were overwhelmingly advantaged. The operations of parties, elections, and interest groups served to reinforce one another to keep the system in place to benefit those interest groups.

Socioeconomic development has been the only notable change that should moderate interest group power in Texas. Because the state has become more complex socially and economically, many new interests desirous of influencing governmental decisions now exist. Although agriculture and the oil business remain quite powerful economically and politically, their declining fortunes have weakened their political clout. The state's minority ethnic groups are becoming more outspoken and aggressive in pressing their demands on state government. In time these changes should moderate the degree to which the traditional establishment interests dominate state politics. Yet much of that change will come about as new groups displace the old ones. In other words, interest groups could, in the future, remain powerful collectively, but some shifting in their relative power and some enhanced competition among them will occur.

Three research projects on the power of interest groups in state politics, executed years apart, confirm both the traditional and the continuing power of such groups in this state. The first of the studies found that in the early 1950s Texas was one of twenty-four states having especially strong interest groups involved in state politics (Zeller, 1954). More recently, Morehouse (1981) and Hamm and Wiggins (forthcoming) found Texas still to be among the states with especially powerful interest groups. The only change from the 1950s was that the list of powerful groups in the state was now lengthier. Hamm and Wiggins, for example, concluded that the most powerful groups in the 1980s were the Texas Trial Lawyers Association, the Texas Medical Association, the Texas Association of Realtors, the Texas State Teachers Association, the "big oil" lobby (which is principally represented by the Texas Mid-Continent Oil and Gas Association), the Texas Motor Transportation Association, the Texas AFL-CIO, the Independent Oil and Gas Producers Association, the Texas Chemical Council, the Texas Association of Business, and the Texas Savings and Loan League.

Interest Groups and Elections

One of the major methods by which interest groups seek to influence government policies is by helping secure the election of candidates for office who are sympathetic to their views. Principally through campaign contributions to such candidates, interest groups hope to ensure that the government will be run by people with their concerns favorably in mind. Naturally, relatively wealthy interest groups with well-heeled members have considerable advantages. The influence of sizable campaign contributions has become especially critical in recent years because of the rising—and astronomical—costs of major election campaigns. A few recent examples will illustrate both the high costs of election campaigns and the key role that major interest groups play in defraying those costs.

Mark White, in his 1982 election to the governorship over the incumbent Bill Clements, spent almost $9 million in his campaign. Although that figure is staggering, Clements spent over $13 million in his losing campaign. Even more interesting, however, is what happened after the election. On election night in November 1982, Mark White was still in debt for almost $5 million in loans used to finance his campaign. Yet by the time he filed his final campaign finance report in January 1983, his loans had been completely paid off. That $5 million debt was eliminated in less than two months because of the rush of business lobbies and interest groups—many of whom had backed Clements before the election—to bring their presence and interests to the attention of the newly elected governor (McNeely, 1983; *Texas Observer*, 1983). The groups sought that attention, of course, by being openhanded with contributions to help eliminate White's debt.

100   *Chapter 5*

One might think such a situation would arise only with a newly elected Democratic governor, but it was repeated in 1986 when Bill Clements ousted White from the governorship. On election day in 1986, Clements's campaign was $4.5 million in debt. But a large number of lobbyists, many of whom had supported White in the campaign, "bought a ticket on the late train" after the election, making substantial contributions to Clements to help pay off his debt. Ann Richards benefited in the same way from lobbyists' generosity after her come-from-behind victory in the 1990 gubernatorial race. She received over $3 million in campaign contributions between election day in November and the end of the year.

Interest groups give funds to candidates for many other offices besides the governorship, of course, and considering how they do so allows us to illustrate another important dimension of their political power. Virtually all interest groups have formed associated organizations called political action committees, or PACs, to meet the requirements of laws regulating their campaign activities. PACs actually make the interest groups' campaign contributions and report them, as necessary, to the state and federal governments. PAC money—and, hence, interest group money—is critically important to candidates for office today. One study of all the members of the Texas Senate, for example, found that they received 50 percent of all their campaign contributions from PACs in 1983 (*Houston Post*, 1984). A more recent study found that members of the Texas Legislature who chaired committees in that body received 62 percent of all their contributions from PACs in 1990 (*Houston Post*, 1991). Some of the latter legislators received over 90 percent of their funds from PACs. We must conclude, then, that the longtime importance of interest groups to Texas politics is considerably reinforced today by the role they play in campaign finance.

| Conclusion |

This survey of the Texas electoral system has shown that, for many years, Texas politics were not very democratic. Indeed, the party system and ultimately the government were dominated by conservative elites with only minimal and virtually ritualistic public involvement. One feature commonly thought to be standard in American democracy—that of regular two-party competition—simply did not exist in Texas or in the rest of the South after the Bourbon Coup. Even today, the extent of two-party competition in Texas state politics is somewhat limited. Thus the two-party pattern is not inevitable or even indispensable, even though it has often been presented in just those terms in civic education courses in the United States.

Recent years have witnessed the operation of powerful forces both encouraging and retarding the breakdown of the Texas one-party system. Political theory concerning the functions of political parties in a democracy suggests that a two-party system is preferable, but change toward a two-party system in Texas is proceeding slowly. To some extent, that change has been driven by social and economic changes in the state, but outside forces like federal government intervention have been equally important.

Yet it appears that the Republican party will continue to grow. Perhaps more important for Texas party politics in the near future, however, will be the internal struggles of the Democratic party. That party cannot be dominated as completely today by a narrow elite as it was even ten or twenty years ago. The state has become far too diverse and far too different from the social and economic circumstances that supported the old system. One result of that diversity has been the appearance of new elite groups whose interests are at times divergent from and at other times common with those of the older elite.

Another important change for the Democratic party has been an increase in the political activity of the state's ethnic minorities. Blacks and Mexican Americans, who have traditionally been left at the bottom of Texas society, are now demanding more of the government—with the clout of large numbers of potential voters behind their demands. The Democratic party's success in resolving its internal divisions and responding to an increasingly diverse society in the state may well decide the Republican party's future success.

References

Barr, Alwyn. 1971. *Reconstruction to Reform: Texas Politics, 1876–1906*. Austin: University of Texas Press.

Bartley, Numan V., and Graham, Hugh D. 1975. *Southern Politics and the Second Reconstruction*. Baltimore: Johns Hopkins University Press.

Davis, Clarice McDonald. 1965. *Legislative Malapportionment and Roll-Call Voting in Texas, 1961–1963*. Austin: Institute of Public Affairs, University of Texas.

Eldersveld, Samuel J. 1982. *Political Parties in American Society*. New York: Basic Books.

Gantt, Fred, Jr. 1964. *The Chief Executive in Texas: A Study in Gubernatorial Leadership*. Austin: University of Texas Press.

Hamm, Keith E., and Wiggins, Charles W. Forthcoming. "Texas: The Transformation from Personal to Informational Lobbying." In Ronald J. Hrebenar and Clive S. Thomas (eds.), *Interest Group Politics in the Southern States*. Tuscaloosa: University of Alabama Press.

Houston Post. 1984. "Texas Officials Got $5 Million in Contributions." April 28, p. A6.

———. 1991. "Panel Chairmen Say PACs Don't Influence Their Actions." March 3, p. A28.

Key, V. O. 1949. *Southern Politics in State and Nation*. New York: Vintage Books.

Kousser, J. Morgan. 1974. *The Shaping of Southern Politics: Suffrage Restriction and the Establishment of the One-Party South, 1880–1910*. New Haven: Yale University Press.

Matthews, Donald R., and Prothro, James W. 1966. *Negroes and the New Southern Politics*. New York: Harcourt Brace Jovanovich.

McNeely, Dave. 1983. "Lobbyists 'Buy Ticket on Late Train' or Risk Being Left Out." *Austin American-Statesman*, January 23, p. C1.

Morehouse, Sarah McCally. 1981. *State Politics, Parties, and Policies*. New York: Holt, Rinehart & Winston.

Rice, Lawrence D. 1971. *The Negro in Texas, 1874–1900*. Baton Rouge: Louisiana State University Press.

Stanley, Jeanie R. 1987. "Party Realignment and the 1986 Texas Elections." *Texas Journal of Political Studies* 9 (Spring–Summer): 3–13.

Stilwell, Hart. 1949. "Texas: Owned by Oil and Interlocking Directorates." In Robert S. Allen (ed.), *Our Sovereign State*. New York: Vanguard Press.

Texas Legislative Council. 1972. *Fourteen Proposed Constitutional Amendments Analyzed*. Austin: Texas Legislature.

Texas Observer. 1983. "Political Intelligence." February 11.

U.S. Bureau of the Census. 1975. *Historical Statistics of the United States*. Pt. 2. Washington, D.C.

———. 1983. *Statistical Abstract of the United States, 1984*. Washington, D.C.

———. 1987. *Statistical Abstract of the United States, 1987*. Washington, D.C.

———. 1989. *Statistical Abstract of the United States, 1989*. Washington, D.C.

Weeks, O. Douglas. 1930. "The Texas-Mexican and the Politics of South Texas." *American Political Science Review* 24 (August): 606–627.

———. 1972. "Texas: Land of Conservative Expansiveness." In William C. Havard (ed.), *The Changing Politics of the South*. Baton Rouge: Louisiana State University Press.

Woodward, C. Vann. 1951. *Origins of the New South, 1877–1913*. Baton Rouge: Louisiana State University Press.

Zeigler, L. Harmon. 1965. "Interest Groups in the States." In Herbert Jacob and Kenneth N. Vines (eds.), *Politics in the American States: A Comparative Analysis*. Boston: Little, Brown.

Zeller, Belle. 1954. *American State Legislatures*. New York: Thomas Y. Crowell.

Chapter 6

The Legislature

The Texas Legislature is the lawmaking institution of the state government. Yet the legislature has several important functions beyond simply making new laws. Its ability to fulfill any of those functions is profoundly affected by constitutional requirements for its structure and by other aspects of its procedures and practices as they have developed over the years. Before we consider those procedures and practices, however, it is worthwhile to review the judgments of a number of other observers about the character of the Texas Legislature.

The Image of the Texas Legislature

The Texas state capitol—the meeting place of the legislature—was built between 1883 and 1888. To pay for the new statehouse, the legislature authorized one of the biggest "horse trades" in history: more than 3 million acres of land in the Texas Panhandle in exchange for the construction of the building. Some historians have argued that the state got quite a good deal out of the trade, because the eventual construction cost of the Capitol far exceeded the value of the land at the time. However, modern-day critics of the legislature might retort that the swap was perhaps the last good deal the legislature secured for the state. And they might add that the wheeling-and-dealing aspect of the exchange has characterized most of the legislature's work ever since. Nor would these problems with the contemporary legislature be the only ones in the eyes of its many critics. As long ago as 1940, for example, the authors of a textbook on state government wrote of the institution:

> *The casual observer witnessing the day-to-day performance of an ordinary legislature receives an impression that the situation in Austin is all but hopeless. He sees what appears to be a maelstrom of impulsive opinions; a blundering procedure of chronic disorder and muddlings that culminate*

invariably in the wreck of constructive legislation, and [that] produce instead a maze of compromise and error which the succeeding session will have to spend much time in undoing before proceeding with its own work. (Patterson, McAlister, and Hester, 1940:59)

The intervening half century since that 1940 observation does not seem to have brought notable improvement to the legislature. The indictment just cited has been echoed by virtually every major textbook on Texas government that has been published since. Likewise, although the Texas Legislature has not been the subject of a great amount of original research by political scientists, the studies that are available typically confirm this dismal view of the institution in one regard or another.

Moreover, the legislature has periodically been the subject of journalistic reports that paint a similar portrait of the body. The most well known of them is *Texas Monthly* magazine's now-institutionalized assessment of the ten best and ten worst individual legislators that is published at the end of each regular legislative session. Though laughable and entertaining, the exploits of each session's "ten worst" members, along with the fierce competition for that dubious designation, are also quite depressing when one considers their importance for state government.

What constitutes this less-than-admirable image of the legislature? Most critics would agree that the Texas Legislature manifests little professionalism; that it is heavily influenced, if not controlled, by special interest groups, mostly from the business sector; and that it has adopted few of the modern procedures of more progressive state legislatures. In consequence, critics would add, the work of the legislature is often poorly carried out, and all too often the broad public interest is sacrificed to the interests of powerful lobby groups.

These are serious charges that strike at the very purpose of the legislature. Students of Texas government should be able to draw their own conclusions about the accuracy of these charges, and to make that possible, the present chapter brings together the major research findings on state legislatures in general and the Texas Legislature in particular. The chapter will, as well, offer our own assessment of these matters in the conclusion. As a beginning point for this subject, however, it is worth considering just what legislatures are intended to do in the political system. Knowledge of the essential functions of legislatures will provide a set of benchmarks against which to assess the performance of the Texas institution.

The Functions of Legislatures

The four functions of legislatures—lawmaking, oversight, representation, and criticism—provide a starting point for our consideration of the Texas Legislature.

In the remainder of this chapter we will examine the aspects of the legislature that assist it in the pursuit of these functions and the aspects that constrain it. The conclusion will draw together the strands of evidence on these matters, assess the overall performance of the legislature, and then relate that assessment to the image of the legislature discussed earlier.

Lawmaking

The principal job of a legislature, as was noted in the introduction to this chapter, is that of lawmaking. That is, a legislature is empowered by the constitution with the writing of new state laws and the revision of old ones. Of course, the legislature does not monopolize all of the lawmaking power. Some of it is shared with the governor, who has the right to propose legislation and to veto bills passed by the legislature.

Students of the lawmaking function should be familiar with the process that textbooks traditionally label as "how a bill becomes a law." This phrase refers to the step-by-step institutional procedure through which a proposed law, or bill, must pass if it is to win the approval of the legislature and then the governor before becoming law. Figure 6-1 is a schematic diagram of the major aspects of that process in Texas. The diagram identifies both the principal approval points for bills and the order in which a bill must pass through those points. Lawmaking in Texas—as in all American legislatures—is a complicated process. But that aspect of the process of lawmaking is far less important to a legislature's performance than are several other characteristics—such as the nature of the membership and the leadership of the body, the professionalism and expertise in the legislature, and the dispersion of power within it. These matters are the concerns of the rest of this chapter.

Oversight

The second major task of the legislature, after lawmaking, is what political scientists have come to call oversight of the executive branch. Once the legislature has created new laws or government policies, they are implemented by the executive branch. An important task of the legislature then becomes overseeing the job done by executive (that is, administrative) agencies. Legislators want to know that their intentions as embodied in the original laws are being carried out. They also want to learn, in the exercising of their oversight, whether unanticipated problems have arisen in the process of policy implementation that call for a revision of the original law. Oversight, then, is an ongoing task of the legislature.

Two other major tasks are to be performed by this institution, but before describing them we should first note some important difficulties of lawmaking and oversight today. A useful perspective for understanding these difficulties is to contrast present-day legislative duties with those of the late nineteenth century—for example, shortly after the ratification of the constitution of 1876.

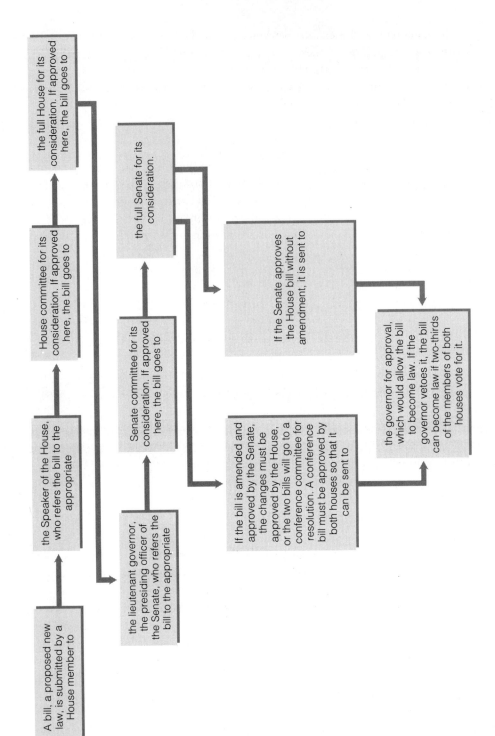

Figure 6-1 | The lawmaking process: how laws are made in Texas

The Legislature

109

In Chapter 4, we explained how the authors of the 1876 constitution, like the majority of Texans at the time, wanted a very limited state government. They eliminated a number of state agencies that had been created under Reconstruction, and they returned a variety of powers to local governments. Moreover, through the nineteenth century and well into the present one, state governments throughout the United States were rather limited in their powers (at least relative to the powers they exercise today). One might say, once again, that state governments followed reasonably closely the political philosophy of laissez-faire—the notion that government should be charged with only a very limited range of responsibilities.

Proponents of laissez-faire would say that state government should provide only the most basic public services—those that cannot be efficiently or safely provided by the private marketplace. Among these services would be some policing, probably some public health functions, limited protection of the state's natural resources, and a limited public education system. Beyond these and a few other essential services, such people would argue, reliance on the private sector to fill society's needs is preferable.

Under a limited government like the one in Texas in the late nineteenth century the tasks of lawmaking and oversight are relatively simple when compared with state government of the present day. Back then, there were not many state agencies, not many laws, and not many challenging tasks facing government. Thus the time and effort required by legislative responsibilities in that period were minimal.

Today, however, the state of Texas—like every other state—has moved far beyond laissez-faire government. The social and economic problems of the twentieth century, the demands of the citizens of Texas for certain kinds of government action, and even demands from the federal government that states initiate certain kinds of action have brought about a fundamentally different state government. Today the state of Texas has taken on a wide range of responsibilities—in education, social welfare, environmental regulation, public health, crime control, and regulation of business and the professions, to name only the most obvious examples. Nor is it simply the range of responsibilities that is important here. Increasingly, the policy problems in many of these areas have become technically complex as never before. Just what kinds of environmental control efforts are likely to be most successful and at what costs are complex issues about which even experts in the subject disagree. The same is true for problems in public education, social welfare, and all the other major policy areas now the responsibility of state government.

Political scientists refer to a governmental system that has taken on such a broad array of responsibilities as a positive state, meaning a government that has assumed positive—or activist—responsibility for the resolution of a large number of society's problems. Under such a system, the tasks of lawmaking and oversight become much more complicated than under the laissez-faire system. In making new laws, legislators must now attempt to master complex, often highly technical issues that may have far-reaching effects on the state, and they must often contend with the conflicting judgments of different experts on some of these policy issues. Because any government policy in many of these areas will have considerable effects on the society or economy of the state, legislators also must contend with vigorous lobbying efforts by groups that stand to gain or lose by their decisions.

Similarly, the job of the legislator has become more complicated because, under the positive state, the number of public agencies charged with the responsibility of executing state policy is much larger. Thus the oversight function becomes more challenging. And oversight, like lawmaking, often revolves around technical questions as legislators attempt to assess just how good a job executive agencies are doing at their assigned tasks. In short, the nature of the times in late twentieth-century America has revolutionized the character of these first two legislative functions.

Representation

As was noted above, the third task of legislatures is representation. This task is linked to the fact that legislators are popularly elected to make public policy decisions in the name of their constituents. Thus, in the processes of lawmaking and oversight, lawmakers should be representing those who elected them. Certainly in the era of the positive state this third task becomes more difficult. Facing a number of complex issues, even the most well-intentioned legislators might be uncertain about the preferences of their constituents on many of those issues. Moreover, because public opinion polls have typically shown that the average citizen often has very limited knowledge of many complicated policy issues, the constituency may actually have no clear preference that might guide the legislator on some of the issues.

The task of representation would be complicated under any circumstances because it can sometimes demand, simultaneously, entirely different actions on the part of the legislator. Political scientists have noted at least two representational roles of the legislator that may be contradictory. One is that of the **delegate**, the elected representative whose goal is to make policy decisions exactly as the majority of his or her constituents would prefer. The other role is that of the **trustee**, whose goal is to make the policy decisions that are in the best interests of his or her constituents, even if those constituents might not recognize the wisdom of such decisions.

Research on individual legislators has shown that some try to achieve one or the other of these two roles, whereas others attempt to move back and forth between the two roles, depending on the policy issue at stake. Looking at this question from a slightly different perspective, one might guess that some legislators are merely driven by self-interest—attempting to make the decisions they think will best help them stay in office. At times legislators might do what they think the majority of their constituents desire. At other times, however, they might follow the interests of only those constituents who belong to their political party, or they might follow the interests of those groups or individuals who helped them most in getting elected in the first place. Whatever strategy legislators individually follow, the task of representation is never simple.

Criticism

The last function of the legislature is in some sense a collective one that relates to the successful operation of democratic government. The legislature ought to be a public forum for criticism of existing government policy. In a democratic system such criticism is expected to come largely from the political party or parties out of power—that is, those not in a majority in the legislature or who are not represented by the governor. Yet disaffected or factional elements in the majority party may at times also provide some of this criticism. The importance of out-group criticism for the healthy functioning of a democratic society cannot be overemphasized. It ensures that policy issues are fully debated before government action is taken; it helps expose shortcomings in proposed and existing policies; and it keeps the public far better informed about public issues and policies than they otherwise would be. In short, such out-group criticism simply keeps the in-group of government leaders on their toes.

Criticism of government policy does not have to arise only in the legislature, but the legislature is a particularly important place for it to do so. The legislature is the principal institutional forum where policy questions will, of necessity, be debated. It is essential that minority or out-group points of view be represented in those debates. The legislature commands a number of institutional resources, such as research expertise, access to information, and legal authority that can be used by minority interests to help publicize their cause. And the legislature is one institution that, because of its prominence, ensures that policy criticism voiced within it will receive media coverage and public attention. Thus whether the public at large ultimately agrees or disagrees with criticism of government policy on any given issue, the goals of democratic government are furthered by its existence.

The Reality of the Texas Legislature

Because the four basic legislative functions are to some degree technical tasks, we begin our review of the Texas Legislature by analyzing its technical competence

112

Chapter 6

as it relates to those functions. Fortunately, a comprehensive analysis of these matters is available. That analysis, completed in 1970 by a nonpartisan group, the Citizens Conference on State Legislatures, and published in a book entitled *State Legislatures: An Evaluation of Their Effectiveness* (1971), offers a fascinating comparison of the legislatures of the fifty states. We will review those findings, detail some of the shortcomings of the Texas Legislature revealed in that study and elsewhere, and then offer a contemporary assessment of how the Texas body rates in terms of technical competence.

The Citizens Conference on State Legislatures adopted five broad criteria by which to evaluate individual legislatures:

1. **Functional Capability** The legislature should have adequate time, research and support staff, facilities, and managerial methods to carry out its duties with competence.

2. **Accountability** The structure of the legislature should be publicly comprehensible and publicly accessible, information on the legislature and its decisions should be publicly available, and the leaders of the legislature should be accountable to the membership.

3. **Information-Handling Capability** Legislators should have sufficient time, staff, and procedures to collect and analyze the information they need to discharge their duties.

4. **Independence** The legislature should be able to determine its own agenda and meeting times, it should be sufficiently independent of the executive branch to function as a partner in the governmental process, and by various procedures and public information processes the legislature should be freed from undue pressure by outside lobby groups.

5. **Representativeness** Members of the legislature should be sufficiently identified with their constituents, provided with sufficient technical resources and legislative opportunities, and sufficiently diverse in their personal characteristics (age, profession, ethnicity, gender, and so on) to ensure that they do represent public preferences.

Rating the Texas Legislature

For each of these five criteria the Citizens Conference developed a long checklist of specific features that would strengthen the legislature's ability to perform well in that area. All fifty state legislatures were analyzed on the checklists and were then ranked from the most to the least well structured in the terms of each criterion. The major results of this research effort were, then, rankings of the fifty states on the five criteria of legislative capability, along with a summary ranking based on the five individual ratings.

How did the Texas Legislature compare? The results are certainly nothing to brag about: Texas ranked thirty-eighth overall and rated poorly on four of the five component scales (Table 6-1). Texas's ranking was especially poor on functional capability, information handling, and independence. Only on the representativeness scale did the Texas Legislature score well in comparison with the legislatures of other states. What were the major criticisms that led to this poor showing for Texas in 1970? And which of those criticisms still hold today?

Constitutionally Mandated Short and Infrequent Sessions Today the Texas Constitution still limits, as it did in 1970, the regular sessions of the legislature to biennial meetings (once every two years) of only 140 days' duration. (Regular sessions begin on the second Tuesday in January of odd-numbered years.) That limitation is quite important because, with the growth of the positive state, the work load of the legislature has expanded both in size and in complexity. A 140-day session might have been adequate to carry out all the necessary business when the constitution was adopted in 1876, but today it seriously compromises the quality of lawmaking and oversight. Similar restrictions were common in many other states earlier in this century, but today forty-three states have annual legislative sessions with, therefore, considerably more working time available to handle their duties.

Inability to Call Itself into Special Session Only the governor can call a special session of the Texas Legislature, and the body must, in such sessions, consider only the issues the governor places on its agenda. Special sessions are also limited by the constitution to only thirty days' duration. Thus the legislature cannot use the device of special sessions to give itself more time for consideration of regular legislative business.

Too Many Members in the House of Representatives The Citizens Conference believed that the optimum size of the lower house of a state legislature is 100 members. Beyond that number, it argued, the functional capability of a legislative body is compromised. By that standard the Texas House of Representatives with its 150 members remains much too large.

Shortcomings of the Committee System In addition to the study by the Citizens Conference, a considerable body of other research suggests that the committee systems of the Texas House and Senate are considerably outmoded. It is widely accepted that legislatures should have so-called standing committees with separate policy responsibilities (for education, law enforcement, natural resources, and so on). The task of those committees is to do the first-round review of proposed new laws when the legislature meets in regular session. Most students of legislatures believe, as well, that a well-structured committee system is essential to the effective

Table 6-1 | Citizens conference rankings of state legislatures, 1970

		Ranking				
Overall Rank	State	Functional Capability	Accountability	Handling Capability	Independence	Representativeness
1	California	1	3	2	3	2
2	New York	4	13	1	8	1
3	Illinois	17	4	6	2	13
4	Florida	5	8	4	1	30
5	Wisconsin	7	21	3	4	10
6	Iowa	6	6	5	11	25
7	Hawaii	2	11	20	7	16
8	Michigan	15	22	9	12	3
9	Nebraska	35	1	16	30	18
10	Minnesota	27	7	13	23	12
11	New Mexico	3	16	28	39	4
12	Alaska	8	29	12	6	40
13	Nevada	13	10	19	14	32
14	Oklahoma	9	27	24	22	8
15	Utah	38	5	8	29	24
16	Ohio	18	24	7	40	9
17	South Dakota	23	12	15	16	37
18	Idaho	20	9	29	27	21
19	Washington	12	17	25	19	39
20	Maryland	16	31	10	15	45
21	Pennsylvania	37	23	23	5	36
22	North Dakota	22	18	17	37	31
23	Kansas	31	15	14	32	34
24	Connecticut	39	26	26	25	6
25	West Virginia	10	32	37	24	15

Table 6-1 | Citizens conference rankings of state legislatures, 1970—cont'd

Overall Rank	State	Ranking				
		Functional Capability	Accountability	Handling Capability	Independence	Representativeness
26	Tennessee	30	44	11	9	26
27	Oregon	28	14	35	35	19
28	Colorado	21	25	21	28	27
29	Massachusetts	32	35	22	21	23
30	Maine	29	34	32	18	22
31	Kentucky	49	2	48	44	7
32	New Jersey	14	42	18	31	35
33	Louisiana	47	39	33	13	14
34	Virginia	25	19	27	26	48
35	Missouri	36	30	40	49	5
36	Rhode Island	33	46	30	41	11
37	Vermont	19	20	34	42	47
38	**Texas**	**45**	**36**	**43**	**45**	**17**
39	New Hampshire	34	33	42	36	43
40	Indiana	44	38	41	43	20
41	Montana	26	28	31	46	49
42	Mississippi	46	43	45	20	28
43	Arizona	11	47	38	17	50
44	South Carolina	50	45	39	10	46
45	Georgia	40	49	36	33	38
46	Arkansas	41	40	46	34	33
47	North Carolina	24	37	44	47	44
48	Delaware	43	48	47	38	29
49	Wyoming	42	41	50	48	42
50	Alabama	48	50	49	50	41

Source: Citizens Conference on State Legislatures (1971:40).

116   *Chapter 6*

working of the whole institution. A good committee system is particularly important for the technical quality of lawmaking and oversight. The Texas Legislature has standing committees and did so in 1970, but there were several problems both then and today with the ways in which those committees operate. (The standing committees of the 1991 legislative session are shown in Table 6-2.)

The biggest problems with the committee systems of the Texas Legislature relate to how individual legislators get to be members of different committees and how the chairpersons of those committees are chosen. In the Texas Legislature both of these matters are effectively controlled by the presiding officers of the separate houses. That is, the Speaker of the House and the lieutenant governor, as the presiding officer of the Senate, control the selection of both committee members and chairpersons. A limited **seniority system** does exist that determines some of a legislator's committee memberships. In other words, legislators get to choose some of their committee assignments, and a rule of seniority (or length of service

Table 6-2 | Standing committees of the Texas Legislature, 1991

Senate Committees

Administration	Intergovernmental Relations
Criminal Justice	Jurisprudence
Economic Development	Natural Resources
Education	Nominations
Finance	Redistricting
Health and Human Services	State Affairs

House Committees

Agriculture and Livestock	Judicial Affairs
Appropriations	Judiciary
Business and Commerce	Labor and Employment
Calendars	Liquor Regulations
Corrections	Local and Consent Calendars
County Affairs	Natural Resources
Criminal Jurisprudence	Public Education
Cultural and Historical Resources	Public Health
Elections	Public Safety
Energy	Redistricting
Environmental Affairs	Retirement and Aging
Financial Institutions	Rules and Resolutions
General Investigating	Science and Technology
Government Organization	State Affairs
Higher Education	State, Federal, and International Relations
House Administration	Transportation
Human Services	Urban Affairs
Insurance	Ways and Means

in the legislature) is employed to determine which members will get the most highly sought-after committee assignments. Yet the seniority system determines only a limited number of all committee assignments, and the bulk of those assignments remain in the hands of the presiding officers.

One consequence of leader control of committee assignments is that there is no guarantee of continuity of membership on the committees. The Speaker of the House and the lieutenant governor can and do make many changes in assignments from session to session. Even the chairpersons are changed with some frequency. To make matters worse, a number of individuals who lost committee chair positions in the House of Representatives under the speakership of Gib Lewis in the 1980s and 1990s were told by Lewis or one of his assistants that they lost their positions for failing to support the Speaker's legislative program.

Continuity of membership and leadership on legislative committees is important because it allows legislators to specialize in the issues handled by their committees. They can become more expert about the subject and more knowledgeable about government programs and policies. A good seniority system or some other method by which legislators can influence their own committee assignments can also enhance the quality of legislative work. On the one hand, when legislators can influence their own committee assignments, they are more likely to be placed on committees in which they have great interest and on which they will be willing, therefore, to work especially hard. On the other hand, committee assignment rules that allow the more senior members to get the most prestigious committee appointments create incentives to remain in the legislature. Thus experience and, one would hope, expertise in legislative work are rewarded.

A committee system that has high turnover and is controlled, as well, by the presiding officers has several potentially unfortunate consequences. It becomes particularly difficult in such a system for members to develop expertise or even much background knowledge of the subject matter of their committees. They will have little incentive even to attempt to do so, for in the next regular session they might be placed on entirely new sets of committees. The inability of members to choose their own committee assignments also means that members have little guarantee that they will get to serve on the committees whose subjects they already know well or care about the most.

Finally, the fact that the presiding officers control the committee system means that those two leaders can stack committees with certain members to control the decision making that goes on in those groups. Even the reforms that created the limited seniority system and brought about other changes in the committees in 1972–1973 have not cut appreciably into that control. Despite certain restrictions on the presiding officers' committee-stacking powers, those powers remained quite strong even after the reforms (Moncrief, 1979). Indeed,

118 *Chapter 6*

changes in the internal rules of the House of Representatives in 1983 and 1985 increased the Speaker's committee appointment powers even further (Price, 1985). Among the traditional powers of the presiding officers are the rights to determine the jurisdiction of individual committees, to assign bills to individual committees, to appoint the members of conference committees, and to control a number of other legislative resources important to the operation of the committee system.

The Citizens Conference cited a number of other problems in the committee structures of the two houses of the Texas Legislature. The details of those criticisms are not of great importance at present, but it is worth noting that only in one or two instances has any notable progress been made since 1970 in terms of responding to those charges. As for the major problems of the committee system, little substantial change has been made since the Citizens Conference report—and some of the changes that have come about, like those strengthening the committee-control powers of the Speaker of the House, have aggravated rather than solved the problems of the committee systems.

Scheduling Problems Another major problem cited by the Citizens Conference was the matter of scheduling debates over proposed legislation after it had received committee approval and been sent to the full House or Senate. The Citizens Conference proposed that an automatic calendar be instated to guarantee that each bill would be debated and that the debate would occur on a certain date. The calendar existing in the Texas Legislature in 1970 and still used today is too complicated and is subject to manipulation by the presiding officers. In the House there are eight different calendars to which different bills can be assigned. But in both houses the presiding officer controls the assignment of bills to calendars, and both of those officials have a number of parliamentary powers that enable them to manipulate the calendars or simply ignore them.

At first glance this subject of calendars might appear to be just a trivial detail of procedure. Yet two significant problems arise out of this issue. One is that without an automatic calendar—and under the time pressure of the short 140-day session—the legislature inevitably falls far behind schedule in working its way through each session's body of proposed legislation. The early days of the session are largely taken up with organizational work and then the initial committee hearings. Toward the end of the session, on the other hand, and particularly in the last few days, the pace of debating and voting on bills becomes frantic. There is always a logjam of legislation that must be considered in the final days. A large number of bills are therefore pushed through the legislature with little time for debate. Bad bills—and even devious ones—can be approved in that atmosphere, because the quality of lawmaking is inevitably compromised under such conditions.

The Legislature 119

Moreover, because the presiding officers can manipulate the calendar, those officials have enormous discretionary power over the ultimate fate of many bills. The Speaker or lieutenant governor can ensure that certain bills are brought up for debate at the time when they are most or least likely to be passed—in accordance with the presiding officers' own preferences for the fate of the bill. The two leaders can also hide controversial bills in the logjam of legislation that is rammed through the legislature in the closing days of the session. They can even kill a bill by seeing that it never comes up for debate. An excellent discussion of just one of the parliamentary powers that make this situation possible is offered in the *Houston Post* editorial on pages 120–121. The character of the scheduling system, at first glance a seemingly minor institutional detail, has enormous importance for both the quality and the kind of legislation that comes out of the Texas Legislature.

Inadequate Legislative Salaries The Citizens Conference also noted that in Texas, like many other states, the salaries of legislators were far too low. The conference recommended that lawmakers be paid something that at least approaches a full-time annual salary so that more people can consider running for the legislature and so that, once elected, legislators can devote all their time to that job.

The salaries of Texas legislators are set by the constitution and thus can be raised only by constitutional amendment—another problem in the eyes of the Citizens Conference, because of the typical difficulties associated with the amendment process. In 1970 the Texas Constitution stipulated annual legislative salaries of $4,800 a year plus $12 a day for expenses when the legislature was in session. Those salaries have been raised subsequently, but even today Texas legislators earn only $7,200 in annual salary plus a $30 per diem expense allowance for the first 120 days of regular sessions and for each day of a special session. In other words, legislators earn about $9,000 per year in total compensation.

A 1991 legal opinion by the state's attorney general makes it possible for legislators to increase their effective total compensation, but it is not clear that all members will take advantage of the opportunity. The attorney general ruled that it was legal for legislators to receive an additional living allowance, in addition to the constitutionally mandated $30 per diem, for those days they are in session. The Speaker of the House established an $85 a day maximum for that new allowance, but because the new benefit was so controversial, only a minority of legislators applied to receive it during 1991. The typical cost of maintaining a second residence in Austin while the legislature is in session, however, is likely to consume both of the two per diem allowances legislators might receive. Thus even with the new benefit, legislators will be serving for remarkably little remuneration.

The consequences of low pay should be obvious. Only certain kinds of people—the wealthy or those in unusually fortunate professional circumstances— can even contemplate running for the office. And many of those who are elected

120   *Chapter 6*

can devote only a limited part of their time to the job. Even when the legislature is in session, many of the members are forced to carry on their private professions at long distance from Austin, supplemented by weekend trips home to do as much business as possible. The time and effort that ought to be devoted to lawmaking, oversight, and so on are, of course, compromised.

Senate Should End Calendar Trickery

Felton West

AUSTIN—Tourists briefly visiting Senate sessions this year may leave with the idea that creating a Texas-flag flower bed at the Capitol is the Senate's next item of business.

Right there at the top of the Senate calendar, printed daily in a little green booklet, is Senate Bill 123, by Sen. Roy Blake of Nacogdoches, "relating to the creation and maintenance on the grounds of the State Capitol a permanent flower bed depicting through appropriate design and flower selection the Texas flag."

Blake is chairman of the powerful Senate Administration Committee, so his bill—up there first in line to be considered by the full Senate—ought to move fast, right?

Wrong.

His bill is not going anywhere. By agreement with Lt. Gov. Bill Hobby, Blake will never try to pass it.

SB123 is just a serious joke, the session's blocking bill. Its whole purpose is to ensure that the calendar, which is officially the "regular order of business," or ROB, is never followed. Since Blake will not try to pass it, no bill beneath it on the calendar can be considered by the Senate unless its author has rounded up an extraordinary majority of votes to suspend the ROB.

A sponsor may have 16 or 18 votes committed for his very good bill—enough to pass it in the 31-member Senate—but it won't ever be passed unless he can muster a two-thirds majority of those present to suspend the ROB so it can be brought to the simple-majority passage vote. The two-thirds-of-those-present majority is 21 votes if there's a full house.

First the sponsor must get recognized by the presiding officer (the lieutenant governor) to make a motion to suspend the ROB. If he is recognized and wins the two-thirds majority for his motion, his bill is brought up, explained, debated, possibly amended, and tentatively approved. Then, if the author can muster a four-fifths majority of the membership (25 votes) to suspend a constitutional rule requiring final passage on another day, the bill may be finally passed and sent to the House the same day.

If the four-fifths majority can't be achieved, then on another day the sponsor must get the ROB suspended again by a two-thirds majority, after which the bill may be passed by a simple-majority vote.

If you ask me, it's terribly undemocratic and the Senate should have a better way to regulate traffic. But this has been the Senate system for as long as anybody there can remember. Lieutenant governors and most senators like it. It enhances a lieutenant governor's control and helps senators obscure their stands on hot-potato bills. It "works both ways," preventing passage of bad bills as well as good ones, its admirers say.

But if a bill has simple-majority support, as long as it is not shown to be unconstitutional, it should become law. Merit, not tricky rules, should determine whether it is passed; this should not have to wait for years until the majority support has grown bigger.

Senate bill traffic could be regulated instead by having committees, which already study bills closely, decide which have enough merit to be voted on at all by the full Senate.

Blake, who seems fond of flower bills, used the same flower-bed bill to block the calendar in the regular legislative session in 1983. The State Purchasing and General Services Commission even wanted to help pass it—until Blake explained.

In 1981, he introduced a bill to prohibit importation of diseased camellias. But whatever dangers foreign camellias threatened us with, Texas evidently remains unprotected from them, because that was just the 1981 calendar-blocking bill.

Cute, eh? But such a system has a profound effect on our laws.

(*Houston Post*, 1985)

Limited Staff Support The Citizens Conference also found that Texas legislators were provided insufficient staff support to carry out their duties appropriately. Texas legislators are provided monthly staff and office expense allowances, but most observers believe that those funds are adequate only to cover basic office and clerical functions. They are not sufficient to allow legislators to hire professional research personnel to aid in the information gathering and analysis that is so important to lawmaking and oversight today. To compound this problem, the staff funds of the individual standing committees are also limited. In some states, by comparison, far more generous staff resources are provided to both individual legislators and the committees.

The Lieutenant Governor Problem Texas, like several other states, was also criticized by the Citizens Conference because the lieutenant governor—a publicly elected executive-branch official in theory—wields considerable power as the presiding officer of the Senate. In effect, the lieutenant governor is an official of the legislative branch, not the executive branch. Unlike the vice president of the United States, the Texas lieutenant governor does not assist the chief executive in implementing policy and supervising administrative agencies. The lieutenant governor acts in that capacity only when assuming the position of acting chief executive, in largely ceremonial fashion, when the governor is out of the state. Instead of assuming a significant role in the executive branch, the lieutenant governor works in the legislative arena to make laws and policy. Because of that position, the lieutenant governor is a powerful official.

If Texans recognize the reality of the lieutenant governor's role, then at least they will not be misled by the arrangement. But many citizens probably do misunderstand the office and assume that the lieutenant governor's role is like that of the vice president of the United States. Thus they do not realize that the lieutenant governor is so independent and powerful and really functions more as an official of the legislative branch than of the executive branch. As J. William Davis (1967:18–19) has written:

The analogy of the Vice President of the United States is not appropriate to the office of the lieutenant governor of Texas. The Vice President has similar constitutional functions, presiding over the Senate and succession to the presidency, but the realities of the office are quite different. The Vice President runs on the ticket with the President, as a member of the "team." They are elected together and are expected to work together at all times. At the President's request and direction, the Vice President may substitute for the President on many occasions and serve as his spokesman, not only in the Senate, but before the nation and the world. . . . This is not true of the lieutenant governor in Texas. He and the governor are elected separately, each running his own race. . . . Persons elected to the two offices may conceivably be of different political leanings. The lieutenant governor rarely substitutes for the governor as his representative or spokesman. Even though he may make many public appearances, he does so as the lieutenant governor, not as a spokesman for the governor. The governor and lieutenant governor usually work together in many ways, but they are not necessarily a part of the same team.

This arrangement for the role of the lieutenant governor means that the distinction between the legislative and executive branch is blurred and, moreover, that the Senate is not able to choose its own leadership. The situation is ill-understood by the average Texan, and many citizens are thereby misled about the actual distribution of power in state government. Beyond that, the arrangement weakens the traditional independence of the legislature in a way that many political observers find objectionable.

Consequences of the Legislature's Shortcomings

Some implications of the various problems with the Texas Legislature have already been mentioned, but the major difficulties bear reiteration because they are all related. One major impact is on the character and quality of the membership of the legislature. The low pay, the personal demands arising from spending about five months every two years in Austin—typically leaving one's family, friends, and professional life back home—and the limited opportunities for professional advancement and technical specialization in the current committee system mean that the people who are elected to the legislature are often little better than amateurs. The incentives are too few, in other words, to attract very many of the most highly qualified potential candidates. Indeed, the best people have far more attractive alternatives in both the private and the public sectors. Furthermore, those who are elected have few incentives to stay in the body, so turnover is relatively high. (Turnover, tenure, and related aspects of the membership of the legislature are discussed in more detail in the section entitled "The Legislators Themselves," below.)

Another consequence of Texas's legislative system is that the presiding officers of the House and Senate have become enormously powerful. Their control over the committee system and the calendar has already been discussed. Yet we should remember that, in their actions when presiding over debates, they have considerable additional power over the fate of legislation. The Speaker of the House and the lieutenant governor also control many of the research and staff resources of their respective houses. They even control the membership of conference committees that must meet to work out compromises between conflicting bills passed by the two bodies.

Based on the powers of the presiding officers and the relative weakness of the individual members, one can make a strong case—as many observers have—that the Texas Legislature is hardly a democratic body. Instead it is something like two feudal monarchies, dominated by the presiding officers who control the agenda and the majority of the legislature most of the time by their power to distribute favors and rewards to those who accept their leadership. Little that is opposed by the presiding officer will ever come out of either house. Some observers have even shown that the powers of the presiding officers have actually grown substantially since the time of the Citizens Conference analysis of state legislatures (Pettus, 1980; Price, 1985).

But the most important result of these various problems is that the quality of the legislature's functioning—whether in lawmaking, in oversight, in representation, or even in policy criticism—is seriously compromised. The time for legislative work is too limited. The quality of the membership is too low. The incentives to remain a legislator are too meager to prevent high turnover. The resources available to the members for research, information gathering, and analysis are too limited. The committee system stifles the development of policy expertise. Finally, a number of the individual problems combine to increase the power of the presiding officers over that of the individual members.

Current Ranking of the Texas Legislature

Our discussion to this point has relied largely on the 1970 comparative study of state legislatures. Even though the current situation in the Texas Legislature has been noted on a number of separate points, one might wonder how that body would fare today in an overall comparison. Although no such study has recently been executed, it is still possible to estimate with some certainty how the Texas Legislature would rate in such a study.

It is possible to make such an estimate because from approximately 1965 to 1980 considerable reform was achieved within state legislatures in the United

States. The Citizens Conference study was only one example of the widespread criticism of existing legislative institutions and procedures. As a consequence of that widespread interest in reform, many states revised their legislative systems in one respect or another. In a number of states, constitutional limitations on legislatures—on their meeting times, frequency of meeting, salary levels, and even on their lawmaking authority—were relaxed. Many states adopted annual instead of biennial sessions. Most states raised legislative salaries. Staff and research resources were expanded dramatically in many states, and many states adopted new scheduling systems to reduce logjams and to streamline the flow of legislative work.

Texas, however, made only modest changes in its legislature during that period. Most of its original constitutional limitations on the body have been left intact. Biennial sessions and limited special sessions were retained. The system of strong presiding officers was retained and, as was noted above, even strengthened. The problems of scheduling and the end-of-session logjam remain. The incentives for professional legislative work are still quite low. There were, it is true, some positive achievements—an increase in legislators' salaries in 1975, some reforms in the committee system, some increases in staff support and in oversight activities. Yet Texas made only limited progress in modernizing its legislature—even in the areas where there were changes—while many other states were taking considerable strides. These facts suggest that if the Citizens Conference study were replicated today, the technical competence of the Texas Legislature would rate even lower now than in 1970 when compared with the legislatures of the other states.

The Legislators Themselves

We turn now to an examination of the elected members themselves: how they get elected, what sorts of individuals they are, and the reasons they enter and leave the institution. The state constitution requires a member of the House of Representatives to be at least 21 years of age, a citizen of the United States, a qualified voter in the state, and a resident of the state for two years, and of the House district for one year, preceding the election. The requirements for Senate eligibility are essentially the same except that the minimum age is 26 and the state residency requirement is five years. Elections to the House are held in November of even-numbered years, and House members serve two-year terms once elected. Senators serve four-year terms, and half of them are elected in November of each even-numbered year. Beyond these formal requirements for membership, however, are some practical requirements that determine who will seek office in the legislature.

The Legislature 125

Practical Requirements for Election

The most obvious requirement is that one must have sufficient interest in politics to seek an office that will require campaigning for the better part of a year, suffering through both a primary and a general election, spending about half the year after the election living in Austin participating in the legislative session and possibly a special session, and then devoting the succeeding year and a half to at least some interim activities and service for constituents—all for about $9,000 a year in total compensation.

Yet that hurdle of interest in politics might be overcome for any number of reasons. In terms of political culture, some legislative hopefuls surely are motivated by something like the moralistic orientation of political life in the public interest. Others probably follow the individualistic idea that politics can aid one's personal career. The salary of a legislator will not itself make a great contribution to one's personal success, but some hope to use their experience in the legislature to seek higher and more lucrative political office. Others frankly hope to use their time in the legislature to make business associations, learn the ins and outs of state government, become acquainted with representatives of the major lobby interests, and then retire from the legislature into an enhanced private career. The latter route can be particularly useful for young professionals in business, law, insurance, and real estate. Finally, some legislative hopefuls probably get their ambition from family or friendship ties with others seriously involved in political life. Many people reared in a highly political family are socialized to believe that it is natural and even expected of them to enter that life. Thus, sufficient interest in politics to get over the first hurdle can arise for a number of reasons.

A second practical requirement is that one must be a self-starter and probably even a self-nominator. Political parties and other formal organizations are not as deeply involved in the initial recruitment of new candidates for the legislature as one might first guess. Many candidates thus recruit themselves to run for the office. Lawrence W. Miller (1977:123–125) found, for example, that in a study of individuals who entered and left the legislature between 1969 and 1976, some 43 percent were self-recruited to run for office. Only 13 percent had been recruited by political party organizations. (The remainder were influenced in their decision to run for office by one or another private, nonparty organization.)

A third practical requirement is that one must be in a personal and professional situation that allows running for an office that pays so little and yet demands so much time—even if pursued on a part-time basis. In short, a person must either be independently wealthy or have a job that can become a second part-time position while he or she is in the legislature. Besides people who are independently wealthy, those who are self-employed are typically better able to meet this requirement. The point is that the financial and time demands of a legislative career,

126   *Chapter 6*

even a short one, constitute a hurdle that only a small and select group of Texans will be able to get over.

One must also be able—by one's own wealth, by having the right connections, or by hard campaign work—to raise sufficient funds to pay for a political campaign. A survey of campaign expenditure reports for the 1984 election year suggests that serious candidates for the Texas Senate probably spent at least $150,000 in their campaigns. Candidates in competitive House races typically had to spend at least $80,000. Even a veteran representative running unopposed for reelection in a small-town district would have probably spent $10,000 to $20,000 in his or her campaign. Each succeeding election year, of course, requires another round of such spending—and the search for campaign contributions necessary to support it.

Who Gets Elected?

From those who get over the practical hurdles and seek election to the legislature, what kinds of people are typically elected today? Some information on that question can be gleaned from a breakdown of the demographic characteristics of legislators in 1991 (Table 6-3). That information indicates that the legislature is overwhelmingly composed of male, Anglo, well-educated business people and lawyers. The only other notable demographic characteristic of the legislative body concerns the occupational data. The occupations listed in Table 6-3 refer to the primary occupation reported by the lawmakers, but a remarkable number of the lawyers and business people reported that they were also engaged in farming or ranching. This fact attests, on the one hand, to the breadth of the business interests of the legislators and, on the other hand, to the continuing salience of those traditional occupations among the state's elected leaders.

Why Legislators Leave

As is true in all state legislatures, the rate of membership turnover from election to election has been declining in Texas over most of the present century. In the last twenty or so years, average turnover at elections has been in the range of 20 to 25 percent in the Senate and 20 to 30 percent in the House. Yet these figures indicate only the percentage of freshmen elected in a given year. Average tenure in office is also important. After the 1991 elections, as an example, the average tenure was 5.3 years in the Senate and 6.2 years in the House. Thus the average senator had served only one and a third terms, and the average representative three terms. These figures indicate that the typical member does not remain long in the House or the Senate. If one thinks of the legislator's job as requiring the development of specialized knowledge and expertise, the average member will probably not have advanced far in that regard before he or she leaves the institution. This

The Legislature 127

Table 6-3 | **Characteristics of members of the Texas Legislature, 1991**

Characteristic	Senate (%)	House (%)
Sex		
Male	87	89
Female	13	11
Education		
Less than college	3	7
Some college or bachelor's degree	42	43
Advanced or graduate degree	52	50
Ethnicity		
Anglo	77	78
Black	6	9
Mexican American	16	13
Occupation		
Law	40	30
Business	33	43
Ranching or farming	10	5
Education	3	6
Medicine	3	3
Homemaker	3	1
Retired	—	1
Other	7	10

Source: Texas State Directory (1991).

problem is, fortunately, moderated a bit by the fact that most freshman senators served in the House before election to the Senate. Yet even in the Senate the average member does not have a long career.

Why is it that most members leave, and what might we learn from their reasons for leaving? Not much research has been done on this question for the Texas Legislature alone, but research on state legislatures in general suggests some probable answers. First, of course, some members seek but fail to be reelected. Miller (1977:43–45) found that in the early 1970s about one-third of those who left the Texas Legislature did so because of failure to win reelection. But of even greater interest are those members who retire voluntarily. If we remember that most people enter the House with no prior experience in elected office, and we keep in mind the financial, personal, and time demands of the office, the likely reasons for voluntary retirement should be clear. (In Miller's study, 25 percent of those who left the legislature during the period that was examined did so voluntarily.)

The principal reason for voluntary retirement is probably the financial strain of the job. Miller (1977:67–69) found that two-thirds of those who retired voluntarily in the early 1970s reported finances to be a major factor in their decision. And no other single reason was mentioned by even as many as 20 percent of the volunteer retirees.

Another probable reason for voluntary retirement might be called one of psychological fitness for political life. Because most legislators are serving in public office for the first time, it should not be surprising that some of them find they are unsuited for the demands of such a position. The rigors of campaigning, of continually having to ask people for financial contributions during the campaign, of enduring the occasional highly bitter election campaign, of having one's private life open to the scrutiny of the mass media and campaign opponents, of sacrificing one's career and family life to the demands of the office—these costs seem greater than the rewards to some legislators.

Once again, the low pay and the relatively low status and lack of professional opportunities in the legislature mean the rewards that might offset some of the demands are particularly meager in Texas. Thus it should not be surprising that the average tenure in the House, particularly, is not long. Even many of those who can put up with the costs of political life may not want to do so for long. Because of the higher status of their office, and because most of their number were experienced in politics before running for the Senate and thus understood the demands of the politician's life, senators often are willing to serve a longer time in office—provided they continue to get reelected.

Another reason some legislators retire is their private career ambitions. Some young professionals, as we mentioned earlier, serve a term or two mainly to make business connections that will aid their careers. Their motivation for being in the legislature, therefore, has little to do with the job itself. One must be skeptical about how devoted such people are to the tasks of lawmaking, oversight, and representation if their primary interest is in their personal careers.

Some other legislators retire because of public career ambitions. That is, they seek higher and probably better-paying public office. (Miller found that 42 percent of those who left the legislature in the early 1970s ran for another office.) The state legislature, particularly the House of Representatives, is a good starting place for a political career, and many people attempt to use it as a stepping-stone to a Senate seat, a seat in the U.S. Congress, or even a local position in city or county government. The financial and other costs of membership in the legislature probably influence the decisions of such legislators, for even many local government offices pay far better salaries than does the legislature. This reason for retirement suggests that politically ambitious members will not want to remain long in the legislature. One might fairly suspect that retirees in this category are often the most capable legislative members.

Implications of the Patterns of Membership

After considering the diverse reasons for legislative recruitment and retirement, we can draw a portrait of the typical state representative when first elected. That person will be a well-educated white male, either near the start of a business or professional career or at a later, more established career position. He will be inexperienced politically. His primary motivations will vary, and some of them will have little to do with the tasks of the legislature. He most likely will find little reason to remain long in the legislature, retiring after only two or three terms. Election defeat, voluntary retirement, or departure to seek higher and more attractive political office will end his career in the Texas Legislature.

Although we can point to several different reasons why the typical representative will retire voluntarily (either to leave politics entirely or to seek a more attractive public office), the work life, low pay, and other characteristics of the legislator's job are such that several of those reasons may interact to bring about a member's decision not to run for reelection. That is, the nature of the job imposes all of those burdens on almost all the members of the House, regardless of their motivations to remain there and their stamina to put up with them.

Another important conclusion concerns the characteristics of the legislature that attract certain kinds of new legislators in the first place, particularly in the House of Representatives. The high costs and low rewards of House membership explain why the individuals who typically seek election there are relatively wealthy and also are the mostly politically inexperienced. Institutional characteristics explain in large part why the legislature is so unrepresentative of the citizens of Texas and why the members—again particularly in the House—are relative amateurs. The same institutional characteristics help explain the high turnover and low average tenure in the body. The high costs and low rewards ensure that most people will not stay long and that their limited experience will not be greatly enriched by technical legislative skills acquired during their time in office. Thus, institutional characteristics weaken even further the technical competence of the membership as a whole.

The typical state senator suffers many of the same difficulties created by the institutional system. Yet most senators, at least, have served in the House before moving on to the Senate. They should have developed some of the technical skills and some of the detailed understanding of government policy that would be desired for legislators. Presumably they also understand the costs and rewards of continued membership in the legislature and have accepted those facts of political life. The higher prestige of Senate membership may explain part of this willingness to continue to serve in the legislature. At the same time we should also recall that the average tenure of senators in 1991 was shorter than that of representatives. Thus the rewards of service in the Senate may not, in fact, be particularly more attractive. One could well conclude, therefore, that the costs of time spent in the Senate must be much the same as those for the House.

130 Chapter 6

Special Interest Groups and the Legislature

Another major concern of this chapter is the role that interest groups play in the legislative process. In discussing the image of the Texas Legislature, we noted that many critics believe that special interests are inordinately powerful in that body. If they are so powerful, how do they make their influence felt? There are five principal means that might be employed by interest groups to influence any legislative body. All five are now used or have been used in the past.

Bribery

Many people seem to believe that outright bribery is the principal means of legislative influence. Certainly bribery has been important at times in all levels of American politics. In the nineteenth century and in the first half or so of the present one it may even have been the primary means of influence. Yet most students of the subject believe that the incidence of this practice has fallen off dramatically in recent decades—in part because of more-aggressive journalistic reporting of bribery when it is discovered, in part because of changing public mores on the subject, and in part because of new and more vigorously enforced laws against it. One might also conclude that most lobbyists no longer need resort to bribery. Most have other resources that are not only more potent but legal as well.

One should not discount the notion, however, that from time to time bribery still occurs. Just how serious such problems can be is indicated by the scope of the so-called Sharpstown Bank scandal, which was uncovered in 1971 by the U.S. Securities and Exchange Commission. Houston banker Frank Sharp, head of the Sharpstown Bank, attempted to influence state banking legislation by bribing a number of state officials with bank stock from which they could gain handsome profits. Governor Preston Smith, Speaker of the House Gus Mutscher, and some of Mutscher's closest supporters in the House were implicated. Mutscher and two other legislative officials were eventually convicted of conspiracy to commit bribery as a result of their role in the affair.

The Social Lobby

Another traditional means of lobby influence of legislators has been what is called the social lobby, or the regular practice of a number of interest groups and their representatives of entertaining state legislators. Many of such organizations maintain regular hospitality suites in hotels near the Capitol where a legislator can get a free meal or a drink in a relaxed, informal setting—and where someone from the lobby can casually discuss the organization's interest in pending legislation at the same time. The social lobby also provides a good number of free meals at lavish restaurants; gifts of food, liquor, or other things; and even weekend trips for

The Legislature **131**

deep-sea fishing, for hunting, or simply for a party at someone's ranch away from Austin.

Some people may look upon the social lobby as a subtle form of bribery, and some legislators may even succumb to it just as if it were that. But above all it creates an implicit atmosphere of indebtedness on the part of many lawmakers. They have accepted favors and thus they cannot complain if favors are requested of them at a later time by the lobbyist involved. Moreover, the social lobby simply provides special opportunities—in relaxed, amiable settings tinged with a sense of indebtedness—for certain groups to press their political demands upon legislators.

The representative of a less well-heeled organization or the individual citizen wishing to advocate a particular point of view must fight for space on the crowded daily calendar of his or her legislator. Such a person might get only a few minutes of the legislator's time as the member hurries from one meeting to another—or, worse, the person might receive only a form letter written by a secretary in the legislator's office. Thus the social lobby creates a unique and especially favorable environment for communicating political interests—for those who can afford to pay for the opportunity.

Many observers have concluded that the social lobby is no longer as important, or as flagrant, as it once was. It is said that the days when the standard tools of the approach were "booze, blondes, and beefsteaks" have waned considerably. That judgment is probably accurate, if for no other reason than that journalistic reporting of the practice has made lobbyists more circumspect. Yet the social lobby remains important. Inquisitive news reporters still turn up juicy examples of the practice (Ellis, 1981). Even in its more circumspect contemporary form, the social lobby still provides unique opportunities to influence the legislature.

One of the reasons the social lobby remains important is the unusual social circumstances in which lawmakers find themselves when the legislature is in session. The typical legislator has left his or her family, friends, and job—and hence regular social and professional life—to move to Austin from January through May at the least. Even though most legislators travel home for many weekends, their regular lifestyles are entirely disrupted. Many of them are also living in Austin on a modest budget because of their low pay as legislators and because of the professional sacrifices required to hold their elected position. They often live in inexpensive motels or join together in groups to share the rent of a house.

The relative poverty and the disrupted social circumstances of legislators in these conditions heighten the importance of the social lobby. Here are people offering a free drink, a free meal, free tickets to a sporting or cultural event, or a free weekend for barbecue and relaxation at someone's ranch in the Hill Country. Here are people, in other words, who offer a free and sometimes quite elaborate substitute for the legislator's missing social life. It is not surprising, then, that the social lobby persists and that, even if subtly, it constitutes an important avenue of influence by special interest groups.

132   *Chapter 6*

Campaign Contributions

Another powerful and legal means for influencing legislators is to assist them in meeting the expenses of running for office. Typical campaign costs were noted earlier, and it would be a rare individual who could pay them personally. Thus outside contributors are critically important to virtually every candidate.

State campaign finance laws have, since 1973, made it illegal for certain special interests, specifically corporations and labor unions, to contribute directly to candidates' election campaign funds. Yet that provision means only that the contributions of major special interest groups must be made either by individuals or by political action committees (PACs). We explained in Chapter 5 how important PAC and interest group contributions are for state legislators. Recall that candidates for legislative office typically receive more than half their campaign contributions from interest groups, with some legislators receiving more than 90 percent of their campaign funds from such groups. The heavy dependence on special interests, then, makes lawmakers highly susceptible to the persuasive efforts of such organizations.

Research Material on Policy Issues

Lobbies sometimes exert another, entirely different means of influence by functioning as an information and research source for legislators. The research resources of the legislators themselves are poor because of their limited professional staff, limited personal time, and the difficulties of developing expertise when turnover is high and seniority rules limited. Legislators frequently are unable to pursue, by their own resources, careful research into policy problems and solutions. But the better-funded interest groups have customarily provided information to fill that gap. Many of these groups maintain high-caliber, professional research staffs to carry out just such research. Many other interest groups can draw upon the technical expertise of their members or their member organizations to provide such research. Of course, such information always takes the point of view of the group that prepares it.

The legislator working on a major policy problem can always depend on both the availability of such information and its inevitable bias. If a legislator is favorably disposed toward the position of the interest group, of course, he or she will also have the same bias. Thus legislators who work closely with well-funded interest groups will have no shortage of well-prepared material to support their legislative arguments. Those who work, alternatively, for less wealthy or less well-organized groups or who simply want to adopt an entirely independent perspective on legislative questions will have considerable difficulty in developing equally detailed material to support their point of view.

The weak research resources of the Texas Legislature, then, create an additional opportunity for certain interest groups to gain disproportionate influence. Many students of legislatures argue that this information-providing function has become one of the most important techniques of special interests. The era of the positive state and of technically complex policy problems has brought with it a serious need for sophisticated information to aid the lawmaking function. If a legislature cannot fill this need on its own, self-interested groups are both ready and eager to help it out.

Going to the Top

The last and perhaps most important technique of special interest group influence is to go straight to the top—that is, to spend a disproportionate amount of one's time and resources getting the most influential legislators, the lieutenant governor and the Speaker of the House, on one's side. This technique is effective because of the great power of these two officials, a situation well understood by sophisticated lobbyists. If a group has the presiding officers (and hence their teams of supporters) backing its interest, that group is in a strong position indeed. The presiding officers, then, themselves become the lobbyists for that interest group— for they use their clout in the legislature to persuade the other members to support that group's preferences, as well.

| Conclusion |

This chapter began by observing the low esteem that many political scientists and journalists have for the Texas Legislature. A detailed examination of this political body—its institutional characteristics, its technical competence, its internal politics, its membership, and the special interest forces acting upon it— offers considerable evidence as to why that unfortunate reputation is well deserved.

The Texas Legislature is an amateur body with poorly developed technical capabilities. It is highly controlled by its presiding officers, a situation that certainly varies from typical expectations about democratic institutions. That situation, as well, makes the work of the legislature highly dependent upon the presiding officers' skill, honesty, fairness, and concern for the public interest. Individuals of laudable character in the positions of lieutenant governor and Speaker of the House can shape laudable governmental policies. But those of lesser character will also have considerable power to create unfortunate policies.

A number of the institutional and membership characteristics of the legis-

134   *Chapter 6*

lature also strengthen certain kinds of special interest group influence on state government policy. A fundamental tenet of democratic government is that citizens should have the right to lobby their government and attempt to influence its decisions. Yet the situation is such in Texas that wealthy establishment interests have disproportionate opportunities to do so. Other groups, often with equally legitimate interests, have far weaker opportunities to make their cases effectively before the legislature.

Finally, it should be clear how these various legislative characteristics compromise all four of the major functions of the Texas Legislature. Lawmaking, oversight, representation, and the providing of a forum for critical policy debates are all carried out in a far less satisfactory manner than is desirable. Regardless of whether a person desires liberal or conservative policies from the state government, he or she will not be well served by the current legislative system. A few individual and group interests will no doubt be well served. But the public interest will often suffer in the process. One can only conclude that public misunderstanding of the Texas Legislature—along with a false sense of economy that equates cheap government with good government—allows this situation to continue. Surely with the Texas Legislature the old adage is true: You get what you pay for.

References

Citizens Conference on State Legislatures. 1971. *State Legislatures: An Evaluation of Their Effectiveness.* New York: Praeger.

Davis, J. William. 1967. *There Shall Also Be a Lieutenant Governor.* Austin: Institute of Public Affairs, University of Texas.

Ellis, V. 1981. "Legislators Hunt Doves and the Chemical Lobby Pays." *Dallas Times Herald,* September 27, p. C3.

Miller, Lawrence W. 1977. "Legislative Turnover and Political Careers: A Study of Texas Legislators, 1969–1975." Unpublished Ph.D. dissertation, Texas Tech University.

Moncrief, Gary. 1979. "Committee Stacking and Reform in the Texas House of Representatives." *Texas Journal of Political Studies* 2 (Fall): 44–57.

Patterson, Caleb Perry, McAlister, Sam B., and Hester, George C. 1940. *State and Local Government in Texas.* New York: Macmillan.

Pettus, Beryl E. 1980. "Escape from Modernization: Legislative Institutions out of Synchronization with Environmental Changes." *Texas Journal of Political Studies* 2 (Spring): 27–41.

Price, Jorjanna. 1985. "Texas House Amends Its Rules Despite Warning, Criticism." *Houston Post,* January 10, p. B7.

Texas State Directory. 1991. Austin: Texas State Directory, Inc.

West, Felton. 1985. "Senate Should End Calendar Trickery." *Houston Post,* January 20, p. B2.

Chapter 7

The Governor

The governor is the highest elected official in the state executive branch. That official has a number of important powers and functions, which we will review in this chapter. Equally important, however, are public beliefs about the power of the governor, which we refer to as the image of the office. To understand fully the political and administrative roles of the governor, it is useful to consider first the character of that public image.

The Image of the Governor

If we were to ask the proverbial man on the street what the job of the governor is, the most typical response would probably be that the governor is just like the U.S. president except that the governor's powers are limited only to this state. In other words, the average Texas citizen might respond that the governor is the head of the executive branch, the boss, the leader of the civil servants who work in the executive branch agencies of the state government. A loquacious citizen might go on to say that the governor also has an important legislative role, just as the president does. This citizen would be thinking of the president's powerful role in the lawmaking process in contemporary America. The president has been allowed by the Congress to initiate policy and the lawmaking process on many important issues. In fact, the Congress has come to expect that the president will adopt that role, although members of Congress still guard their own power to revise or expand upon the president's policy recommendations. Thus many average Texans might assume that their governor has an analogous relationship with the Texas Legislature. The image of the governorship, in other words, is shaped considerably by the assumption that all governmental chief executives are much like the president.

The image of the governor described above is, however, seriously in error. As J. William Davis and Ruth Cowart Wright (1976:112–113) have expressed it: "It is with regard to the power of the governor that the average Texan probably suffers

138 Chapter 7

the greatest misconception of his state government. The governor is highly visible. His election is hotly contested. It appears that he must be a powerful chief executive, the counterpart of the president on the state level. Not so." In reality, the governor of Texas is a quite weak public official with powers that fall far short of those the average citizen probably believes the governor has. This fact has been reiterated by scholars and critics of Texas government for decades.

As long ago as 1933 a state legislative investigation of the executive branch of government concluded:

> It might be logically assumed that the duties of the governor, in his capacity as chief executive officer of the state, would closely resemble the duties of the general manager of a large business enterprise. This is not at all the case, however. There are a great number of independent agencies in the state government, and the executive heads of most of these agencies are beyond the scope of the governor's direct authority, due to the methods of selecting them. The pressure of routine business, most of it of detailed character, keeps the governor from devoting much time to duties of an executive nature. There are too many administrative departments, boards, commissions, and other agencies for him to keep in touch with them all. (Joint Legislative Committee on Organization and Economy, 1933:2)

More-recent scholarly discussions have pointed out that all of a Texas governor's formal powers, not just those of a strictly administrative nature, are quite limited. Many governors themselves have complained about the situation. Consider, as examples, the remarks of four governors who held the office in the twentieth century:

> The governor of Texas, under the present apportionment of governmental responsibility, hardly has the opportunity to form a policy and is without power to enforce departmental efficiency. (Dan Moody)
>
> If the governor asks them [a state executive branch agency] to do something they don't want to do, they can tell him to go jump into the lake. (W. Lee O'Daniel)
>
> The governor of Texas is something of a paper tiger. (Allan Shivers)
>
> Nobody works for the governor. They all work for their boards. Administrators won't volunteer anything—I never know anything except by hearsay. They volunteer nothing. (John Connally)

A major task of this chapter will be to explain why the preceding remarks are correct. In the process we will also examine the role that governors can play in state politics and discover the resources that determine their success in that role.

Before proceeding to the details of how the office operates, however, it will be helpful to consider the functions of governors and executive branch agencies more generally and to learn how public expectations of those institutions have changed.

The Functions of Governors

The role of an American governor in the politics and administration of his or her state is the result of several separate factors: public expectations about governmental responsibilities at different times in the history of the state, efforts to expand or to limit those responsibilities through constitutional reform, and alternating periods of competition and cooperation with the state legislature over how much power that body would allow the chief executive. Obviously the history, development, and politics of each state have been sufficiently distinctive that the governorship may have assumed a somewhat distinctive character in every state. Yet one can detect common patterns of state political development, as well. By tracing the historical evolution of those patterns, we can see quite clearly the ways they have affected the governorships of almost all states.

The evolution of what we might call the **public philosophy** that defines the role of governors—indeed, that defines in some sense the role of the entire administrative branch of government—was brilliantly described by Herbert Kaufman (1956). The idea of a public philosophy about chief executives and executive systems may sound highly abstract and academic. Yet when we explore exactly what is meant by this phrase, we find that it refers to practical and important matters about how government is to be run.

Representativeness

Kaufman noted three historical eras when different public philosophies were dominant. In the first of those eras, lasting roughly from the founding of the American nation to the late nineteenth century, the dominant philosophy stressed a goal of **representativeness** to be served by the executive branch of government. That is, this philosophy sought great public control over the executive branch. The practical results of the pursuit of this goal were, first, that early in the history of the United States, state governors were typically given a position subordinate to the legislature, itself the preeminent representative body. The governor's weak position was weakened further during the first third or so of the nineteenth century when a second dimension of representativeness was widely adopted. This second feature was the expansion of public control of executive officials by making the majority of their positions elective. Thus many states adopted a plural executive, whereby not just the governor but also most major state offices were filled in separate elections.

Chapter 7

Texas's first state constitution, that of 1845, gave the governor more power than any of its successors, although even then a stringent limit was placed on the number of terms a governor could serve in office. Each successive new constitution adopted more constraints on the office, in keeping with the philosophy of representativeness (Gantt, 1964:15–39). Even the 1869 Reconstruction constitution was in that tradition, but the Republican-dominated legislature gave a wide array of statutory powers to the governor that offset the general orientation of the document. It was the abuse of those statutory powers by Governor Edmund Davis and their association with Republican rule—as was described in Chapter 4—that led to the even more restrictive constitution of 1876. Put another way, the 1876 constitution was the product of a desire to rid the state of the "unrepresentative" Republican leaders and to weaken the powers of the governor so that no future incumbent could be the autocratic ruler that Governor Davis had been. Even today the office of the governor is greatly constrained by the provisions of the Texas Constitution of 1876.

Late in the nineteenth century, however, some of the institutional features established in the pursuit of representativeness fell into disrepute nationally. One reason for the disenchantment was the abuse of power by political bosses who controlled state or city administrations with political party machines. In many eastern seaboard cities such machines were based on the manipulation of new immigrants, because machine officials would supply jobs or other favors to the immigrants in exchange for their votes at election time. Yet widespread corruption among elected political leaders—in legislatures as well as in the executive branch—and a sense that elected officials often lacked the technical competence to carry out important governmental tasks also led to a new public philosophy. Kaufman called this second philosophy the search for **neutral competence** in government. That is, reformers sought to place control of many governmental functions in the hands of professional experts who were themselves insulated from political influence.

Neutral Competence

At the level of state government, neutral competence was sought by the creation of a variety of independent boards and commissions given the power to carry out specific governmental functions. These agencies were to be staffed with specialists whose expertise would shape agency decisions. Typically, heads of the agencies would be appointed by the governor with the approval of the legislature. But once those officials were in office, the governor could not control their policy making or fire them. In addition, the terms of office of the members of these boards and commissions did not coincide with the governor's term. Rarely would a single governor have the power to appoint even a majority of the members of a board. These various institutional arrangements, it is easy to see, did in fact insulate the experts who headed such agencies from very much political control by either the governor or the legislature.

Thus in the late nineteenth century a variety of such agencies was created, some of them sparked by the regulatory commission movement. In Texas a number of agencies were established in the period 1890–1920. Most of them were intended to regulate either a single business field, like banking or insurance, or a single profession, like law or medicine.

As Kaufman pointed out, neutral competence remains a highly valued goal for public bureaucracies. It is seen in the development of merit systems for public employment, in the desire to eliminate patronage employment systems, in increasingly advanced educational requirements for public jobs, and in periodic controversies over elective versus appointive systems of choosing executive officials. The 1984–1987 controversy in Texas over whether the State Board of Education should be appointed or elected is an excellent contemporary example of the last situation. In 1984 the legislature passed a law converting the board from an elected to an appointed one. The intention of the law was to allow a new team of neutrally competent board members to oversee the initiation of the sweeping educational reforms passed in 1984, or House Bill 72. Proponents of the appointed board had argued precisely that the existing, elected board was not competent for the task. The 1984 law mandated this change in the board for only four years, but a referendum on the 1987 election ballot allowed voters to indicate their preference between the two systems. The majority endorsed the election alternative. Representativeness prevailed over neutral competence.

Even many of the supporters of the philosophy of neutral competence admit that problems can arise in government because of this system. In fact, such problems have been hotly debated in the twentieth century as more and more government agencies were structured under this philosophy. The creation of a variety of independent boards and commissions under no central authority led to fragmentation in governmental effort. The multiple, elected executive system that was created in the search for representativeness had similar effects, and the independent agency movement exacerbated that tendency. Thus the coordination of policy efforts across agencies became quite difficult. At times different agencies in the same state worked at cross-purposes. Elected chief executives, the public at large, and even the legislatures that created the agencies did not have as much influence over agencies as they often desired.

The lack of coordination became more pronounced and far more important as state governments moved steadily away from laissez-faire toward positive state responsibilities, as was described in previous chapters. Government was becoming much more powerful, it was attempting to regulate many more aspects of social and economic life, and each separate governmental function was becoming ever more expensive. In those circumstances it is hardly surprising that governors and state legislatures desired to curb the independence of many agencies and integrate all their activities.

Executive Leadership

The disenchantment with the worst aspects of the independent agency system in the twentieth century led to the spawning of a third public philosophy for executive systems. Kaufman called this third philosophy the desire for **executive leadership**—meaning control and coordination of the entire executive branch by a single chief executive. Progress toward this third goal—which requires greatly increased gubernatorial power—has been slow in many states because of legislative fears about losing power to the executive, as well as the resistance of independent agencies to political control. Yet in this century a number of reforms have extended the authority of the governor in many states. The earliest of those measures increased the length of the term of office, allowed governors to run for more than a single term, and gave them greater appointive, budgetary, and policy coordination powers. In the last few decades, the period of extensive reform of state legislatures, the powers of many governors were also greatly extended, in particular by granting them new organizational controls over the executive branch (Sabato, 1978:63–96; Beyle and Muchmore, 1983).

In Texas, only a few of the reforms associated with the drive toward executive leadership have been accepted. The constitution of 1876 had no restriction on the number of terms a person could serve in that office, but its requirement for only a two-year term was changed to a four-year term by amendment in 1972. However, none of the other major reforms consistent with the notion of executive leadership has been adopted in Texas. Yet Texas is not entirely alone in its reticence to pursue this philosophy. The executive systems of many states still retain features of all three of the philosophies cited by Kaufman. Features of each new system were typically adopted piecemeal, so the net result has been an administrative hodgepodge with no single dominant rationale. The result for states like Texas is that the most recent philosophy, executive leadership, is the least well represented.

Despite the slow evolution of the philosophy of executive leadership, some states have advanced quite far in the pursuit of such a system. In those states there is considerable truth in the analogy between the powers of the president and those of the governor. Such states have accepted the idea that, in the era of positive government, control of the state's executive branch should be concentrated in the hands of a single chief executive who is accountable to the people through elections and through the legislature. Furthermore, to give that executive the ability to carry out the leadership tasks the public expects today, those states have expanded the formal powers of their governors in several vital areas—policy making, budgeting, and the activities of the executive branch.

The Reality of the Texas Governor's Powers

The powers that have been bestowed on governors in states wishing to strengthen executive leadership are **formal powers** prescribed either in the constitution or in statutory laws passed by the legislature. Virtually all governors have some powers in policy making, budgeting, and executive branch activities, of course. It is the relative extent of their authority in each area that distinguishes the weak from the strong. Yet because every governor's formal powers are set out in state law, they can be easily compared with those of the governors of other states. Thus one can assess the relative position of the governor of Texas vis-à-vis the powers of other governors and against the theoretical standard of executive leadership.

Rating the Governor's Principal Formal Powers

The most recent, relatively comprehensive assessment of the relative formal powers of American governors is that offered by Beyle (1983), following in the tradition of earlier work by Beyle (1982), Beyle and Dalton (1981), Ransone (1982:27–47), and Schlesinger (1965). Beyle distinguishes five areas of formal power for governors:

1. **Tenure potential**, based on the length of the term of office allowed the governor and the limitations, if any, on the possibilities of reelection to the office

2. **Appointive powers**, based on the percentage of major offices filled by gubernatorial appointments and the extent to which such appointments are limited by other arrangements (such as a requirement that the governor's nominees must be approved by the legislature)

3. **Budget powers**, based on the extent of the governor's control over the budget-making process

4. **Organization powers**, based on the extent of the governor's powers over executive branch agencies (powers that might range from directing the programs and policies of agencies to reorganizing large portions of the administrative system)

5. **Veto powers**, based on the governor's power to veto bills by the legislature and the legislature's power, in turn, to override such a veto

Beyle rated the fifty governors in each of these five areas, assigning scores of 1 to 5—the higher the score, the greater the power in the particular area. In addition to rating these individual powers, Beyle calculated a summary index of power based on all five areas combined (Table 7-1).

How did the governor of Texas compare? Out of a possible total score of 25,

Table 7-1 | **Combined index of formal powers of governors, 1981**

State	Tenure Potential	Appointive Powers	Budget Powers	Organization Powers	Veto Powers	Total Index
New York	5	5	5	4	5	24
Hawaii	4	5	5	4	5	23
Maryland	4	4	5	5	5	23
Massachusetts	5	5	5	5	3	23
Minnesota	5	5	5	3	5	23
New Jersey	4	4	5	5	5	23
Pennsylvania	4	5	5	4	5	23
Utah	5	4	5	4	5	23
California	5	5	5	2	5	22
Connecticut	5	3	5	4	5	22
Illinois	5	5	5	2	5	22
Michigan	5	2	5	5	5	22
South Dakota	4	3	5	5	5	22
Wyoming	5	4	5	3	5	22
Arizona	5	3	5	3	5	21
Colorado	5	3	5	3	5	21
Delaware	4	4	5	3	5	21
Idaho	5	3	5	3	5	21
Iowa	5	4	5	2	5	21
Alaska	4	1	5	5	5	20
Maine	4	4	5	5	2	20
Montana	5	3	5	4	3	20
Tennessee	4	4	5	3	4	20
Missouri	4	1	5	4	5	19
Nebraska	4	4	5	1	5	19
Ohio	4	3	5	2	5	19
Virginia	3	4	5	4	3	19

Table 7-1 | Combined index of formal powers of governors, 1981—cont'd

State	Tenure Potential	Appointive Powers	Budget Powers	Organization Powers	Veto Powers	Total Index
Wisconsin	5	3	5	3	3	19
Florida	4	1	5	3	5	18
Georgia	4	2	5	2	5	18
Kansas	4	2	4	3	5	18
Kentucky	3	4	5	2	4	18
Louisiana	4	4	4	1	5	18
North Dakota	5	1	5	2	5	18
West Virginia	4	3	5	2	4	18
Alabama	4	3	5	1	4	17
Arkansas	2	4	5	2	4	17
New Mexico	3	4	5	2	3	17
Oklahoma	4	2	5	1	5	17
Washington	5	2	5	2	3	17
Indiana	4	5	5	1	1	16
Oregon	4	1	5	3	3	16
Rhode Island	2	4	5	3	2	16
Vermont	2	4	5	3	2	16
Nevada	4	3	5	1	2	15
New Hampshire	2	1	5	4	2	14
North Carolina	4	5	3	2	0	14
Mississippi	3	2	1	1	5	12
Texas	**5**	**1**	**1**	**1**	**3**	**11**
South Carolina	4	1	1	1	3	10
Average score	4.1	3.2	4.7	2.9	4.1	19.0

Source: Gray, Jacob, and Vines (1983:458–459).

the governor of Texas received only 11 power points, making Texas's governor the second weakest in the entire nation in terms of formal powers. Why does the chief executive of Texas rate so poorly? To answer that question, we must examine the formal powers in each of the five component areas.

Tenure Potential The governor of Texas was rated as very strong in tenure potential, along with the heads of seventeen other states, principally because there is no limit on the number of terms an individual can serve. In theory a governor can, if reelected, remain in office long enough both to learn the ropes and to carry out an extended policy program. Yet the actual execution of such a program depends on other powers besides just tenure, and in those other areas the governor of Texas is far weaker.

Appointive Powers Beyle rated the governor of Texas among the eight weakest in the ability to appoint heads of major state agencies. The power to hire and fire agency heads, as the president of the United States has with a large number of federal agencies, would give a governor considerable control over the policies of those agencies. But the Texas governor is severely limited here because many of the most important agency heads are separately elected, including the comptroller of public accounts, the treasurer, the commissioner of the General Land Office, the attorney general, the commissioner of agriculture, the members of the Texas Railroad Commission, and the members of the State Board of Education.

The only major offices the governor can fill by appointment are the secretary of state, the adjutant general, the executive director of the Department of Community Affairs, and the director of the Office of State-Federal Relations. The secretary of state is a glorified keeper of certain state records, and the adjutant general is the head of the Texas National Guard. The executive director of the Department of Community Affairs coordinates a number of joint federal-state programs and administers certain federal programs run by the state. The director of the Office of State-Federal Relations is the state's lobbyist in the nation's capital. What is striking about this list of the governor's "major" appointees is that none of them has, in fact, a major policy-making position and none of them heads a truly major state agency.

The governor has the power to appoint the members of more than 100 boards or commissions, but that power is severely limited in accordance with the intentions of the philosophy of neutral competence. Some of the appointees must be drawn from certain professions or particular regions of the state; all of them serve overlapping terms of office of more than four years to limit the number of members of any given agency that a single governor might appoint; and once in office, they are outside the control of the chief executive.

Budget Powers Beyle rated the governor of Texas among the three weakest governors in the nation in terms of budget-making power. Although the constitution requires that the governor submit a proposed budget to the legislature at the beginning of each session, the Legislative Budget Board—an agency created in 1949 and controlled by the presiding officers of the legislature—prepares and submits to the legislature its own budget. That document has become by custom the definitive budget for legislative action.

Organization Powers In the area of organization powers the governor of Texas was once again rated as being very weak—in fact, as one of the nine weakest governors in the nation. The Texas governor has virtually no power to reorganize or consolidate agencies or their functions, nor does the governor even have clear authority to control the actions and policies of individual agencies. The constitution implies that the chief executive should have some control over executive branch agencies.[1] In practice, however, the governor has little control because of the independent constitutional status of so many agencies and the governor's limited power to hire or fire agency heads.

Veto Powers The governor of Texas scored a moderate power rating in veto powers. The constitution provides the governor with the power to veto bills passed by the legislature and to veto line items in appropriation bills. For a bill to become law over the governor's veto, it must be approved by two-thirds of the members of each house of the legislature.

Beyond the explicit constitutional details of the veto power, there are practical circumstances that both strengthen and weaken that power. Often the mere threat of a veto, if argued with enough force by the governor, can result in amendments to a bill before it is passed by the legislature. As the preceding chapter indicated, getting a bill through the legislature can be difficult enough in the first place, and the pressures of time can be so severe as to limit the prospects of getting it through both houses a second time should it be vetoed. Thus a sufficiently creditable threat of veto can often lead to a successful compromise that amounts to a victory for the governor.

The veto power is also strengthened by the fact that so many bills are passed in the last few days of the 140-day legislative session. Many bills arrive on the governor's desk for approval after the legislature has closed down and its members have gone home for another year and a half. Should the governor veto one of those bills, the legislature cannot override the veto, simply because it is not in session. Thus the legislature's inability to keep to a timely schedule, a problem discussed at some length in Chapter 6, limits its ability to control the lawmaking process vis-à-vis the governor. The governor's veto can be absolute with all of the end-of-session measures. A study of the use of the governor's veto power from 1876 to 1968 indicated that more than two-thirds of all vetoes exercised by governors during that period came after the legislature had adjourned (Gantt, 1969).

Finally, certain practical matters limit the governor's veto power over appropriations items. For example, the line-item veto must be all-or-nothing. The governor cannot say, "I believe this item is 10 or 15 percent too high, so I will reduce it by that amount." Instead the item must be accepted entirely or vetoed entirely. Often that means the governor must accept line items that he or she believes are too generous because at least some level of spending on that item is critical to the functioning of the agency concerned. It means, as well, that agency heads may be able to circumvent the item veto by clever budgeting practices. By combining controversial and noncontroversial items or by otherwise lumping items together—and getting them through the legislature, of course—they can often avoid the threat of a veto.

Governor Ann Richards has complained vehemently about the growing practice of lump-sum budgeting arising out of the combined efforts of the legislature and executive branch agencies. When Richards received the 1992–1993 biennial appropriations bill from the legislature, she found that the entire budgets for a large number of executive branch agencies were included in single-line items. Thus she had no choice but to accept those parts of the budget without any effective possibility of using her line-item veto power.

Other Formal Powers

Beyond the formal powers considered by Beyle, three other powers of the governor deserve some discussion: military powers, intergovernmental relations powers, and legislative powers.

Military Powers The constitution designates the governor as the "commander in chief of the military forces of the state" and empowers him or her with calling "forth the militia to execute the laws of the State, to suppress insurrections, repel invasions and protect the frontier from hostile incursions by Indians or other predatory bands." Given the unlikelihood of a border war with Mexico or a sudden uprising of the state's few Native Americans, this power is not consequential. The state militia may prove useful from time to time in helping preserve order after natural disasters, but the military powers of the governor do little to help him or her run the state government or shape its policies.

Intergovernmental Relations Powers Of far more consequence are the powers granted the governor in relations with other states and the federal government. The constitution charges the governor with conducting the state's business with these other governments, and that position as broker or spokesperson with the federal government can be critical. If the governor is an effective spokesperson for the state in its relations with the federal government, his or her credibility and prestige with the people and the legislature will rise.

Of even more practical consequence under this heading is that the governor is a key figure in dispensing to local governments funds that are provided by federal or state programs. A number of federal programs and grant distribution policies require the governor to act as the state's central planning and grant-dispensing officer. For example, the governor's office directly administered over $30 million in such monies in 1988 (mostly for criminal justice and regional planning activities) and is involved in the planning, funding, or implementation of local government activities in a variety of other ways.

Legislative Powers The constitution gives to the governor four major powers in the lawmaking process:

1. It directs the governor to deliver a message to the legislature at the start of each legislative session on the "condition of the State."
2. It empowers the governor to "recommend to the Legislature such measures as the governor may deem expedient."
3. It allows the governor to convene the legislature in special session and to set the agenda of such sessions.
4. It allows the governor to veto bills passed by the legislature (along with the item veto over appropriations measures) subject to an override if two-thirds of the members of both legislative houses overturn the veto.

These legislative powers are undeniably important. They illustrate that American constitutions typically provide for the sharing of legislative, executive, and judicial power among the branches of government rather than a literal separation of powers. Yet the formal legislative powers given the governor of Texas have not evolved as far as have those of the president or those of some other governors. The Texas Legislature has seldom been willing to regard the governor's ideas as more than mere recommendations. And unlike Congress and its relationship with the president the Texas Legislature has shown little willingness to allow the governor to initiate policy proposals. In other words, the status of the governor's proposals is far lower in the eyes of Texas legislators than is that of the president's proposals in the eyes of members of Congress. As we will see later in this chapter, Texas governors must rely heavily on informal powers to heighten the status of their proposals. Even using those informal powers, many governors must work hard simply to get a serious hearing in the legislature for their ideas.

The Governor's Staff

To assist in the execution of gubernatorial responsibilities, the governor is provided—in the Office of the Governor—a professional staff of notable size. In fiscal year 1992, for example, the Office of the Governor under Ann Richards was

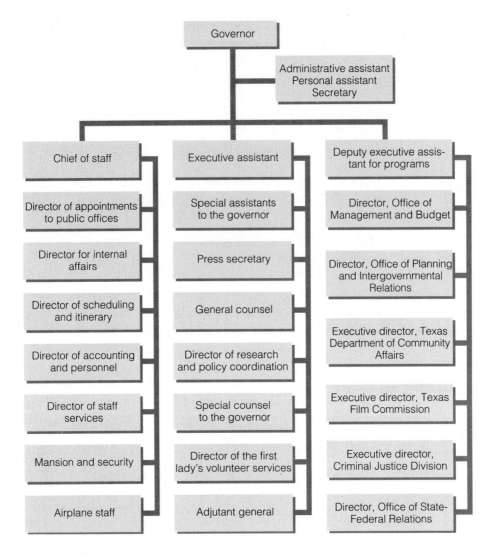

Figure 7-1 | Office of the Governor of Texas, 1985

budgeted $8 million for its principal operations. A typical organization chart for the office under the tenure of Mark White in 1985 is provided in Figure 7-1.

The Governor's Informal Powers

In addition to the powers fixed in law and described above, governors can draw on a few informal sources of political strength. The most important of these informal powers arise from the governor's duties as chief of state and leader of his or her political party and from the strength of his or her political personality.

Chief of State

The role of the governor is enhanced beyond that implied by the formal powers simply because he or she is the highest elected official in the state and that position carries considerable public and political prestige. Some of that prestige arises because the governor functions as the chief of state. Fred Gantt (1973:25) has described this aspect of the governor's job in the following passage:

> *In his role as head of state (which Constitution writers in 1876 viewed as what probably should be his major role), he represents the state on ceremonial occasions. He shakes hands with thousands of persons each year; he travels tens of thousands of miles to appear at public functions; he makes hundreds of speeches; and he is photographed with scores of groups or individuals. His presence at any meeting adds a sense of importance and dignity that would be lacking if he were not there, for he symbolizes the state and its authority. He issues numerous proclamations, calling upon citizens to observe such diverse occasions as Blackeyed Pea Week, Buy-It-Made-in-Texas Month, Multiple Sclerosis Month, and Save Your Vision Week—thus adding his prestige and backing to the observance.*

Acting in the role of chief of state, the governor has the opportunity to develop an important informal source of power, mainly because many citizens confuse appearance with reality. That is, they may assume that the appearance of power—as it arises in the role of chief of state—implies that the governor has equally prominent political and administrative power in the government at large. If people think the governor is powerful or important, then he or she will be able to draw upon that misplaced prestige to obtain additional power. Even other public officials over whom the governor has little or no formal power must grant him or her at least some deference because of the prestige of the office.

Some of the governor's formal powers—such as being spokesperson in Texas's relations with the federal government and with other state governments—arise from the role of chief of state. In exercising those formal powers, the governor can gain even more prestige. Again, if he or she is seen by the public and other state officials as carrying out prestigious duties in negotiating with these outside powers, the governor will become more important in their eyes.

Head of Party

By tradition the governor has been seen as the nominal head, at least, of his or her political party. That is, the governor is the party's chief spokesperson, typically leading the party's delegation at state and national political conventions as well as some of the fund-raising efforts of the party. This role is another that has developed informally and is not required of the governor. Yet most governors have desired the opportunity to lead their party because of the potential benefits to their own position and career. Like the chief-of-state activities, party leadership enhances the prestige, visibility, and apparent importance of the governor.

These benefits arise even though many of the governor's party leadership activities are more ceremonial than anything else, mainly because the party organization itself plays so limited a role in campaigns and elections. It does not monopolize the recruitment of candidates to run for office. It does not monopolize fund-raising efforts. (Most candidates, as we have noted, raise the bulk of their funds independently.) Nor does the party force candidates who run for office under its banner to accept a common set of policy positions. Despite those limits to the organizational powers of the major parties, they retain considerable prestige and importance that are bound to be shared by whoever is seen as their leader.

Political Personality

The main source of informal power the governor can draw upon—indeed, some would say, the most important source of all of the governor's powers—is personality. In other words, the governor's personal political skills and the desire to use them to accomplish political objectives determine his or her impact on state government. It is the governor's personal abilities as a politician—powers of persuasion, the ability to sell ideas to the public and to other officials, the ability to negotiate with powerful figures whether they are other public officials or representatives of major interest groups—that determine how effectively he or she will employ both the formal and informal powers of the office.

A governor's political personality is of special importance in Texas because of the severely limited formal powers provided to the office. If the office were accompanied by strong administrative, budgetary, and policy-making authority, then even a governor of limited personal political abilities could leave a mark on state government. In the absence of such powers, however, every governor must work diligently and resourcefully to leave a record of notable accomplishment. Personal political skill constitutes, therefore, the most important asset upon which any governor of Texas can draw.

The Governors Themselves

The remarks of the preceding section about the personal political abilities of governors lead naturally to a discussion of other factors relevant to that office—

above all, the requirements for the office and the kinds of people elected to it. Just as is the case for membership in the legislature, the constitution prescribes certain requirements for holding the office of governor. The candidate must be at least 30 years of age, must be a citizen of the United States, and must have lived in the state for at least five years immediately preceding the election.

The constitution also establishes certain terms and requirements of service for the governor, although some of those conditions have been changed by amendment over the state's history. The constitution, as accepted by the voters in 1876, prescribed a two-year term of office and set an annual salary for the governor of $4,000. In 1936 the salary was raised to $12,000 by constitutional amendment, and then in 1954 the voters accepted an amendment that allows the legislature to fix the governor's salary. By 1992 the legislature had raised the salary to $93,432, one of the highest governor's salaries in the nation. As we noted earlier, another constitutional amendment passed in 1972 changed the term of office to four years.

Practical Requirements for Election

Beyond the formal requirements of office, some practical limitations also determine the kinds of people who can realistically hope to be elected governor of Texas. If one considers the people who have successfully campaigned for the position since World War II, several practical requirements are obvious.[2] The first of them has been—with the one exception for Bill Clements—that the person must be a member of the Democratic party. Another essential attribute has been extensive experience either in the legislature or in another elective state office. Eight of the ten postwar governors have had such experience. The exceptions—John Connally and Bill Clements—had served in high-level administrative positions in the federal government in Washington. Third, every successful candidate for the office since the late 1930s has either been long associated with the conservative establishment elite of Texas or has favored sufficiently conservative policies to have been readily accepted by that elite (Green, 1979:3–21).

Another practical requirement for the office—yet one easily met by candidates who have already passed the three cited above—is the ability to attract a large amount of campaign funds. At least since the end of World War II, contemporary observers have lamented the high cost of campaigns for the office. An estimate of the cost necessary to assure election in the late 1940s was a minimum of $300,000 (Stilwell, 1949:320). That figure translates into about 30 cents per general-election vote cast for the winning candidate in 1948.

By the mid-1960s Gantt (1964:279) estimated that a hard-fought campaign would cost each candidate at least half a million dollars, or 35 to 40 cents per general-election vote for successful candidates in that period. That total spending

154 Chapter 7

figure was far exceeded, however, when John Connally reported spending $699,000 in his successful 1962 campaign.

The most striking increase in costs began in 1978 with the campaign of millionaire businessman Bill Clements. He was willing to spend his own money—and quite a lot of it—along with his outside contributions in order to get elected. In his 1978 campaign Clements spent more than $7.1 million, or about $6 for each general-election vote he received. Then, in the 1982 campaign, challenger Mark White spent $8.9 million, or about $4.20 per general-election vote, in defeating Clements. In the same race, Clements spent about $13.3 million—or $8.94 for each vote he received—in his losing effort. The final White–Clements rematch in the 1986 election saw the combined expenditures of the two candidates top $25 million and those of the winning candidate, Clements, average $6 per general-election vote. In the 1990 campaign, Ann Richards and Clayton Williams together spent about $36 million pursuing the governorship. The campaign spending figures for these recent races provide ample evidence of the importance of this last practical requirement for seeking the office of governor.

Who Gets Elected?

The importance of these practical requirements can be seen in the personal characteristics and backgrounds of the post–World War II Texas governors (Table 7-2). Every governor except one during that period—as well as the overwhelming majority of prewar governors—was a middle-aged Anglo male with substantial business and public-sector experience. All the governors in the postwar era have been college educated, and many—most notably the attorneys—have held advanced professional degrees. Most had served in some kind of state elective office before seeking the governorship. All but one had been successful businessmen or attorneys, as well. All of them save one were elected under the banner of the Democratic party, and all of those Democrats were associated with the party's conservative wing.

The Fate of Ex-Governors

To paraphrase an old saying, ex-governors never die—they just fade away. One might think that experience in the governorship would be an important stepping-stone to higher office. The office undeniably has much prestige, and one might think that service there could embellish any political career. Moreover, most governors have left the office in their middle to late fifties—still at an appropriate age to seek higher office. Yet rarely has a former Texas governor sought another office. Of the twenty-seven individuals who served in the office since 1876 and who did not die in office (as only one did), only fifteen sub-

Table 7-2 | **Personal backgrounds of post-World War II Texas governors**

Governor	Age at Election	Public Experience			College Education	Profession
		Texas Legislature	Other Elective State Office	Federal Elective or Administrative Office		
Coke Stevenson (1941–1947)	53	√	√		√	Banker, rancher
Beauford Jester (1947–1949)	54		√		√	Lawyer
Allan Shivers (1949–1957)	42	√	√		√	Lawyer, businessman
Price Daniel (1957–1963)	47	√	√	√	√	Lawyer
John Connally (1963–1969)	46			√	√	Lawyer, businessman
Preston Smith (1969–1973)	57	√	√		√	Businessman
Dolph Briscoe (1973–1979)	50	√			√	Rancher, businessman
Bill Clements (1979–1983)	62			√	√	Businessman
Mark White (1983–1987)	43		√		√	Lawyer
Bill Clements (1987–1991)	70		√	√	√	Businessman
Ann Richards (1991–present)	57		√		√	Educator, public official

156   *Chapter 7*

sequently ran for higher elective office or even for reelection to the governorship. Only five of those fifteen were successful, the most recent being Bill Clements. He was reelected to the governorship in 1986 after losing an earlier reelection bid in 1982 when he was the incumbent. The last governor to seek higher office successfully was W. Lee O'Daniel in 1941. O'Daniel served in the U.S. Senate after his stint in the governorship, as was discussed in Chapter 5. Fewer than a third of these twenty-six ex-governors have held any other elective or appointive public offices subsequent to their tenure as governor (Gantt, 1964:64–68; Phares, 1976).

It seems fair, then, to draw certain speculative conclusions about postgubernatorial careers. One is that the office is so limited in power—and, hence, political opportunity—that it rarely affords an individual the political success or public esteem necessary to seek higher office successfully. The second conclusion is that more-ambitious politicians recognize the limitations of the office as a stepping-stone to higher ones. Therefore, such politicians seek other routes to satisfy their ambitions and leave the governorship to the less ambitious and perhaps the less able. Either conclusion, if correct, would be a telling affirmation of just how important is the governorship of Texas.

Conclusion

Early in this chapter we discussed the public's image of the office and role of the governor; the public tends to view the governor as a powerful chief executive. Yet the remainder of the chapter has demonstrated how different from that public image the office really is. The formal powers of the office are very limited. Although there are informal sources of gubernatorial power, none of them are unique to Texas nor are they of unusual importance to Texas governors. Hence the office is weak both in an absolute sense and in a relative one when compared with the governorships of other states. Thus the office is very different from what the average Texan believes it to be. It may well be very different, too, from what the average candidate for the office believes it to be during the election campaign. Many candidates make campaign pledges they simply will not, if elected, have the power to fulfill, because of the limitations of the office.

The weakness of the governorship in Texas can be explained in large part by the influence of the philosophy of representativeness on the state's constitution and, hence, on the rest of the state's governmental system. Then the late nineteenth-century philosophy of neutral competence, widely adopted in Texas with the creation of a number of regulatory agencies early in this century, fragmented control of the executive branch even further. The result is an administrative system with little central control.

The Governor

It is also clear that the most contemporary public philosophy—that of executive leadership—has had the least impact on the office of the governor in Texas. Thus the state is attempting to achieve late twentieth-century governmental objectives with an administrative system rooted largely in the early nineteenth century. One should not be surprised that many difficulties arise in that effort.

These conclusions also emphasize the importance of the informal powers and the political personality of the governor of Texas—at least if the governor wishes to leave a mark on the state's public policies or administration. To have such an impact, a governor must be skillful as a politician and must use the informal sources of power boldly. Yet even the most skillful and resourceful of governors should not expect to have enormous influence on the direction of state government. This same set of circumstances explains why individuals with weak personalities and limited political skills are overwhelmed by the office. Such individuals—and Texas has certainly had its share of them as governors—are little more than figureheads exercising no real authority and, in effect, giving over control of the executive branch to the legislature and to the independently powerful heads of individual state agencies.

Notes

1. The constitution does not include a detailed explanation of the governor's executive powers. It does, however, along with a number of other specific grants of power, confer upon the governor the title of "chief executive officer of the State" (Article IV, Section 1) and charge that the governor "shall cause the laws to be faithfully executed" (Article IV, Section 10).
2. For an analysis of the patterns of ascension to the Texas governorship roughly between the end of Reconstruction and World War II, see Schlesinger (1957:74–87).

References

Beyle, Thad L. 1982. "The Governor's Power of Organization." *State Government* 55 (3): 79–87.

———. 1983. "Governors." In Virginia Gray, Herbert Jacob, and Kenneth N. Vines (eds.), *Politics in the American States*. Boston: Little, Brown.

Beyle, Thad L., and Dalton, Robert. 1981. "Appointment Power: Does It Belong to the Governor?" *State Government* 54 (1): 2–13.

Beyle, Thad L., and Muchmore, Lynn R. 1983. "Governors in the American Federal System." In Thad L. Beyle and Lynn R. Muchmore (eds.), *Being Governor: The View from the Office*. Durham, N.C.: Duke University Press.

Davis, J. William, and Wright, Ruth Cowart. 1976. *Texas: Political Practice and Public Policy*. Dubuque, Iowa: Kendall/Hunt.

Gantt, Fred, Jr. 1964. *The Chief Executive in Texas: A Study in Gubernatorial Leadership.* Austin: University of Texas Press.

———. 1969. "The Governor's Veto in Texas: An Absolute Negative?" *Public Affairs Comment* 15 (March): 1–4.

———. 1973. *The Impact of the Texas Constitution on the Executive.* Houston: Institute for Urban Studies, University of Houston.

Green, George Norris. 1979. *The Establishment in Texas Politics: The Primitive Years, 1938–1957.* Westport, Conn.: Greenwood Press.

Joint Legislative Committee on Organization and Economy. 1933. *The Government of the State of Texas: General Executive and Administrative Agencies; and the Militia, Texas Rangers, Highway Patrol, and Examining Boards.* Austin: Von Boeckmann-Jones Co.

Kaufman, Herbert. 1956. "Emerging Conflicts in the Doctrines of Public Administration." *American Political Science Review* 50 (December): 1057–1073.

Phares, Ross. 1976. *The Governors of Texas.* Gretna, La.: Pelikan.

Ransone, Coleman B. 1982. *The American Governorship.* Westport, Conn.: Greenwood Press.

Sabato, Larry. 1978. *Goodbye to Good-Time Charlie: The American Governor Transformed, 1950–1975.* 2nd ed. Washington, D.C.: CQ Press.

Schlesinger, Joseph A. 1957. *How They Became Governor: A Study of Comparative State Politics.* East Lansing: Governmental Research Bureau, Michigan State University.

———. 1965. "The Politics of the Executive." In Herbert Jacob and Kenneth N. Vines (eds.), *Politics in the American States: A Comparative Analysis.* Boston: Little, Brown.

Stilwell, Hart. 1949. "Texas: Owned by Oil and Interlocking Directorates." In Robert S. Allen (ed.), *Our Sovereign State.* New York: Vanguard Press.

Chapter 8

The Executive Branch of State Government

It took Mrs. Harold Thiele about 24 hours and dozens of calls to seven public and private agencies before she got a skunk out of her kitchen. The first call was to the Austin police. Officers feared a shot at the animal cowering behind an oven might hit a gas pipe. The next call was to Austin Animal Control. They did not answer the telephone on Saturday night so Thiele forced the skunk into a small cage. The woman called animal control officers again Sunday morning, but employees there refused to come out and get the captured skunk. Next up on Thiele's telephone list was the Texas Department of Health followed by the Austin City Sanitation Department and Austin Humane Society—all without luck.... [Finally] Austin City Manager Jorge Carrasco... ended the situation by sending an employee from animal control with instructions to "eliminate the problem."

—Associated Press

Whether or not Mrs. Thiele's skunk was the responsibility of a government agency is debatable, but the character of her encounter with these several executive branch agencies is not unusual. Members of the public often have quite satisfying dealings with executive branch bureaucrats, but frustrating and unsatisfying ones like Mrs. Thiele's are routine, too. Such encounters illustrate more than dissatisfaction with executive branch agencies, however. They also underscore how dependent we are on the work of those organizations. Getting rid of a skunk may appear a laughable, minor problem, but securing appropriate assistance from a police officer, a welfare caseworker, a government regulator, and so on is not.

Executive branch agencies and their employees carry out critically important functions and deliver essential services to virtually all Texans. Further, Texans have far more direct dependence on the work of bureaucratic employees—and are far more likely to have frequent, routine encounters with such employees—than with elected officials. Bureaucrats do not deal simply with abstract policy. They make specific decisions about services and policies that often have immediate and consequential effects on the lives of citizens. Thus the quality of the work of

162   *Chapter 8*

bureaucrats, the extent of their power, and the ways that their power is restrained by public and elected officials should be matters of considerable concern to all Texans.

Like ordinary citizens, elected public officials, we should add, often experience frustrations in their dealings with executive branch bureaucrats. Consider the governor, first, in this regard. Many people imagine, as was noted in Chapter 7, that the governor is truly the chief executive of the state's bureaucratic agencies. Yet we explained why that is not the case, and we will amplify that explanation shortly. State legislators, too, can experience frustrations with the executive branch. They may seek information from bureaucratic agencies to assist their lawmaking and oversight functions, and they may attempt to help individual constituents resolve problems or conflicts with state agencies. Doubtless, some of those exchanges will be satisfying and others will not. Such circumstances suggest that executive branch agencies are somewhat independent actors in the public policy process. That is an additional reason why Texans should be concerned with the power of those agencies and how it is restrained.

The Role of the Bureaucracy in a Democratic Society

The preceding observations raise a number of questions that merit detailed consideration. What ought to be the role of executive branch bureaucrats in a democratic government? To what degree and in what manner should they be accountable to elected officials? How much independent control over government policy should bureaucrats be allowed? What are reasonable public expectations for the manner in which individual bureaucrats and their agencies respond to the problems and needs of individuals?

Philosophical Perspectives

Even democratic theorists disagree on the appropriate role for the bureaucracy. Herbert Finer (1941:342), for example, maintains: "The servants of the public are not to decide their own course: They are to be responsible to the elected representatives of the public, and these are to determine the course of action of the public servants to the most minute degree that is technically feasible." According to Finer, bureaucrats should be closely supervised and directed by elected officials. Appointed administrators should be allowed as little discretion as possible. Whenever possible, the judgment of the elected official rather than the judgment of the bureaucrat should prevail on policy issues.

Carl Friedrich (1940) places greater trust in the ability of the administrator to make wise policy choices. Consequently, Friedrich would provide the bureaucracy with considerable latitude in the discharge of its duties. The test of a responsible decision would be the extent to which it is responsive to technical expertise on the one hand and to public preference on the other. According to Friedrich (1940:17), a bureaucratic policy can be called irresponsible if it was adopted "without proper regard to the existing sum of human knowledge concerning the technical issues involved" or "without proper regard for existing preferences in the community, and more particularly its prevailing majority." Friedrich would give bureaucrats a significant degree of independence from elected officials. He would then expect bureaucrats to make policy choices on the basis of their professional expertise. Decisions would be limited only by the requirement that they be generally compatible with the preferences of the majority.

Still another perspective is offered by Joseph Schumpeter (1950:68), who argues that the bureaucracy must be "strong enough to guide and, if need be, to instruct the politician." He continues: "In order to be able to do this it must be in a position to evolve principles of its own and sufficiently independent to assert them. It must be a power in its own right." Schumpeter's perspective is fascinating because it is not only a statement of what ought to be but also a description of what many people believe to be reality as well. That is, many critics of the bureaucracy charge that the bureaucracy is a power in its own right and that it has achieved virtual independence from elected officials. As a result, it is alleged to be both unaccountable and unresponsive.

These three differing perspectives on the appropriate role of the bureaucracy reflect a basic ambiguity about how much independence and power the administrative branch of government should have. Americans have a deep distrust of appointed officials. They fear bureaucratic power because too easily that power can degenerate into abuse and arrogance. American society agonizes over how bureaucrats are to be held accountable and made responsive to the will of the people. At the same time, the extraordinary complexity of modern society requires the dedicated attention of career specialists. Such experts should be protected from political interference so that they can perform their duties competently, fairly, and impartially.

Public Expectations

Average citizens harbor ambiguous, and even contradictory, attitudes about public bureaucracies. Citizens want bureaucrats to administer the law and public programs competently, consistently, and fairly, for example. To accomplish those goals, bureaucracies try to hire professionals who will apply their expertise, the best management tools and scientific knowledge, and the most sophisticated technology.

Americans also want their bureaucrats to be responsive, however. When citizens call or write to complain about a problem, they expect the bureaucracy to take prompt and effective action. Unfortunately, bureaucrats cannot always be

164   *Chapter 8*

fair and responsive at the same time. Fairness suggests that each case is handled on its own merits, without favoritism. If the bureaucracy is to be responsive, however, it has to play favorites. It cannot be responsive to everyone on an equal basis. To be responsive means to pick and choose among competing demands and to give certain ones preferential treatment. To respond to some demands means to ignore others. Unfortunately for bureaucrats, the citizen does not distinguish between fairness and responsiveness. Bureaucrats are expected to accomplish both. When they prove unable to do so, the public is often dissatisfied.

The public also expects efficiency and effectiveness. *Efficiency* is defined as accomplishing a goal with a minimum expenditure of resources. *Effectiveness* is defined as accomplishing the goal successfully. Often there is a contradiction between efficiency and effectiveness. Many citizens are concerned with high crime rates, for example. They want the police to provide better protection and catch more criminals. However, they may be unwilling to shoulder the additional tax burden necessary to fund major increases in police patrols. In this instance, effectiveness (lower crime rates and better police protection) clashes with efficiency (minimal resources required to do the job). Similarly, citizens want better streets and highways and education, but they are frequently opposed to paying more to obtain them. They want effectiveness and efficiency at the same time— and painlessly. When citizens face trade-offs between efficiency and effectiveness, they tend to blame the bureaucracy for its inability to achieve both goals simultaneously.

Yet another contradiction is posed by professionalism and independence on the one hand and accountability on the other. Most citizens want bureaucrats to be free from interference by elected officials and pressure groups and to be fair rather than to show favoritism. Citizens expect bureaucrats to be professionally trained and equipped with the most modern technology and to apply technical competence and professional values to the solution of public problems.

But citizens also want bureaucrats to be accountable to the public. Nothing is more likely to anger the average citizen than the perception that bureaucrats are arrogant and unconcerned with the people's wishes. But if an independent bureaucracy is established to ensure professionalism and impartiality, the government also runs the risk of creating a group of powerful public officials who are essentially free to chart their own course. An independent bureaucracy protected by job security is more likely to be accountable to its own professional values than to any concept of the public interest.

In sum, both scholars and citizens disagree among themselves about the appropriate role for public bureaucracies. Individuals are quite likely, in fact, to express contradictory attitudes on that matter at different times and under different circumstances. Thus, controversies about the role of bureaucracies in government are frequent but are seldom settled to general satisfaction. Consequently, the actual role of public bureaucracies reflects this fundamental disagreement.

The Evolution of the Bureaucratic Role

We could illustrate how the Texas bureaucracy reflects uncertainties about its role in several ways, but one of the easiest ways is based on the three public philosophies for the administrative branch of government articulated by Herbert Kaufman (1956) and discussed in Chapter 7. Recall that the earliest of these public philosophies stressed the goal of representativeness. Developed in the early nineteenth century, that philosophy sought to ensure public control over the executive branch, much in keeping with the argument of Herbert Finer (1941) that bureaucrats should be closely controlled by elected officials. The use of the plural executive in Texas, whereby voters elect a number of the heads of state executive branch divisions (governor, attorney general, land commissioner, treasurer, and so on), is in keeping with the philosophy of representativeness and Finer's argument.

The second public philosophy, that of neutral competence, developed in the late nineteenth century and sought to isolate administration from partisan political influence. Politically neutral experts were given wide discretion to shape public policy, much as Schumpeter (1950:68) argued that the bureaucracy "must be a power in its own right." The independent boards and commissions that run a host of Texas state agencies follow this second philosophy and Schumpeter's maxim.

Finally, the third philosophy is that of executive leadership, which evolved in the twentieth century with a motivation to ensure centralized control over the growing executive branch apparatus. According to Friedrich (1940), an administrator who strikes a balance between professional expertise and public preference in making policy decisions is directed at the same general goal as this last public philosophy. That general goal is also reflected in that portion of the Texas state executive branch in which agency heads are appointed by the governor and serve at his or her pleasure.

The Texas bureaucracy is, then, something of a hodgepodge of different kinds of agencies, created at different times under different philosophies about what their broad role in the democratic process should be. The real structure of the state executive branch, in other words, reflects the ambiguities and contradictions that both scholars and citizens share about that institution.

The Power of the Bureaucracy

We suggested earlier that executive branch agencies are often quite powerful politically, but we have not fully explained how they have achieved their power. Several closely related factors combine to make these organizations indeed a powerful and somewhat independent force in the policy process. First, bureaucrats

166 *Chapter 8*

are essential. Government cannot operate without them. They are crucial to the implementation and enforcement of thousands of state laws, programs, and policies. As we noted above, the typical citizen encounter with state government is most likely to be with an appointed bureaucrat fulfilling his or her responsibilities in that regard.

A second reason for bureaucratic power is implicit in our preceding discussion of the actual character of the state executive branch. The structural arrangements under which many state agencies were created gives them a good deal of independence and, hence, power. Agencies run by independent boards and commissions, for example, can often chart their own course, especially with regard to potential control from the governor, the alleged chief executive of the overall bureaucracy. Those agencies headed by separately elected officials can also resist central control by the governor. The elected heads of such agencies can develop distinctive missions and policies that may run counter to the governor's preferences. Elected bureaucrats are independently accountable to the voters—who are unlikely to reflect upon these issues of general executive branch coordination and the power of individual agencies.

Another major source of bureaucratic power is the discretion that administrators enjoy with respect to how they carry out their duties and even with how they interpret the laws that they are to enforce. Most state laws and programs provide many opportunities for the exercise of such discretion. Few laws are so precisely written that they do not leave a great deal of room for bureaucrats to exercise their own judgment with respect to how the laws should be interpreted or enforced. Often the governor and legislature explicitly give a great deal of such power to bureaucrats. That is, they pass relatively general laws and then charge the relevant bureaucratic agency with filling in the details. In the latter process, of course, the bureaucrats are actually writing part of the law and deciding how those parts adopted by the governor and the legislature will be interpreted.

Individual bureaucrats often have discretion, too, in the day-to-day enforcement of laws and implementation of policies. Highway patrol officers, welfare caseworkers, and regulatory inspectors, as examples, can frequently exercise their independent, supposedly professional judgment about how to enforce laws or apply general policies to the specific clients and individuals they encounter in their work. Even higher-level officials in the highway patrol, welfare bureaucracy, and regulatory agencies have difficulty in limiting such discretionary behavior. When such discretion is exercised, the bureaucrat is determining precisely what will be the law on the street, regardless of what is the law on the books.

Bureaucrats find yet another source of power in the support of clientele groups. Every bureaucracy has clients—the people and groups who use the services provided by the board, commission, agency, or department. Depending on the bureaucracy, the clientele group may be bankers, farmers, real estate agents, schoolteachers, doctors, or the oil or insurance industry. The highway lobby, for example, is one of the most powerful clientele groups in the state. These groups have a direct and vested interest in the decisions of their bureaucracy. They closely monitor its activities. Key members of the clientele group—whether that group is oil or insurance executives, highway contractors, or schoolteachers—develop close personal relationships with top administrators in the agency.

The Public Utility Commission (PUC) illustrates this relationship. Because the PUC approves or rejects requests from utility companies for rate increases, it is easy to see why those companies go to great lengths to influence decisions. The three PUC commissioners and their staffs are visited hundreds of times each year by executives of the utility giants—AT&T Company, Houston Lighting and Power, Southwestern Bell Telephone, General Telephone, Central Power and Light of Corpus Christi, and Texas Utilities Electric of Dallas. Although utility representatives are prohibited by law from discussing specific cases that are under review by the commission, their constant interaction with commission staff members provides numerous opportunities to influence policy outcomes.

Utility company executives also interact with commissioners and their staffs at business conferences. Frequently, the utility companies finance meetings and conferences and pay part of the expenses of state officials in attendance. Because rate increases can easily translate into hundreds of millions of dollars in additional profits, such meetings are taken seriously indeed.

Frequently the public interest takes a backseat to the narrow but much more forcefully expressed interests of the clientele group. When that happens, the bureaucracy is said to have been captured by its clientele group. A capture is most likely to occur when a bureaucracy has responsibility for the regulation of a certain occupational group or industry.

Some bureaucracies are adroit at exploiting the clientele relationship. Just as clients use the bureaucracy, bureaucrats also use the clientele group. If an agency's power, jurisdiction, or budget is threatened, it will call upon its clientele to rally to its support. If that support is sufficiently energetic, it may persuade the legislature to change its plans. This point is discussed in more detail later in the chapter.

The State Agencies

We have referred several times to the different kinds of state agencies. Yet one can get a more complete sense of the nature of the executive branch by reviewing those categories in modest detail, along with the most prominent agencies in each one. As we have described them before, the most important categories are agencies with separately elected heads, agencies with heads who can be hired and fired by the governor, and agencies with multimember governing boards or commissions whose members the governor can appoint but not fire. A general organization chart

168 *Chapter 8*

for the state executive branch, organized in terms of these categories, is provided in Figure 8-1.

Agencies with Elected Heads

Seven major agencies have individual heads or governing boards that are elected by the general public. They are described below.

Attorney General The attorney general performs two major functions. The first is to respond to requests for legal advice and opinions from the legislature and from all state agencies, boards, commissions, and departments. Although the attorney general's interpretations of laws, rules, and regulations are not legally binding, they do carry significant weight. Therefore this officeholder exerts a major influence on the operations of state government through evaluation of the legality of proposed or actual policies, rules, laws, and regulations. The attorney general is also the chief lawyer for the state, representing the state in civil and criminal cases and prosecuting violations of state law.

Comptroller of Public Accounts The comptroller is a powerful state official who directs the collection of taxes and, before each legislative session, issues an evaluation and estimate of anticipated state government revenues. Those estimates (which are issued monthly during the legislative session) are vital to the appropriations process because the legislature is prohibited from spending more than expected revenues provide. The comptroller is not only an auditor, accountant, and tax collector but also a key figure in the appropriations process.

Commissioner of the General Land Office The land commissioner's duties include control over the leasing of state lands (the state either owns or has mineral interests in 22.5 million acres) for grazing and for oil and gas exploration. This official also operates the Veterans Land Program whereby Texas veterans can purchase land with money borrowed from the state; the low-interest loans are made possible through bond sales approved by the voters.

Commissioner of Agriculture The commissioner of agriculture performs a variety of duties: enforcing laws related to agriculture, providing various educational and research services, maintaining standards of weights and measures, and promoting the agricultural products of the state. The commissioner also regulates the use of pesticides, administers consumer protection laws, enforces disease and pest control programs and policies, and provides food inspection services.

State Treasurer The state treasurer is an important financial officer of state government. The treasurer's duties include acting as custodian of state funds

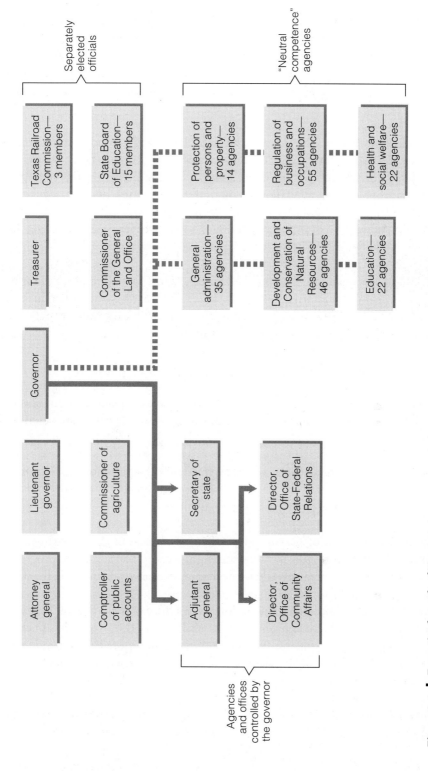

Figure 8-1 Executive branch of Texas state government

and securities, as well as county and municipal bonds; paying the state's bills; and selling cigarette and alcoholic beverage excise tax stamps. The state treasurer is also an ex officio member of the State Depository Board, which decides which banks will receive deposits of state funds, and an ex officio member of the State Banking Board, which reviews charter applications for new banks.

Railroad Commission The three members of the Texas Railroad Commission—who are elected in statewide elections to staggered six-year terms—have responsibility for the regulation of oil and gas drilling activities, the setting of production quotas, the regulation of oil and gas pipelines, and the regulation of coal and lignite mining. Originally established in 1891 to regulate the railroads, this powerful commission continues to oversee the transportation industries in the state, including trucking as well as railroads.

State Board of Education The fifteen members of the State Board of Education are elected from separate regions in the state. The board is the policy-making division of the Texas Education Agency, which supervises local school districts and, hence, public elementary and secondary education.

Appointed Department Heads

Agencies whose heads are appointed by the governor make up another type of state bureaucracy in Texas government. The heads of these four agencies are described below.

Secretary of State The secretary of state is the state's chief election official. Other duties include the issuing of charters of incorporation for businesses and the publication of administrative rules and regulations.

Director, Department of Community Affairs The head of the Department of Community Affairs is responsible for directing and coordinating various programs at both the state and federal level that are relevant to local governments in the state.

Director, Office of State-Federal Relations The Office of State-Federal Relations watches out for the interests of the state in Washington, D.C. The chief function of the director is to provide information to the governor on federal aid and grant programs and on national legislation that is of importance to state and local governments in Texas.

Adjutant General The adjutant general commands the Texas State Guard, the Texas Army National Guard, and the Texas Air National Guard.

Boards and Commissions

The vast majority of state agencies are of the third general type, multimember boards and commissions. Their membership consists of appointments by the governor (the most typical form of appointment) and, in some agencies, ex officio members (who hold the position because of another state office they also hold) or appointments by other state officials. Typically, the members of these boards are appointed to staggered six-year terms. The board makes general policy decisions for the agency and appoints a chief administrator who is responsible for day-to-day operations in accordance with such policies. Some typical examples of such agencies, within particular policy areas, are given below.

Agriculture A number of boards and commissions fall under the general heading of agriculture. A prominent state commission in this functional area is the Texas Animal Health Commission. As its name implies, its main task is to administer programs to fight diseases in livestock. Typically the law specifies that various groups and geographic regions be represented. For example, the nine members of the Animal Health Commission (appointed by the governor with the consent of the Senate to staggered six-year terms) must include hog, poultry, cattle, and horse raisers.

Education A major group of state boards in the policy area of education are the seventeen boards of regents who set policy for the public universities in the state. In addition to these boards of regents, another state agency is important in establishing and monitoring educational policy. The eighteen members of the Coordinating Board, Texas College and University System, have responsibility for administering state aid to community colleges and federal grants to colleges and universities. In addition, the board approves degree programs and has various responsibilities for construction programs and projects. The members of these education boards are appointed by the governor.

Health and Hospitals A nine-member board sets policy for the Department of Mental Health and Retardation. The board appoints an administrator to direct the operations of the department. The department's responsibilities include the operation of various schools, hospitals, outpatient clinics, and rehabilitation centers for the mentally ill and retarded. The department also has licensing authority over mental hospitals in the private sector.

Natural Resources A major board in the area of natural resources is the Water Development Board. Composed of six members (appointed by the governor with the consent of the Senate to six-year overlapping terms), the board sets policy for the Texas Water Commission, an independent commission with three full-time

172   *Chapter 8*

members appointed to six-year staggered terms by the governor. The Water Commission counts among its responsibilities the adjudication of water rights and disputes, the establishment of water districts, and the authorization of water use permits.

Regulation of Occupations A considerable number of state boards exist to regulate and certify qualifications for various occupations and professions. Prospective practitioners in those occupations and professions must obtain a license issued by the relevant board before they can engage in the occupation. The boards can also prescribe requirements for continuing education, testing or other hurdles for renewal of one's license, ethics requirements, advertising practices, and related professional activities. Some examples of such boards are the State Board of Medical Examiners, the State Board of Morticians, and the State Board of Barber Examiners.

One might wonder why state government has chosen to create separate agencies to regulate 55 different occupations and professions. We should add, however, that a considerable number of additional occupations are regulated by other, multipurpose agencies. Thus the total number of occupations under the supervision of the state is much larger than 55. Why, again, are these occupations of such great concern to the state? Is the system an example of big government run amok? In a newspaper editorial on pages 172–173, political columnist Molly Ivins (1992) offered a humorous version of the answer that political scientists give to explain a good deal of this form of regulation and the existence of many of such agencies.

Let's Regulate Some Big Things

Molly Ivins

"Several years ago," writes a longtime reader, "when you claimed that the state of Texas was fixing to regulate interior decorators, I thought, 'Oh, that Ivins, she'll say anything for a laugh.' But now I read in the papers the state is going to do just that. I promise never to doubt you again."

Well, I should hope not.

In fact, the scheme to regulate inferior desecrators has been kicking around for a long time now—pushed not by a government crazed with power, ready to take over every aspect of our lives, unwilling to let The Free Market work its Adam Smith–ish magic—but by, of course, interior decora-

tors themselves. Those on the right, who hold that Gummint Regulation hobbling The Free Market is the root of all evil, need to come study the Texas Legislature to find out how the real world works.

Gummint Regulation is almost never imposed from above by a power-crazed government but is almost always a consequence of some trade or industry begging to be regulated. The purpose, you understand, is not to protect consumers from the malefactors in whatever line of work it is— it's to protect the folks already in that line of work from other folks who would like to muscle in on the action.

The Executive Branch of State Government   **173**

Thus it is that the state is brought in to regulate the lawn-sprinkler installers, watch-repairers, barbers, cosmetologists and a plethora of other toilers and spinners, reapers and sowers, who would just as soon not have more competition, thank you.

These folks always manage to grandfather themselves, exempt from the requirements they lay upon whoever else wants to become an inferior desecrator, lawn-sprinkler installer or watch repair person.

The legislature is apt to go along not only because its committees are presented with endless tales of horror concerning appalling interiors, malfunctioning sprinklers and watches that never work again, but also because the regulatory programs pay for themselves: Those who wish to be licensed to do whatever-it-is have to cough up enough to cover the testing and inspection mandates. With no taxes at stake, the Lege is cheerfully prepared to mandate away. —Reprinted by Permission. Copyright 1992 *The Fort Worth Star-Telegram.*

| The Size of the Executive Branch |

The preceding discussion and an examination of Figure 8-1 could leave one with the impression that the state executive branch in Texas is quite large. There are, indeed, many agencies—both in total and in numerous specific areas of policy. Another way of considering the size of the executive branch, however, is to look at the number of employees there. The state's Legislative Budget Board recently compared Texas in this regard with the other 49 states (Table 8-1).

The board compared the sizes of state bureaucracies in a standard way: the ratio of the number of state employees to the total state population, which they presumably serve. On that basis, Texas ranks forty-fourth among the states; that is, only six other states have a smaller state bureaucracy in these terms. In general the more populous states, like Texas, have relatively low ratios by this measure, but Texas still ranks well below the average for the fifteen most populous states (identified by asterisks in Table 8-1). Thus, although Texas has many state agencies, its executive branch is relatively small. (For a discussion of privatization as a means of reducing the size of the Texas bureaucracy, see the box on pages 173–174.)

Privatization—A Panacea for Big Government?

We have said that a large bureaucracy is inevitable in modern governments. Obviously, such a system is also far more costly than government in earlier times. Considerable problems of inefficiency may arise in a large bureaucratic system, too, as we have suggested. Some critics of modern government have argued that **privatization** could be a partial solution for these problems.

Privatization is granting to private companies the power to produce goods or services that have traditionally been provided by governments. Some typical examples of government services and activities recently privatized in one or another state or local government include tax collection, garbage collection, management of parks or other recreational facilities, operation of correc-

174 *Chapter 8*

Table 8-1 | **Full-time-equivalent state employees, 1988**

Rank	State	Employees per 10,000 Population	Rank	State	Employees per 10,000 Population
1	Alaska	401	26	Kentucky	174
2	Hawaii	401	27	Idaho	170
3	Delaware	294	28	Arkansas	169
4	New Mexico	248	29	Mississippi	169
5	Wyoming	227	30	*Massachusetts	164
6	North Dakota	224	31	*North Carolina	159
7	Vermont	219	32	*New York	158
8	South Carolina	211	33	*Georgia	157
9	Rhode Island	202	34	Colorado	156
10	Montana	199	35	Nevada	154
11	Iowa	197	36	*Indiana	151
12	Utah	196	37	New Hampshire	148
13	Oklahoma	195	38	Tennessee	147
14	Kansas	191	39	Minnesota	143
15	Washington	185	40	*Michigan	139
16	Connecticut	183	41	*Missouri	138
17	Louisiana	183	42	*New Jersey	135
18	Maine	182	43	Wisconsin	134
19	Oregon	182	**44**	***Texas**	**124**
20	Maryland	182	45	Arizona	124
21	*Virginia	181	46	*Ohio	120
22	West Virginia	180	47	*Florida	114
23	Nebraska	179	48	*Illinois	113
24	Alabama	176	49	*California	107
25	South Dakota	175	50	*Pennsylvania	104
				Fifty-state average	147

*One of the fifteen most populous states.

Source: Legislative Budget Board (1990:3–14).

tional institutions, and provision of janitorial services.

The proponents of privatization believe that it can be both a less expensive and a more efficient method of providing government services. If recent estimates from the state comptroller are a good guide, however, privatization does not appear to be a panacea for the Texas bureaucracy. As a part of the Texas Performance Review, the comptroller's office surveyed state operations for possible services and functions that appeared especially appropriate for privatization. After examining the list of possibilities that were identified, the comptroller estimated that, if they were all privatized, the state could save about $30 million annually. Such a savings would represent less than 1 percent of the current 1992 fiscal year's budget, and it would doubtless be an even smaller percentage of future budgets (because they will inevitably be larger). Thus it appears that privatization could have but a marginal effect on the costs of modern government in Texas.

The Executive Branch of State Government

Fragmentation in the Executive Branch

We have alluded to how the structure of the executive branch inhibits coordination of agency effort and, hence, leads to inefficiency and a multiplicity of sometimes conflicting agency goals. An excellent example of this situation comes from the Texas Performance Review, a far-reaching evaluation of state government operations and finances mandated by the legislature and carried out by the comptroller of public accounts in 1991.

The Texas Performance Review considered the character of state agencies and operations in a number of policy fields, one of the most prominent of which was health and human services. The most important state agencies in this policy area are included in the organization chart in Figure 8-2: fourteen state departments, commissions, and councils. Each agency has its separate legislative mandate; governing board, commission, or council; executive director, commissioner, or administrator charged with running the agency; and extended set of agency activities and associated staff.

Of this system (if we dare give it so organized a title), the authors of the performance review observed: "Because there is no incentive for agency boards or agencies to work together, planning and policy-making often occur in a vacuum, all too often resulting in either unnecessary duplication of services or the failure to provide needed services." The performance review concluded:

> [These problems] are largely attributable to the fragmented approach that is taken in developing, administering and delivering health and human services. This fragmentation produces well-documented agency-wide problems such as a failure to maximize federal funds, inconsistency in rate-setting and contracting, and a failure to coordinate client transportation services. However, accountability across agencies is hindered by a lack of common program definitions, outcome measures, and regional boundaries that normally would allow for cross-agency comparisons and analyses of existing and needed services. (Comptroller of Public Accounts, 1991:43)

Nor is this policy field an exception. Indeed, virtually every broad policy area has too many agencies with too many diverse missions and programs to expect that coordination and efficiency are well served (Figure 8-1).

Reorganizing the Texas Bureaucracy

Criticisms of the fragmentation of the state bureaucracy have been made for decades, and various remedies have been offered with equal frequency. The most common proposed reform is one version or another of a reorganization of the

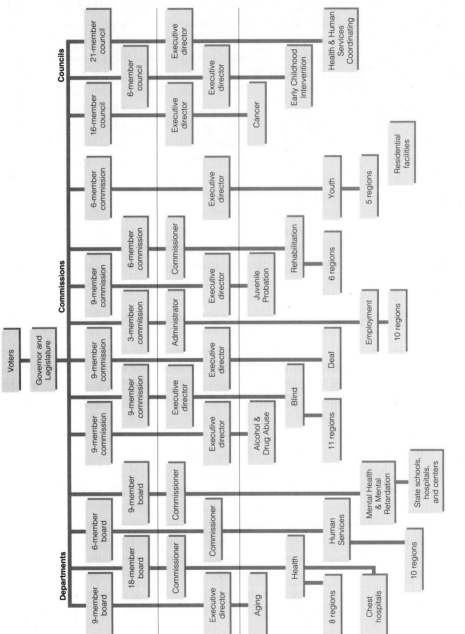

Figure 8-2 | Principal state health and human service agencies in Texas, 1991
Source: Comptroller of Public Accounts (1991:44)

system of state administration and agencies. Typically, such a proposal is made with the idea of collapsing several existing agencies into a single, larger one that would reduce the layers of bureaucracy, overlapping and competing functions, and duplicative administrative structures.

A good example of such a proposed reform comes from the Texas Performance Review. After describing the fragmented system of health and human services agencies (Figure 8-2), the authors of the review proposed a streamlined structure (Figure 8-3). The proposed system would have one governing board and one commissioner for the entire policy area, ensuring coordinated system-wide policy making, planning, and budgeting. The present fourteen major agencies would be collapsed into six departments, and their activities would be further coordinated by the use of common regional structures, field office locations, service delivery routines, client-handling procedures, and information management processes (Comptroller of Public Accounts, 1991:43–47).

The legislature even followed the general recommendation of the Texas Performance Review in this case. Eleven existing agencies were brought under the oversight of the newly created Health and Human Services Commission for purposes of budget and policy coordination. The ultimate success of this reorganization, however, in terms of efficiency and coordination goals cannot yet be judged.

Such proposals for reorganization clearly have an appealing logic. Reorganization is touted, first, for the prospect of eliminating the inefficiency and duplication of effort inherent in the current system of agencies. Under many proposed reorganizations—although not the one in Figure 8-3—accountability would also be increased because individual department heads would be hired and fired by the governor. (The governor was, however, granted the power to appoint the commissioner for the new Health and Human Services Commission created in 1991.)

Under the present arrangement, various agencies, boards, and departments are free to chart their own course. Consequently, different bureaucracies sometimes work at cross-purposes, with little agreement on goals and priorities. The absence of a common purpose, in combination with the absence of uniform personnel and financial practices and procedures, works against the efficient use of resources. Many observers assert that reorganization of the state bureaucracy would change all this. The governor and the governor's staff would set broad policies, and the department heads and agency directors would implement them. Goals and priorities would be clearly articulated, and the various state agencies would work together to achieve them. Setting goals and establishing chains of command and lines of authority, the argument runs, would contribute to the achievement of the goals and to the efficient use of resources in pursuit of policy objectives.

Another alleged advantage of administrative reorganization is that it would

178

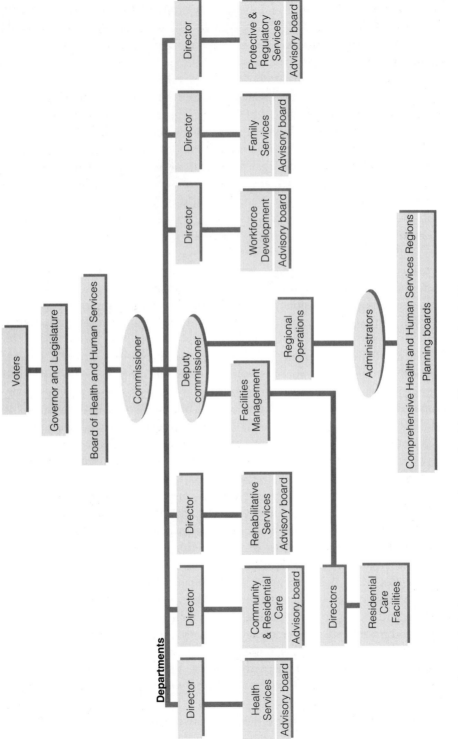

Figure 8-3 | **Proposed administration system for state health and human services in Texas**
Source: Comptroller of Public Accounts (1991:46)

reduce the influence of clientele groups. In the present fragmented bureaucracy, narrow interest groups have many opportunities to develop a preferential relationship with the state board or agency responsible for regulating them. The capture of a state agency by a clientele group ensures that the broad public interest will not be well served. But proponents of reorganization maintain that the consolidation of scattered agencies, boards, and commissions into broad policy areas, in combination with the concentration of power in the hands of the governor, would lessen, if not eliminate altogether, the direct influence of clientele groups. Bureaucratic officials would then be accountable to the governor rather than to a narrow vested interest.

Barriers to Reform

If there are so many criticisms of the fragmented, unaccountable state bureaucracy, and so many advantages inherent in reorganization, why does the state administrative system continue to operate without significant reform? The state constitution is not wholly to blame. Although the constitutional obstacle is indeed one barrier to reform, other, more powerful, forces are also at work.

One source of potential opposition is the legislature, or at least some members of the legislature. Reorganization plans often propose to strengthen the governor's control over the bureaucracy and reduce the role of the legislature in state administration. It is obvious, therefore, why the legislature may be unenthusiastic about proposed reforms. Moreover, many legislators enjoy close relationships with key bureaucratic officials. Those professional associations and personal friendships operate to the advantage of the bureaucrats when efforts are made to reorganize the state administrative machinery.

Bureaucratic officials themselves frequently resist reform. Their opposition is almost certain to occur when the proposed reorganization would eliminate some state agencies and drastically curtail the operations of others. Bureaucrats can be effective opponents. They have the information, experience, and expertise to support their arguments. They maintain that the professionalism of state government will decline and that efficient service delivery will suffer if the proposed reforms are implemented. Because bureaucrats can legitimately lay claim to expert status, their warnings cannot be taken lightly. Career bureaucrats can rely upon their numerous contacts in and out of government to quietly but effectively lobby behind the scenes against reorganization plans.

Some of the most vocal opposition to reorganization comes from elected officials. Any attempt to eliminate or consolidate the administrative functions presided over by the treasurer, comptroller, land commissioner, agricultural commissioner, or railroad commissioners would almost certainly arouse powerful opposition from the incumbents of these offices. And unlike appointed bureau-

180   *Chapter 8*

crats, these elected officials could make their appeals for support to a statewide constituency.

Another source of opposition is the clientele group. Groups that have labored long and hard for decades to develop a relationship with a state board or agency to ensure preferential treatment are highly unlikely to accept fundamental change in that relationship without a fight. Clientele groups are frequently composed of powerful, highly organized, and well-financed business interests. Therefore, their opposition to administrative reorganization is likely to be particularly effective. Given the widespread opposition to bureaucratic reform, then, it should not be surprising that reorganization efforts are frequently feeble and ineffective.

Even the few examples of recent successful reorganizations offer evidence of how seldom this strategy is likely to be employed. The legislature recently brought a number of health and human service agencies under the supervision of a single one, the Health and Human Services Commission, as was noted earlier. Before that, the most notable reorganization created the Department of Criminal Justice out of the old Department of Corrections and some smaller, related agencies. Yet both of those reorganizations were carried out in times when the state was in dire financial need and when the agencies being reorganized were especially costly and under great criticism by members of the legislature. Further, the clients of those agencies—principally the poor and medically needy in one case and convicted felons in the other—have essentially no political clout. These cases suggest that only in exceptionally favorable—and, hence, rare—instances is reorganization likely to be successfully implemented.

Would Reorganization Work?

With so many critics of the state bureaucracy, one might think any change would be for the better. But would it? In fact, the evidence from reorganization efforts made in other states suggests that the results are not always as expected. Kenneth Meier (1980) studied sixteen states that undertook a reorganization of their bureaucracies and compared them with a like number of states that did not reorganize. He found that the reorganized state bureaucracies did not spend less money than the ones that failed to reorganize. Other studies support that conclusion.

Moreover, there is no evidence that reorganized state bureaucracies are more efficient and effective than ones that do not reorganize. *Effectiveness*, we recall, is defined as successfully accomplishing goals and objectives. An efficient organization accomplishes goals with a minimum expenditure of resources (money, personnel, equipment, effort). The problem with the concepts of efficiency and effectiveness is that they are exceedingly difficult to measure. Before we can determine whether a state agency is efficient in the expenditure of resources, we have to determine whether it is effective. That is, does it successfully accomplish its goals? But before we can determine whether an organization has accomplished its goals, a judgment has to be made about what those goals actually are. And organizations seldom have goals that are clearly expressed.

This problem is revealed when bureaucratic officials are asked what the goals of their organization are. They are apt to respond with a broad statement to the effect that their goal is to deliver a particular service or a set of services to the public at the lowest possible cost to the taxpayer. But that goal is so vague as to be essentially meaningless. Deeper probing quickly reveals that each agency and department has a variety of different goals. There are long-term goals and short-term goals, operational goals and symbolic goals, goals for the top-level administrators and goals for the employees, goals for the organization as a whole and goals for the individuals who make up the organization. Moreover, different offices within the bureaucracy pursue different goals. The governor and the governor's staff may have one set of goals for an agency, whereas the director and the agency staff perceive a different set. The problem of determining the true goals of the organization may be further compounded by the contradictory nature of various goals.

Although we do not want to belabor the point, we must emphasize how hard it is to measure the concepts of efficiency and effectiveness. It is often alleged that consolidation of the bewildering array of boards, commissions, and agencies into a much smaller number of departments, with control concentrated in the governor's hands, would greatly improve efficiency and effectiveness. But if we cannot accurately assess efficiency and effectiveness, for the reasons previously discussed, how can we be so certain that reorganization would actually improve them?

Sunset Review of State Agencies

Although efforts at systematic reorganization have not been successful in Texas, one more-limited kind of reform was adopted in 1977 and has been in operation since. That reform is called sunset review, whereby each state agency is periodically subject to an evaluation to determine whether it should be abolished (and, hence, the sun would set on it), maintained in its existing structure, or modified in one or more administrative or programmatic ways.

The Sunset Advisory Commission, an agency of the state legislature, is responsible for the evaluations. The commission reviews a number of agencies each year and then presents the results of those reviews to the legislature in its next session. The legislature must act on the recommendations, but it does not have to adopt the specific proposals of the commission. Agencies included in the annual review are abolished unless the legislature decides to renew them for twelve years. All agencies are evaluated, with the exception of institutions of higher education and those created by the state constitution.

The results of the first sunset review cycle suggested that the new requirements might significantly influence the growth and direction of the state bureaucracy. Of the twenty-five agencies evaluated, eight were abolished, another was discontinued and its activities taken over by another agency, and two others were combined with existing agencies. In the second review cycle, however, only two of twenty-eight agencies were allowed to die and three others had their functions taken over by existing agencies.

The subsequent recommendations of the Sunset Commission confirm the observation that the review process has not in fact had a significant impact upon the state bureaucracy. The number of agencies abolished each cycle has remained low. More important, the agencies terminated have never been among the most significant and influential. For example, one agency terminated during the 1985 review cycle was the Texas Health Facilities Commission. Agencies abolished in earlier evaluation periods included the Pink Bollworm Commission, the Board of Tuberculosis Nurse Examiners, the Texas Navy, the Stonewall Jackson Memorial Board, the Board of Examiners of Social Psychotherapists, the Burial Association Rate Board, and the Board of Library Examiners.

Most of the abolished agencies have either been insignificant or inactive. Sometimes they are both. A tuberculosis nurse has not been graduated in the state since 1961, for example. Indeed, the only school that trained such nurses shut its doors that year. Therefore, elimination of the Board of Tuberculosis Nurse Examiners (which licensed tuberculosis nurses to practice) cannot be considered a major reform of the bureaucracy. In fact, the Sunset Commission has even maintained some agencies that should have been abolished. The Burial Association Rate Board had its functions transferred to another board, it is true, but the Burial Association Rate Board has not even met in fourteen years.

Earlier we noted that bureaucrats and their clients can offer powerful resistance to efforts to abolish or alter an existing agency. That seems to be the case with respect to the reform goals of the Sunset Commission. Powerful, well-entrenched agencies can employ a variety of resources to escape termination. The inconsequential agencies that serve no useful purpose, that have few employees, and that enjoy the support of no powerful clientele group are the agencies that will be scheduled for elimination.

Powerful legislators can also manipulate the sunset process to punish agencies of which they are critical or to protect those with which they have close ties (Curry,

1990). Despite that negative aspect, Curry argues that the sunset review process has produced positive results by increasing the scrutiny of individual agencies and by suggesting particular management and policy improvements. In our judgment, however, the benefits have been relatively modest because political influences sometimes overwhelm the process and because the small size of the Sunset Advisory Commission staff limits the depth of its reviews of agencies.

| Conclusion |

It is a practical reality that large bureaucratic organizations are necessary for the executive branch of modern governments. Yet the desirable role of the executive branch of government in the policy-making process is a controversial matter—for all levels of government, not just the state level. How to govern bureaucratic organizations most effectively and democratically and how to appropriately limit their role in the policy process are problems that no modern government has resolved to everyone's satisfaction.

The bureaucracy of the state of Texas amply illustrates the problems. The several different perspectives on the role of the bureaucracy are all represented to some degree in the actual structure of the executive branch. The imprint of the constitution of 1876 is evident, as well, as we explained briefly in Chapter 4. Furthermore, attempts to control the bureaucracy and to minimize its organizational problems seldom rise above the contradictory attitudes that both citizens and elected officials share about these organizations. Political considerations as well as rational calculations often affect the reactions that legislators, citizens, and the governor have toward proposals for reorganization or reform. The sunset process is similarly plagued. Even the public's general expectations for the executive branch—efficiency, effectiveness, responsiveness to particular problems, or whatever—are mixed and often conflicting. In other words, we can readily point to problems of inefficiency, redundancy, and limited central control of the executive branch, but it is far more difficult to propose solutions that would be widely endorsed.

Regardless of whether the problems inherent in the current organization of the executive branch can be solved, Texans should at least understand the character and implications of those problems. And Texans must recognize the role and power that executive agencies have in the public policy process. For good or ill, those agencies play a major role in the shaping of government policy. Thus they are not simply neutral instruments to be used by the governor and the legislature to execute legislative policies blindly. The agencies are active, somewhat independent actors in the policy-making process and, hence, in the determination of how Texans are governed.

References

Comptroller of Public Accounts. 1991. *Breaking the Mold, New Ways to Govern Texas: A Report from the Texas Performance Review*. Vol. 1. Austin.

Curry, Landon. 1990. "The Politics of Sunset Review in Texas." *Public Administration Review* 50 (January–February): 58–63.

Finer, Herbert. 1941. "Administrative Responsibility in Democratic Government." *Public Administration Review* 1 (Summer): 335–350.

Friedrich, Carl J. 1940. "Public Policy and the Nature of Administrative Responsibility." *Public Policy* 1: 3–24.

Ivins, Molly. 1992. "Let's Regulate Some Big Things." *The Fort Worth Star-Telegram*.

Kaufman, Herbert. 1956. "Emerging Conflicts in the Doctrines of Public Administration." *American Political Science Review* 50 (December): 1057–1073.

Legislative Budget Board. 1990. *Fiscal Size Up: 1990–91 Biennium Texas State Services*. Austin.

Meier, Kenneth J. 1980. "Executive Reorganization of Government: Impact on Employment and Expenditures." *American Journal of Political Science* 24: 396–412.

Schumpeter, Joseph A. 1950. *Capitalism, Socialism, and Democracy*. New York: Harper & Row.

Chapter 9

The Court System

The judicial system of Texas has surely come a long way since the days when Judge Roy Bean would open court in his courtroom-cum-saloon in Langtry in the 1880s with the following announcement: "Hear Ye! Hear Ye! This honorable court is now in session, and if anybody wants a snort before we start, step up to the bar and name your poison" (Lloyd, 1967:63). This chapter reviews the present character and operations of the state's court system with particular emphasis on how the functioning of the system corresponds with the public's understanding of it. Before beginning that review, however, it will be useful to consider the role of the court system in state government.

The Functions of State Court Systems

The Texas Constitution specifies that the judicial power of the state shall be vested in its court system. That power is principally one of applying the constitutional and statutory laws of the state to civil and criminal disputes. That is, claims are brought into the court system by private citizens who believe that disputes arising in their civil affairs fall under provisions of state law and by officers of the state who are charged with enforcing civil and criminal laws. The courts provide the institutional setting in which such claims will be heard. Judges sit as arbiters, presiding over the hearing of such disputes. And juries—panels of ordinary citizens—may be employed to evaluate the facts, the resolution, and the settlement appropriate to each dispute.

Much of the courts' work is routine application of the law to specific cases. An individual is or is not guilty of a traffic violation or burglary or a violation of the local building code. A divorce should or should not be granted to a particular couple. A deceased person's will is probated according to established procedures. The overwhelming majority of court cases are of this routine character—although, of course, any such case can be of great consequence to the parties involved.

188 *Chapter 9*

Other judicial decisions, though certainly only a small percentage, are far from routine. The law itself may be unclear on some points. The facts of some cases may be sufficiently complicated to obscure whether they indicate illegal behavior. And some laws may conflict with constitutional provisions. The courts are called upon to resolve such intricate matters as these. Court decisions in such instances can have far-reaching consequences that are hardly routine. When the courts decide how to unravel the law's tangles, they are deciding in effect what the law is. When they decide whether certain complicated facts fall within the purview of the law, they are defining the limits of the law's applicability. When they resolve conflicts between two or more laws, they are also deciding which law should prevail. In other words, in such instances the courts can make law and public policy.

The Role of the Courts in the Public Policy Process

One dimension of the functions of the courts in Texas politics today is especially remarkable as a change from the courts' role in past times. Selected state and federal court decisions since the late 1970s have dramatically affected the policy priorities of state government, and they have mandated equally dramatic additions to state spending. Those court decisions have even led some observers to argue that the courts—not the governor and legislature—are really determining major state policies.

The most prominent of these court decisions include the following:

1. *Ruiz* v. *Lynaugh* (formerly known as *Ruiz* v. *Estelle*), a federal court case that required sweeping reforms in and significantly increased spending on the state's prison system

2. *R.A.J.* v. *Jones*, a federal court lawsuit over conditions in state hospitals and the treatment of the mentally ill that forced the state to expand and improve its programs in that area substantially

3. *Lelsz* v. *Kavanagh*, a federal court case that challenged the conditions in state schools and the treatment of the mentally retarded and led to increased spending and improved programs in those institutions

4. *Edgewood* v. *Kirby*, a state court suit over inequities in the system of funding local school districts, in which the state's funding system was declared unconstitutional. Although no constitutional system has been developed as of late 1992, the state has already had to increase its financial support of local schools as a result of ongoing efforts toward that goal.

5. *League of United Latin American Citizens* v. *Richards*, a state court case that found that the state's system of funding higher education unconstitutionally discriminated against Hispanics. This recent case was appealed to

a higher court, and the final outcome is therefore uncertain. If the original decision is upheld, the state might have to invest substantial new resources in educational facilities in South Texas.

Some people have criticized these court decisions on the grounds that they have imposed unreasonable burdens on the state. Others argue that the courts are merely forcing the state to abide by its own laws and those of the U.S. Constitution. According to this second argument, those groups and individuals who could not get their rights ensured through the legislature or the governor have used the courts to do so. Regardless of one's viewpoint, however, a practical consequence must be recognized. Through decisions like those listed above, the judicial branch today plays an active role in the making of state public policy. In those cases, too, the courts' work is hardly routine, and the decisions clearly have far-reaching consequences. These facts are simply more reasons why it is important for us to understand the judicial branch of state government and how it functions.

The Image of the Court System

The nonroutine aspects of the judicial function are certainly the ones that are most widely discussed in the mass media and in scholarship on the courts. They are, after all, the more interesting aspects of the judicial role. The public also probably has greater interest in the nonroutine aspects of the judicial system (except when members of the public find themselves involved in a "routine" legal dispute). Yet a preoccupation with the sensational side of the judicial system has important consequences for our understanding of the system as a whole. It leaves Americans with images or perceptions of the courts that are not entirely accurate.

First, Americans have the widespread perception that judges are impartial, professional umpires in the system—that is, technical experts of a certain kind. Thus the average citizen probably expects all judges to be technically qualified and to be isolated from politics so that their decisions might not be biased by partisan leanings or ideological disposition. Then, in their perceptions of the court system, most people accord to judges a crucial role in the system. Judges are, after all, the neutral technical experts who sit at the center of court decision making. Finally, the average citizen probably believes that the nonroutine aspects of judicial decision making described here are the most important ones. Thus that citizen would focus attention on the highest courts in the system, the so-called supreme courts, because of the belief that more of the nonroutine and, hence, more important decisions take place there.

There is good reason to question the accuracy of these and many other public perceptions of the courts. A nationwide poll has shown, for example, that Americans admit they are less familiar with the courts than they are with the two other

190   *Chapter 9*

branches of their government (Bennack, 1983). That same survey also revealed some widely held but fundamental misperceptions of the operations of courts. In this chapter we will consider the accuracy of perceptions of the court system as they might apply in Texas. Although there is some truth in all of them, each perception can also lead to a misunderstanding of how Texas courts really operate. After examining the structure and operations of Texas courts, we will reconsider these public perceptions and their relevance for the reality of the court system.

Organization of the Texas Court System

A citizen's understanding of the court system ought to begin with the basic structural details of the system of courts, the geographic distribution of courts in the state, the method of selecting judges, and the role of juries. Thus we will first look at those aspects of the Texas court system.

Basic Structure of the System

The court system of Texas shares certain features with courts of all the states. The system is a kind of hierarchy in which higher courts handle appeals from lower ones. In this arrangement the lower-level courts are ones with **original jurisdiction**—that is, the authority to hear the initial legal action in certain kinds of disputes (depending on the subject matter handled by each court). In other words, it is in the courts of original jurisdiction that witnesses are heard, evidence is presented, and verdicts are rendered.

The higher-level courts in the system are **appellate courts**, usually with no original jurisdiction and only with the authority to hear appeals of decisions of lower-level courts. The appellate courts of Texas have been described in this way:

> *Appellate courts do not try cases, have jurors, or hear witnesses. Rather, they review actions and decisions of the lower courts on questions of law or allegations of procedural error. In carrying out this review, the appellate courts are usually restricted to [reviewing] the evidence and exhibits presented at the trial-court level. (Office of Court Administration, 1990:5)*

Within this general framework Texas, like every other state, has a fairly elaborate set of courts. The most important of those bodies, along with their relationships to one another in the court hierarchy, are portrayed in Figure 9-1. The three lowest levels of the courts are the ones with **limited original jurisdiction**. The two lowest levels, the justice of the peace courts and the municipal courts, have jurisdiction limited to minor civil and criminal actions. Municipal courts, for example, hear traffic cases as well as cases under city ordinances for zoning, fire

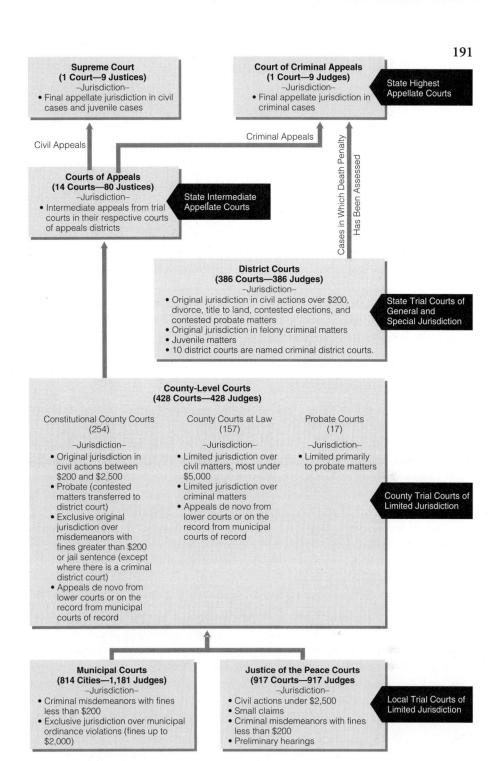

Figure 9-1 | **Court structure of Texas, 1990**
Source: Office of Court Administration (1990:9)

safety, public health matters, and the like. The criminal jurisdiction of the justice of the peace courts is limited to offenses for which the maximum punishment is by fine alone and that not to exceed $200.

Typically these two lowest courts are not **courts of record**. That is, no transcript of the actual court proceedings is maintained for future reference (as in appeals of the decision). Court records at these levels include only the nature of the original charge or complaint, the names and addresses of the parties involved, the plea of the defendant, and the final decision of the court.[1]

The second level in the system is that of the **county courts**. The Texas Constitution requires that there be one county court in each county, but the legislature is also empowered to create more county courts "as it may deem necessary." Thus by 1990 the legislature had created 254 constitutional county courts and 174 statutory county courts. Most of the statutory courts are located in major metropolitan areas because of the heavy caseloads in such places. Many statutory courts are also specialized bodies handling only civil, criminal, probate, or juvenile cases.

Constitutional county courts have jurisdiction over certain civil and criminal matters as set out in the constitution, whereas the jurisdiction of each statutory court is defined in the legislation that created it. Essentially, however, county courts also handle relatively minor legal disputes—only misdemeanor criminal cases, for example. In civil disputes over monetary matters their jurisdiction is limited to cases in which the amount in dispute is $2,500 or less for constitutional county courts and $5,000 or less for statutory courts. County courts also hear appeals of rulings from municipal courts and justice of the peace courts. County courts, like all those above them in the Texas system, are courts of record.

The third, and most important, level of trial courts is that of the **district courts**. These bodies have original jurisdiction in all felony criminal cases and in a number of civil areas. Generally, district courts have original jurisdiction over the more important legal disputes.[2]

The number of district courts has been increased over the history of the state in an effort to keep pace with the increase in caseloads. By 1990 there were 386 such courts, all limited in their authority to specific geographic areas. In certain large metropolitan areas, as well, some of these courts are specialized bodies hearing only selected kinds of cases. Despite the increased number of such courts, they have had trouble keeping up with the growing volume of judicial business. In Harris County in 1985, for example, the time between the filing of a civil suit in a district court and the trial of that case was projected to be thirty-seven months (Kennedy, 1985).

The first level of appellate courts in Texas is that of the **courts of appeals**. Each of these fourteen courts has responsibility for a specified geographic area. Eighty judges serve at this level. Each of the courts has one chief justice and from two

The Court System   193

to twelve associate justices. These courts hear only appeals from district and county courts (appeals of death penalty verdicts in the district courts go directly to the court of criminal appeals above this level, however). Hearings in the courts of appeals are decided either by all the judges on a given court sitting together or by three-judge panels.

Above the courts of appeals Texas has an unusual system in that it has two "supreme" courts. The one that is named the **Texas Supreme Court** hears only civil and juvenile case appeals of decisions made in the courts of appeals. It is a nine-member body whose entire membership sits together to decide each case before it. One of the judges is elected to the position of chief justice; the others are designated justices.

The **Court of Criminal Appeals** hears appeals of criminal case decisions of the courts of appeals and death penalty appeals from the district courts. This second supreme court also has nine judges who hear cases in Austin. Capital punishment cases are heard by the full court; others may be heard by three-judge panels.

The Texas Supreme Court has some organizational control over the entire Texas court system. It develops the rules of civil procedure—that is, the procedural rules under which civil cases are processed by Texas courts. It also formulates rules for the administration of various lower courts, manages the case distribution of the several courts of appeals to equalize their work loads, supervises the State Bar and its rules, and oversees the disciplining of judges for misconduct.

Geographic Distribution of Courts of Original Jurisdiction

Metropolitan areas have a great many courts and a greater specialization of courts because of their larger volume of legal disputes. The response of the court system to its ever-expanding caseload is considered in detail later in this chapter, but the location of various courts is an important element of that response. Thus it is useful at this point to illustrate the differences between the separate court systems of different parts of the state. In Table 9-1 the state and local courts are compared for three quite different Texas counties: Blanco County, an almost entirely rural county west of Austin; Lubbock County in the lower Panhandle, which is the location of the city of Lubbock; and Harris County in Southeast Texas, which includes most of the Houston metropolitan area.

The court systems of the two less populous counties in Table 9-1 have relatively small numbers of courts and judges. Even in Lubbock County, with about two dozen judges, most of the judges serve in the relatively less important justice of the peace courts and municipal courts. Harris County, in contrast, has a large number of courts at all levels and those courts are more specialized. In light of the number and variety of courts in large metropolitan areas like Harris County,

194 *Chapter 9*

Table 9-1 | Court systems of three Texas counties, 1990

Court	Blanco County (Rural and Small-Town)	Lubbock County (with a Medium-Sized City)	Harris County (Highly Urbanized)
Courts of appeals	None	None	First and Fourteenth districts—18 courts of appeals judges
District courts	1	6	59
County courts	1 constitutional	1 constitutional 3 county courts at law	4 civil 14 criminal 4 probate 1 constitutional
Justices of the peace	2	7	16
Municipal courts	1 town	6 cities and towns	33 cities and towns

Source: Office of Court Administration (1990).

it is easy to understand why many people admit to limited familiarity with the court system.[3]

Selection of Judges

All judges in Texas, with the exception of municipal court judges, are elected in partisan elections held on the November ballot in even-numbered years. District court judges and all other elected judges below them serve four-year terms and are elected by the voters in their geographic district. Appellate judges serve six-year overlapping terms and are elected on statewide ballots. When vacancies occur in district court or higher positions—typically because of death or retirement—governor-appointed replacements who must be confirmed by the Senate in its next regular session serve until the next election.

Partisan election of judges was favored in many states during the period of Jacksonian democracy of the middle 1800s, when representativeness in government was desired (see Chapter 7). In the twentieth century, however, a variety of other selection systems have been promulgated with the hope of isolating the judicial bench from partisan politics and increasing the number of professionally competent judges. Thus in some states the legislature bases judicial appointments on the professional abilities of the judges. Even more popular in recent times have been various systems whereby governors appoint judges from lists approved by a nonpartisan review committee intended to screen candidates according to their merit and competence. To retain their posts, the appointed judges in some of those systems must run for voter approval in an unopposed election after a certain initial term of office. Thus the public is allowed the opportunity to evaluate such judges on their records. It should be noted, however, that about a dozen states continue to use partsian election systems and that a nearly equal number use nonpartisan elections (*Book of the States, 1990–1991*, 1990:210–212).

Partisan elections have been widely criticized in recent years for several reasons. Such election systems are thought to discourage the candidacy of many highly qualified individuals who are averse to getting involved in politics and the rigors of election campaigns. Indeed, some people have argued that the individuals attracted to those aspects of the system might be the very people one would not wish to see on the bench.

It has also been argued that the focus on party labels and the general partisan atmosphere of elections divert the voters' attention from what ought to be important: the professional qualifications of judicial candidates and the actual judicial records of incumbent judges. The typically low voter participation in such elections—arising because many people vote only on elections at the top of the ballot and fail to cast votes in lower races, like those for judgeships—is said to undermine the degree of public control through the representative electoral mechanism. Yet it should be noted that all the various systems of judicial selection have their critics (Dubois, 1980:3–35) and that political science research on their character and consequences has not been able to demonstrate that any particular system is clearly superior or inferior to the others.

In Texas the system of partisan elections has been criticized from time to time for all the reasons indicated above. Some of that criticism has become particularly sharp recently. Public interest in the issue has typically been low, but some members of the legal profession have been actively promoting a change in the method of selecting judges. A 1983 poll of members of the State Bar, with about half of the membership responding, found overwhelming support for changing to a nonpartisan election system (*Texas Bar Journal*, 1983:463). (Only two choices were offered in the poll: keeping partisan elections or changing to nonpartisan ones.) The state legislature held hearings on the subject in 1984 and 1985 but adopted no changes. Then in 1986 several prominent state officials, including Chief Justice John Hill and Lieutenant Governor Bill Hobby, endorsed a plan for judicial appointments by the governor from lists provided by a nonpartisan review panel. Despite such support, many members of the bar and many sitting judges continue to favor and lobby for the current system, and the legislature has given no serious attention to a constitutional amendment to change the way the state's judges are chosen.

Grand Juries

All charges for felony offenses must arise out of a grand jury's deliberation over the facts of the potential case (although the accused can waive his or her right to

196   *Chapter 9*

the hearing and accept an indictment forthwith). **Grand juries** are twelve-member panels of lay citizens who serve individual district courts to review such cases, typically for a three-month or six-month term. These juries deliver an indictment when at least nine of their members believe that sufficient evidence is available to proceed with indictment and trial. If at least nine members are not so persuaded, the grand jury will issue a **no bill** and no indictments will be issued.

Grand juries are intended to provide a point in the legal system where average citizens can play a role to ensure the quality of justice. Grand juries throughout the United States, however, have come under notable criticism in recent years (Frankel and Naftalis, 1975). Although not much is known systematically about grand juries in Texas because of the limited research on them, two of the concerns cited by Frankel and Naftalis were found to be of great relevance to Harris County grand juries in a fascinating case study by Carp (1974). One of those concerns was that grand juries are seldom representative of the community at large; instead they are dominated by high-income, high-status individuals. Carp found that Harris County grand juries were overwhelmingly composed of male, Anglo, middle-aged, high-income business people and other professionals. In other words, the juries were far from representative of the Houston community.

Moreover, grand juries have often been criticized as being controlled by district attorneys—whose recommendations about whether to indict often are the predominant influence on the jury's decisions. Carp found that in 1971 the various Harris County grand juries sitting in that year spent an average of only five minutes on each case in deciding whether to indict—including the time necessary for the prosecuting attorney to present the case and the evidence. That finding, along with several others that emerged in the study, led Carp to conclude that the decision making by the juries was heavily controlled by the prosecuting attorneys and their representations. Typically the grand jury moved quickly through the facts of each case, simply rubber-stamping the prosecuting attorney's recommendation about whether to bring an indictment. To the extent that a similar pattern of decision making characterizes other Texas grand juries, one would have to conclude that they provide little public control of the judicial process. One would also have to conclude that the prosecuting attorney, instead, turns out to be the key figure in the indicting process and that the attorney's opinion of individual cases is seldom constrained by a grand jury.

Trial or Petit Juries

Criminal defendants and disputants in civil proceedings are constitutionally guaranteed a trial before a lay jury if they desire it. If the criminal defendant or both parties in a civil case agree, however, the case can be heard by the judge in a so-called **bench trial**. In the latter instance, the judge determines both the final decision and whatever criminal penalty or civil settlement is appropriate. District court juries are twelve-member panels. Petit juries in the county and lower courts are six-member panels.

The Work Load of Texas Courts

To understand fully the character and operations of state courts, in addition to understanding their structure, one needs a sense of the kinds and amount of business they do—the work load or caseload of various courts. Several aspects of the work load are relevant here.

Cases Heard by Courts of Original Jurisdiction

Because it is the lowest courts that hear legal cases at their inception, the courts of original jurisdiction are of particular interest. Indeed, the work load of the appellate courts is, to a large degree, a product of what occurs in the lower courts. The lowest courts in the Texas system—the justice of the peace courts and municipal courts—have caseloads heavily weighted with traffic offenses. For example, about 90 percent of municipal court cases arise from parking and traffic citations. Justice of the peace courts also hear large numbers of traffic cases along with a variety of others for misdemeanor crimes, small claims suits, foreclosures, and recovery of possession of personal property. County courts, too, have work loads heavily oriented toward relatively minor legal matters. Those courts hear, as prominent examples, large numbers of cases involving traffic offenses, driving while intoxicated, bad checks, personal injury, and debt claims.

As we indicated earlier, the district courts are the most important trial courts because they hear the more serious cases. A breakdown of the composition of the cases heard at this level in the most recent year for which complete data are available is presented in Figure 9-2. Although all cases involving serious criminal offenses are heard in district courts, such cases constitute only about a quarter of the district courts' total work load. In fact, more divorce cases than criminal cases are heard in a typical year. Among the criminal cases, the most typical ones are for theft, burglary, and drug-related offenses (Figure 9-2).

Growth of the District Court Caseload

Another important aspect of court work loads—and one that has caused considerable strain in all court systems—has been the great increase in the numbers of cases in recent decades. Although this phenomenon has occurred in all levels of Texas courts, it can be most appropriately illustrated for the district courts, again primarily because of their importance to the overall system (Table 9-2).

The state of Texas has tried to keep pace with the increasing district court caseload by increasing the number of district court judges. But even with a near

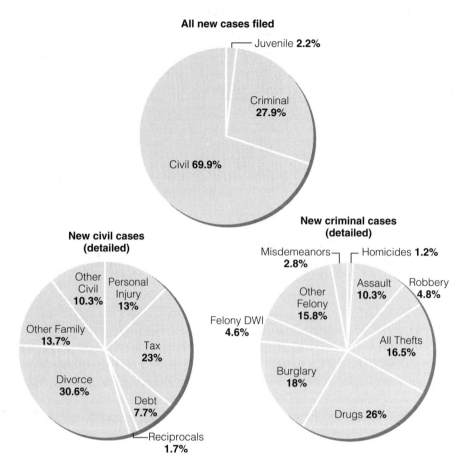

Figure 9-2 | Cases added to Texas district court dockets, 1990
Source: Office of Court Administration (1990:165)

doubling of the judges during the period covered in Table 9-2, the number of new cases filed annually per judge has increased by over a third. Thus judges are forced to hear more cases per year, and one has to suspect that the quality of justice might often be compromised under that kind of pressure.

How are district court judges able to handle the growing volume of work? If the typical judge worked five days a week for fifty weeks in 1990, he or she would have had to dispose of more than six cases per day on average to meet his or her share of the 1,697 cases settled per judge that year. Obviously, the average case must not have required much of the judge's or the court's time for resolution. One might fairly wonder about the quality of this fast-moving justice.

The Court System 199

Table 9-2 | Growth of Texas district court caseload, 1970–1990

Caseload	1970	1980	1990
New cases added to docket	260,171	427,871	676,985
Cases disposed of	249,829	373,355	651,643
Cases pending at year-end	259,847	473,191	664,643
Number of judges	211	310	384
New cases per judge	1,233	1,380	1,763
Cases disposed of per judge	1,184	1,204	1,697

Source: Annual Report of the Texas Judicial System (various years).

Most cases that begin at the district level of the court system also end there. That is, only a small proportion of district court decisions are appealed to a higher court. In 1990, for example, 8,062 cases were filed with the courts of appeals—the appellate court immediately above the district courts. In addition, 42 death penalty appeals went directly to the Court of Criminal Appeals. These two sets of appeals taken together, however, represented only a tiny fraction of the more than 1 million cases settled annually by the district and county courts in recent times. Thus, once again, the character of district court decision making becomes of special interest because the district court is, in fact, the "supreme court" for most cases.

Disposition of District Court Cases

We can see how the district courts get through their voluminous work load by examining in detail the ways in which cases are disposed of at this level (Table 9-3). In criminal cases, virtually all defendants either were found guilty or had their case dismissed. More than 60 percent of all the criminal cases settled ended in convictions or deferred adjudication, which is granted in selected cases in which a defendant pleads guilty and the judge places the person on a rigid probation and defers the entering of a guilty verdict. Almost a third of all the cases were dismissed or revoked, but that figure is somewhat misleading; in many of those cases the defendant had been convicted of another charge. (This circumstance arises because statistics are kept on the basis of cases instead of persons charged, and some individuals are charged with several cases in this system.)

Most notable in Table 9-3, however, is that only 1 percent of all district court criminal cases ended in acquittal. The explanation for this remarkable figure lies in a second statistic: the percentage of guilty pleas among all cases that were not dismissed. As considerable research on other states has also demonstrated, in the overwhelming majority of criminal trials the defendant pleads guilty at the start and is quickly sentenced. There is no trial as one might think of a trial in the

200   *Chapter 9*

Table 9-3 | **Disposition of Texas district court cases, 1990**

Disposition	Number of Cases	Percentage of Total
Criminal Cases		
Total dispositions	188,730	100
Convictions	90,607	48
Placed on deferred adjudication	24,383	13
Acquittals	1,318	1
Dismissed or revoked	53,257	28
Other dispositions	19,165	10
Number of convictions in which the defendant pleaded guilty	86,483	
Guilty pleas as a percentage of total convictions		95
Civil Cases		
Total dispositions	448,360	100
Judgment after jury trial	3,560	1
Judgment after bench trial	126,378	28
Default judgments	37,520	8
Agreed judgments	53,735	12
Summary judgments	5,170	1
Dismissed for lack of prosecution	66,495	15
Dismissed by plaintiff	72,137	16
Other dispositions	83,365	19

Source: Office of Court Administration (1990:168–169).

conventional way—that is, as an adversarial hearing before a jury with both sides presenting independent evidence.

It is difficult to know precisely how this pattern of the disposition of criminal cases affects the quality of justice. It might signify that the criminal justice system pursues only cases in which the evidence is entirely clear and overwhelming. In other words, all those individuals convicted in the district courts in 1990 were undoubtedly guilty if that speculation is correct. Of course, there might have been many guilty individuals among the third of the cases that were dismissed, perhaps because of the weakness of the prosecution's evidence.

Many critics of the criminal justice system question the universality of these conclusions. These critics point to the widespread use of the plea bargaining system, whereby prosecutors bargain with defendants to induce them to plead guilty, usually to a reduced charge, to avoid the time and expense of a full trial. The critics believe that many defendants are not fully informed of the consequences of accepting a plea bargain. Glick and Vines (1973:74) note:

The Court System   201

> *There is no element of due process in the system, and the defendant is convicted without formal procedures or checks guaranteeing constitutional protections. . . . There is no judicial review of the propriety of the bargain, and not only does the process take place clandestinely, but in the sentencing stage there is often a pretense that no bargaining took place in order to reach the guilty plea.*

Whether this system is just or not in most instances, it certainly helps explain why most cases end at the district court level. Because the overwhelming majority of those convicted of criminal offenses plead guilty in the first place, they have few grounds on which to support an appeal of their own conviction.

A similar pattern is evident for civil cases, as well. Only 29 percent of these cases were settled by complete trials. About one-third of all civil cases were dismissed, often after the parties had reached out-of-court settlements. The remainder of civil cases were also settled in ways that required little court time or effort.

The preceding observations indicate how the court system is able to handle the volume of cases that it does—even though the backlog of pending cases still is rising in Texas district courts. These observations are important in another sense, as well. They indicate that in only a minority of cases does the court system operate in the way the average citizen probably assumes it does. One could say the average citizen probably accepts the Perry Mason model of the justice system: all defendants are innocent until proven guilty, and they get to confront their accusors before a jury of their peers—with the privilege of brilliant counsel.

Yet the typical state court case proceeds in a far different fashion (Blumberg, 1967; Eisenstein and Jacob, 1977). Both criminal and civil cases are more likely to be settled out of court by private negotiations between parties. In other words, no adversarial confrontation before an impartial court and jury takes place. For criminal cases, the pattern of actual decision making indicates, as well, that the prosecuting attorney is far more important to the outcome than is the judge—for it is the prosecuting attorney who arranges the plea bargain, just as it is the same individual, one should recall, who dominates the grand jury and the indictment process. Finally, once an out-of-court settlement is reached, there is no appeal of its terms. The criminal defendant who pleads guilty effectively gives up that right, and the civil litigant who settles privately must do so as well, as a condition of the settlement.

Appellate Court Caseloads

Although we have argued here that the court of original jurisdiction is, in reality, the "supreme court" for most cases, it is still important to consider the work load of the appellate courts. Every defendant who loses a case in the district or county

202   *Chapter 9*

courts is guaranteed by the state constitution the right to appeal the outcome in the courts of appeals. As we noted above, currently only a small percentage of lower-level court decisions are so appealed.

Courts of Appeals In the 1970s the backlog of as-yet-unreviewed criminal appeals grew considerably—because of more-liberal rules about defendants' rights and because many more individuals convicted of criminal offenses were encouraged to appeal. Before 1981 those appeals went directly to the Court of Criminal Appeals. In other words, the intermediate court of appeals heard only civil cases. But the growing criminal appeals backlog forced the state to reorganize the system. By a constitutional amendment that took effect in 1981, criminal as well as civil appeals were first directed to the newly expanded courts of appeals.

After that reorganization, the courts of appeals made steady progress toward reducing the backlog of unreviewed cases for a number of years, but by 1990 the backlog began to grow again. In that year these courts disposed of more than 8,000 cases and ended the year with the backlog about 3 percent larger than at the first of the year. That end-of-year backlog amounted to more than 6,000 cases waiting to be reviewed.

Of additional interest are the results in the 8,000-plus cases settled. In 37 percent of the appeals the decision of the lower court was affirmed, and in another 19 percent the appeal was simply dismissed. In only 15 percent of the appeals was the lower court decision reversed in any way. (The remainder of the cases were settled in other ways without a decision by the courts of appeals.) Thus most of the time the courts of appeals accepted the decision of the lower court as appropriate.

Court of Criminal Appeals After the 1981 reorganization, individuals convicted of criminal offenses whose appeals were not found to be meritorious by the courts of appeals could request a rehearing by the Court of Criminal Appeals. The latter court has discretion, however, in what cases it chooses to hear. That is, those appealing to this court are not guaranteed a rehearing there.

The caseload statistics for 1990 offer a typical portrait of Court of Criminal Appeals decisions since the 1981 reorganization. The court received 1,380 petitions to review lower court decisions, 42 death penalty appeals, 2,078 applications for writs of habeas corpus, and more than 1,000 other motions (for example, for the rehearing of appeals denied earlier). The court added only 405 of those cases to its docket for consideration of the lower courts' decisions, and during 1990 it disposed of 457 such cases.

Supreme Court Since 1981 the Texas Supreme Court has heard only civil appeals from decisions of the intermediate courts of appeals. As a result its work load, though growing steadily, has been more manageable than that of the Court of

Criminal Appeals. For example, in 1990 the state supreme court received 876 appeals of lower court decisions. The court accepted 158 such cases and disposed of 154. The court also received more than 1,000 other applications for various writs and motions in the same year.

The Judges Themselves

At the beginning of this chapter, we observed that most Texans probably accord judges a particularly important role in the court system. We have by now pointed out some ways in which that view is both inaccurate and misleading. Yet no survey of the court system would be complete without a more detailed review of the requirements of judgeships, the processes of judicial selection, and the resultant character of the bench.

Statutory Requirements for Office and Salaries

State law prescribes certain qualifications necessary to run for election for some of the judgeships available in Texas. To qualify for a district judgeship or higher, one must be an American and a Texas citizen, must be licensed to practice law in the state, and must have spent a certain number of years either in legal practice or serving as a judge (with the experience requirement increasing for the higher positions). To run for election to one of the constitutional county courts, it is required only that a candidate "be well informed in the law." In other words, formal legal training and a license to practice law are not necessary. Service on a statutory county court may, however, require professional legal experience if it was written into the law creating the court in question.

There are no formal educational or experience requirements that justice of the peace candidates must fulfill before seeking election. In 1973, however, the state legislature required that nonlawyers newly elected to these positions must take forty hours of college study in the law within one year and then twenty more hours annually as long as they hold office. The educational requirements for municipal judges vary from city to city, but the majority of judges at that level—just like the majority of both county court judges and justices of the peace—are not trained in the law or, therefore, licensed to practice law.

The base salaries of the district court and higher-level judges are set by the state legislature. Counties where courts of appeal and district courts hold session may, however, supplement the base salaries of judges at those two levels, and many counties do so with widely varying supplemental amounts.[4] Salaries at the lower-level courts are set by the appropriate local governmental jurisdiction and, hence, also vary widely. Base and supplemental salary information for these various positions in 1990 are presented in Table 9-4.[5]

204 *Chapter 9*

Table 9-4 | Judicial salaries in Texas, 1990

Court	Salary	Comments
Texas Supreme Court and Court of Criminal Appeals		
Chief justice	$91,875	
Justices	$89,250	
Courts of Appeals		
Chief justices	$80,850	Some counties supplement
Associate justices	$80,325	these salaries with an additional $5,000 to $8,000 per year
District Courts	$76,309	Some counties supplement these salaries with as much as $10,000 more per year
County Courts	Varies by county	Determined by each county
Justices of the Peace	Varies by county	Determined by each county
Municipal Courts	Varies by city	Determined by each city

Source: Office of Court Administration (1990:10–11).

The salaries of Texas judges compare reasonably well with those of the judges in other states. In a recent survey the salaries of Texas Supreme Court associate justices ranked sixteenth in the nation among all state supreme courts (*Book of the States, 1990–1991,* 1990:221). Salaries of Texas district court judges ranked twenty-first, but that comparison was made only on the base figure for the Texas judges. Those Texas district judges earning the highest salary supplements indicated in Table 9-4 would have ranked among the top trial court judges in the nation.

More important, however, is a comparison of salaries of Texas judges and those of their professional colleagues who have remained in private practice. In a 1989 survey sponsored by *Student Lawyer* magazine, the average nonpatent law firm partner in Dallas and Houston, as examples, earned over $200,000 a year. One must suspect, of course, that the especially capable and successful law firm partners in Texas—those who are professionally well above the average—earn far more than these average incomes. Thus in terms of attracting highly capable legal professionals to state judgeships, Texas's judicial salaries fall far below what such capable individuals can earn in private practice in the state.

Judicial Elections and Appointments

Little research has been carried out on the typical election and campaign experiences of candidates for judgeships in Texas. As an example, little systematic

The Court System   205

information is available on how competitive or how expensive these races are. Nor is it known how the typical candidate decides to run, or is recruited to run, for office. Certainly these elections are quiet, typically featuring modest campaign budgets, low public interest, and low voter turnout. The turnout is low for these races because they are usually listed far down the election ballot, and many voters quit voting before they reach those positions on the ballot.

For the mid-1950s, Henderson and Sinclair (1964:22) have shown that in about 90 percent of the elections for district and higher judges, the Democratic candidate ran unopposed. That figure attests to the low political salience of these posts. By the 1982 election some 83 percent of the judicial candidates were still running for election unopposed. Yet in Dallas and Houston, where the Republican party is particularly strong, 51 percent of such races featured two-party competition (Bush and Coffee, 1982:1512). Thus in recent times the Republican party has begun to field a more vigorous campaign effort in some parts of the state, but only in some parts. We are reminded, once again, of the difficulties faced by the Republican party in its efforts to expand and provide a viable alternative to the dominant Democratic organization.

Characteristics of Judges

If more research on the election process were available, it might indicate some of the informal requirements for judicial positions. However, it is possible to learn some of those informal criteria, and a good deal more besides, by examining information on the personal backgrounds of Texas judges, collected by the Texas Judicial Council (Table 9-5).

Included in Table 9-5 are several revealing pieces of information, from which a portrait of the typical state judge can be drawn. Clearly women and young individuals are quite rare on the bench. The overwhelming majority of the district or higher-level judges are middle-aged males who have spent some time in private practice and in either a lower-court judgeship or a prosecuting attorney post. Although the data from the Judicial Council do not include information on ethnicity, black and Hispanic judges are rare in Texas.[6]

Positions in the three lowest courts are also predominantly filled with middle-aged white males. At the same time, lawyers are rare in the lowest courts. Other data from the Judicial Council indicate that fewer than half of the judges in these three courts even graduated from college.

Another quite interesting statistic here is the large percentage of judges who first gained their positions by appointment. The percentage varies across the various kinds of courts, but it is of notable magnitude for all of them. Because judges are publicly elected, these figures might seem puzzling. Their explanation lies in the relative frequency with which the governor gets to fill vacancies on the

Table 9-5 | Personal characteristics of Texas judges

Characteristic	Supreme Court	Court of Criminal Appeals	Courts of Appeals	District Courts	Constitutional County Courts	Statutory County Courts	Justices of the Peace	Municipal Courts
Number on the Bench	9	9	80	374	254	174	949	1,191
Average Age	50	53	56	52	55	50	56	53
Sex (%)								
Male	100	100	91	90	—	—	—	—
Female	0	0	9	10	—	—	—	—
Law School Graduates (%)	100	100	100	99	28	90	7	30
Percentage Licensed to Practice Law	100	100	100	100	26	100	6	48
(Percentage of total reporting education data)	(100)	(100)	(94)	(95)	(58)	(85)	(70)	(45)
Percentage Reporting Previous Experience as								
Prosecutor	22	44	26	45	—	42	—	—
Private attorney	100	89	82	80	—	71	—	—
Lower court judge	33	22	41	25	—	18	—	—
Percentage Who Came to Present Judgeship by								
Election	66	77	47	41	73	39	59	—
Appointment	33	22	52	59	26	61	41	—
(Percentage of total reporting how they entered present position)	(100)	(100)	(100)	(100)	(97)	(94)	(82)	—

Source: Office of Court Administration (1989:90, 736–751).

bench. Gubernatorial appointees who want to remain on the bench must seek reelection at the next regular election date, but by that time they are incumbent judges who can profit from public exposure, incumbency status, and—if they are competent—a positive reputation among other lawyers and judges.

No research has been done on judicial retirements and the motivations that lead judges to retire and, hence, create the possibility of so many gubernatorial appointments. Yet one might speculate that at least two factors are at work in the process. Because so many judges are in their middle age or later, many of them may be ready to retire completely after eight or ten years on the bench. On the other hand, some judges may decide that they cannot afford to remain on the bench very many years. When they compare their state salaries to those available in private practice, many may choose to return to the more lucrative alternative after a few years. Certainly a highly competent attorney working only part-time in private practice could still earn more than many judges. That alternative might look more and more attractive to aging judges, tired of the heavy work load, inflexible hours, and repetitiveness of their duties on the bench.

Conclusion

Early in this chapter we considered the average citizen's image of the court system. The average citizen probably thinks of judges as professional, nonpolitical experts, believes that judges and juries are crucial figures in the settling of all legal disputes, and thinks of the appellate courts as the most important courts in the system.

Although that image of the court system is accurate to some degree, it is also misleading. In light of the actual structure and operation of the Texas court system, several qualifications must be noted with regard to that image. The professional expertise of many Texas judges is only that which they have gained by experience in the office—because many of the lower-level judges are not trained as lawyers. Furthermore, almost all the state's judges are inevitably caught up in politics and partisan influences, given that they must stand for election on partisan ballots. Nor does the election system, as was explained earlier, contribute much to the voter's ability to evaluate candidates for judgeships on their professional merit and ability.

Although the preceding remarks about Texas judges are important, the present chapter has also indicated why judges are not as central to the outcome of most legal disputes as many citizens think. The increasing caseloads, the pressure on criminal defendants to plea-bargain, the pressure in civil cases for out-of-court settlements, and the powerful role of the prosecuting attorneys all indicate why the role of either the judge or the jury is often quite limited—or even virtually nonexistent.

Finally, this chapter has suggested why one should not place too much emphasis on the role of the appellate courts either. The vast majority of cases begin

Chapter 9

and end in the same place: the court of original jurisdiction. The nature of the typical legal outcome—with mostly guilty pleas in criminal cases and out-of-court settlements in civil cases—also helps explain why those cases cannot be appealed. These findings indicate why all the components of the courts of original jurisdiction—the professionalism of their judges, the fairness and concern for justice of their prosecuting attorneys, and the time spent in settling individual cases—are critically important to the quality of justice in Texas.

Notes

1. None of the state's justice of the peace courts is a court of record. Only 10 of 828 cities—Austin, El Paso, Houston, Longview, Lubbock, Marshall, Midland, San Antonio, Sweetwater, and Wichita Falls—maintain their municipal courts as courts of record. This circumstance becomes important when someone appeals a decision of one of these courts to a higher level. When the appeal is of a decision of a non-court-of-record body, the case must be completely retried, or tried **de novo**, in the higher court. That fact, and the added expenses associated with such rehearings, means that in most appeals from such courts the case is dismissed by the original judge so that his or her jurisdiction can avoid those expenses.
2. The jurisdictions of the county and district courts overlap somewhat: in civil suits with financial controversies in which the amount at issue is between $200 and $5,000. The district courts have jurisdiction when the amount at issue is $5,000 or more.
3. Public understanding of the complete American court system is complicated by the existence of the state and local system described in this chapter as well as the federal court system, which is not covered here.
4. These salary supplements are limited by state law so that the maximum possible annual salary for judges at one court level is always at least $1,000 less than that of judges at the next level.
5. No single official source lists the salaries of all lower-court judges in Texas. Toombs (1983), however, has shown that the salaries of justices of the peace, many of whom are only part-time officials, are rather low, especially outside major metropolitan areas. In 1979, according to Toombs's data, almost half of all justices of the peace earned annual salaries of less than $7,000. Only 15 percent of them earned $16,000 or more.
6. This portrait of the typical contemporary judge is virtually identical to that drawn by Henderson and Sinclair (1964) for the typical Texas judge of the mid-1950s.

References

Bennack, Frank A. 1983. "The Public, the Media, and the Judicial System." *State Court Journal* 7 (Fall): 4–13.
Blumberg, Abraham S. 1967. *Criminal Justice.* Chicago: Quadrangle Books.
Book of the States, 1990–1991. 1990. Lexington, Ky.: Council of State Governments.
Bush, Bob, and Coffee, Gordon. 1982. "The Partisan System and the Search for Alternatives." *Texas Bar Journal* 45 (December): 1511–1513.

The Court System 209

Carp, Robert A. 1974. "The Harris County Grand Jury—A Case Study." *Houston Law Review* 12 (October): 90–120.

Dubois, Philip L. 1980. *From Ballot to Bench: Judicial Elections and the Quest for Accountability.* Austin: University of Texas Press.

Eisenstein, James, and Jacob, Herbert. 1977. *Felony Justice: An Organizational Analysis of Criminal Courts.* Boston: Little, Brown.

Frankel, Marvin E., and Naftalis, Gary P. 1975. *The Grand Jury: An Institution on Trial.* New York: Hill & Wang.

Glick, Henry Robert, and Vines, Kenneth N. 1973. *State Court Systems.* Englewood Cliffs, N.J.: Prentice-Hall.

Henderson, Bancroft C., and Sinclair, T. C. 1964. *Judicial Selection in Texas: An Exploratory Study.* Houston: Public Affairs Research Center, University of Houston.

Kennedy, Tom. 1985. "Individual Docket May Aid Case Load." *Houston Post*, March 18, p. B1.

Lloyd, Everett. 1967. *Law West of the Pecos: The Story of Roy Bean.* San Antonio: Naylor Co.

Office of Court Administration. 1989. *Texas Judicial System Annual Report, 1989.* Austin: Texas Judicial Council.

———. 1990. *Texas Judicial System Annual Report, 1990.* Austin: Texas Judicial Council.

Texas Bar Journal. 1983. "State Bar Activities: Referendum Results Announced." Vol. 46 (April): 463.

Toombs, Dennis L. 1983. "The Part-Time Lay Justice of the Peace in Texas." *Public Affairs Comment* 29 (May): 1–7.

Chapter 10

The Political Economy of the Metropolis

The urban areas of Texas have been particularly affected by the economic developments described in Chapter 1. In fact, the evolution of the state's economy over the last century has profoundly shaped the character of all cities in the United States, along with the problems of governing those cities. At the beginning of the century the great cities of the nation—New York, Chicago, Pittsburgh, and so on—already had been transformed by the growth of the industrial economy, and those cities of the early industrial era reflected the requirements of the time in a number of ways. All the major elements necessary for the success of that economic system had to be near each other: workers, management, transportation, capital, and raw materials. Both raw materials and finished products were heavy and took up space. Plastics and lightweight alloys were not available, and transportation systems for the movement of materials were limited. Interstate freeways, trucking, and jet travel were nonexistent. Industrial centers were heavily dependent upon water and rail transport.

Because the age of the automobile, freeways, and suburbs had not yet dawned, workers had to live close to the factory. Because of the nature of assembly-line production, management had to be nearby to supervise and control labor. The limited communications system ensured that banking, marketing, and distribution services and facilities would be located near production and manufacturing centers. In short, the industrial city was much more compact than cities today. The limitations of transportation, communications, and technology demanded a close-knit and geographically concentrated urban area.

The modern city is vastly different. A drive through one of the great urban areas of Texas reveals few factory smokestacks. Instead there are mazes of freeways, unending suburbs, and towering glass and chrome skyscrapers. The Texas city reflects the changing economy. Although some manufacturing and production are still done (petrochemical production, for example), Houston, Dallas, Austin, and San Antonio are increasingly centers for economic activity other than industry. Those activities are concentrated around the processing of information in edu-

211

212   *Chapter 10*

cation, financial management, banking, high technology, communications, computers, research and development, medical services, insurance, government, and tourism. The modern Texas city is highly decentralized and geographically dispersed.

Several developments account for these changes in the shape of the metropolis. One major force was the automobile and the extraordinary mobility it provided. The car and the freeway made the suburbs possible. Now people could work in the central city and live in faraway communities. Another major force was the changing economy. Texas cities no longer have a central business district. Instead they have several centers of economic activity distinguished by groups of skyscrapers clustered here and there against the skyline. This dispersal of economic activity was made possible by the advances in communication and transportation. Now labor can be located in one place (even in a foreign country), management in another, capital in another, raw materials in another, and research and transportation in still another. Leaps in technology make possible the control and coordination of all these dispersed functions.

The growth of large metropolitan areas in Texas has created new policy problems for government. At the same time, the evolving character of the areas has created new hurdles for the resolution of those problems. In this chapter we will discuss how Texas urban areas have changed in recent decades and then relate those changes to problems of governance. Our emphasis will be on entire urban areas rather than on individual cities. Each large metropolitan area in Texas is divided into a number of individual municipalities—and numerous other local government units like counties, school districts, and other special districts. These separate governing units are simultaneously independent by law but interdependent by necessity because they share many problems that none of them can solve alone. Thus, to understand the relevance of contemporary urban life for state and local government, we must concentrate upon the entire urban area.

Metropolitan Texas

As we learned in Chapter 2, population growth has been especially rapid in urban areas of the state in recent years. That phenomenon has undermined some of the myths about Texas held by many outsiders and residents. Texas has long been thought of as a rural and small-town state. Many people's images of the state have been shaped by fiction and movie portrayals of life in small Texas towns like those in Larry McMurtry's *Last Picture Show* and *Texasville*. Foreign visitors and even visitors from other states often expect Texans to be countrified cowboy and farmer types. When *Texas Monthly* magazine asked a number of famous Texans in 1989 to write short essays about their favorite Texas places, many of them wrote about a rural or small-town spot.

Yet in reality the majority of Texans live in cities—and in big cities, as we indicated in Chapter 2. Texas is even more urbanized than the United States as a whole and has been so since the 1950s. Today, more than 80 percent of Texans live in urban areas. Big cities are doubtless attractive: they can offer exceptional opportunities for work, family life, entertainment, and general social advancement. Yet big cities also create remarkable problems that inevitably arise when large numbers of people live and work in proximity. Large cities have particularly difficult problems of crime, transportation, public health, sanitation, and environmental degradation, as but a few examples. Thus the growth of large metropolitan areas in Texas has exacerbated the depth and complexity of such problems—which must be addressed by state and local governments.

In Chapter 2 we also explained that a second recent trend in urban areas is rapid **suburbanization**: the growth of suburban areas outside the traditional city center. Since the 1970s such areas have grown considerably faster in population size than have the central cities. Each of Texas's major cities is today only the original core area of a large, sprawling metropolitan complex that includes many suburban areas on the periphery. Some of those suburbs are in the jurisdiction of the core city; some have been incorporated into separate, smaller cities; and some are in unincorporated fringe areas. Suburban growth has been spurred, in part, by limited opportunities within the central city, where the costs of land, homes, and business development sites are typically high. But suburban growth has also been promoted by the flight of many former central city residents. Those who can—or can afford to—have often chosen to leave the high crime, pollution, crowding, and related problems of the core city for the less-threatening haven of the suburb.

Generally, only relatively wealthy families and mobile businesses can escape to the suburbs. Left behind in the central city are disproportionate numbers of the poor, the working class, and the marginal and immobile businesses. Thus central cities have experienced a loss of wealth and tax base while they retain the typical problems of large, sometimes decaying neighborhoods and industrial areas. The wealth flees and the problems remain. That means, of course, that central cities today have an especially difficult time responding to the many problems of urban growth we listed above. The pattern of growth has complicated the efforts to deal with the unfortunate consequences of growth.

Efforts to respond to central-city problems are further complicated by the ethnic pattern of urban growth and migration. The populations of Texas's central cities are increasingly black and Hispanic in their ethnic composition (Table 10-1). In 1980 each of Texas's five largest central cities had sizable black and Hispanic populations, and each of them experienced notable growth in the percentages of those ethnic groups subsequently. Indeed, in Dallas, Houston, and San Antonio, the "minorities" are now the majorities.

214   Chapter 10

Table 10-1 | **Hispanics and blacks in Texas's major cities, 1980 and 1990**

	Percentage of Population That Is Hispanic or Black	
City	1980	1990
Austin	31	35
Dallas	41	50
Fort Worth	36	41
Houston	45	55
San Antonio	61	68

Sources: U.S. Bureau of the Census (1983, 1991).

Increasingly, as well, the suburbs are white and wealthy, and the central cities are black, brown, and poor. This segregation by ethnicity and income makes efforts to deal with city problems more difficult. Ethnic tensions are heightened, as are suburban residents' views that city problems are those of other people unlike themselves. Suburban residents lead different lives and experience different problems from those of central-city residents. Thus suburban residents and their elected representatives in city, county, and state government are often uninterested in the problems of the core cities.

Federal Aid and the Development of the Metropolis

Federal financial aid has also had a significant influence on the growth and character of urban areas in Texas, although that influence is not widely recognized. Today, federal aid appears to be of little importance. During the Reagan and Bush presidencies, that aid fell to much lower levels than in former times. Nationwide, federal aid dropped from 14 percent of city government general revenue in 1981, for example, to 5 percent in 1990. But those recent trends do not reflect the long-term importance that such aid has had over the twentieth century.

Houston serves as an excellent example of the significance of federal aid. Although a great deal of attention was given during the 1960s and 1970s to the city's refusal to accept federal money for its police department, the rhetoric concealed a fundamentally contradictory reality: The city has always relied upon federal money to finance projects crucial to its economic growth. At the turn of the century, Houston began to use federal funds to finance the construction of the Houston Ship Channel. Federally funded expansions and improvements of this vitally important world port have continued throughout the twentieth century. Another significant federal project has been the construction and maintenance of the flood control system in the Houston area. Although citizens who are flooded out of their homes after every heavy rainfall might deny that such a system exists, the fact remains that federally funded flood control has moderated the flooding problem.

Houston received another major economic benefit from federal money during World War II. Federal war contracts provided a mighty stimulus to Ship Channel industries, ranging from shipbuilding to steel production. The petrochemical industry was transformed into a major economic activity, as well. Federal support continued after the war for a variety of important projects: the development of municipal water sources (Lakes Houston and Conroe, among others), intercontinental airports, sewer systems and water lines, wastewater treatment plants, roads, and bridges. Federal support of the Manned Spacecraft Center and the Texas Medical Center has also yielded major economic benefits for the area, in terms of more jobs and in terms of a variety of significant high-tech applications and spin-offs.

Local leaders not only accepted federal money but also eagerly sought it. Houston's success in obtaining federal aid can be traced in large part to a highly effective coalition of prominent local business leaders and Texas politicians in Washington. It is difficult to imagine the Houston area enjoying its present degree of economic success without a ship channel and port, a flood control system, a petrochemical industry, an extensive public service infrastructure, a space center, and one of the world's great medical complexes. Yet as late as the 1970s local politicians still pointed out with pride that the police department refused federal aid because it would mean a loss of local control.

Houston has not been alone in its heavy reliance on economic aid. Dozens of other urban areas in Texas have followed a similar route. The motivation has been above all economic. When the federal government pays for something, local taxes do not have to be raised to do so. In addition, these federal projects have been designed primarily to stimulate economic growth. Airports, freeways, bridges, ports, harbors, water and sewer systems—the public services and facilities that are essential to economic development—are typical examples. It is not surprising that federal aid has made a dramatic contribution to the economic growth of the state's urban areas; after all, most cities in the country have vigorously pursued federal money. What is surprising is that local business and political leaders have long championed a myth of self-reliance and fiscal conservatism. The reality of the situation is that great efforts were made to obtain federal dollars for economic development. The serious criticism of federal funding was reserved for social welfare and police programs.

Federal aid has also contributed to the process of suburbanization. In particular, the federally funded freeway systems have made possible the dispersal of huge numbers of people within metropolitan regions. Federal support of a vast service infrastructure without regard for jurisdictional boundaries has encouraged the proliferation of new governments. It has also helped to create new population

216   *Chapter 10*

and economic centers at greater and greater distances from the central city. Thus federal aid has worked in conjunction with changing economic circumstances to make decentralization possible.

Fragmented Government

A principal consequence of the growth of the modern, decentralized urban area has been the fragmentation of governmental power in such areas. In other words, no single unit of government has responsibility for the problems that beset an entire urban area or, for that matter, has the power to respond to all those problems. Instead, governmental jurisdiction is divided among dozens and sometimes hundreds of political units. As examples of this fragmentation, the numbers of governmental jurisdictions in the home counties of Texas's five largest cities are given in Table 10-2. And one must remember that these individual counties contain only a portion of the larger metropolitan area. Each entire metropolitan area includes many more cities, school districts, and special districts—in addition to several county governments.

What are the consequences of such political fragmentation? Some people allege that fragmentation is a good thing, but there are better arguments that it has serious, unfortunate consequences.

One alleged advantage is that fragmentation enhances the citizen's freedom of choice. If people are upset with the governmental jurisdiction in which they

Table 10-2 | Local governments in the principal counties of Texas's largest metropolitan areas, 1987

County and Major City	Municipalities	School Districts	Special Districts	Total[a]
Bexar (San Antonio)	22	16	20	59
Dallas (Dallas)	26	16	38	81
Harris (Houston)	28	24	765	818
Tarrant (Fort Worth)	34	18	19	72
Travis (Austin)	14	8	94	117

[a]Including the county government.

Source: U.S. Bureau of the Census (1988).

The Political Economy of the Metropolis   217

live, they can relocate to another nearby. Thus a family may move to escape high taxes and crime or to find better schools for the children.

Another alleged advantage of fragmentation is that it creates competition among governments within an urban area. According to this perspective, citizens shop among different governmental jurisdictions until they find the right package of housing, taxes, and services at the right cost. Government officials recognize that citizens are discerning shoppers. They realize that if they are to be successful in attracting citizens in a highly competitive environment, they will have to provide the best possible services at the lowest possible cost. Therefore, governments are forced to become both more efficient and more responsive. According to the advocates of fragmentation, government is generally inefficient and unresponsive to its citizens because it enjoys a monopoly. It has no incentive to improve. In a fragmented system, however, it loses its monopoly. One government is forced to compete with other governments for preferred customers. The competition requires it to modify its behavior, and the citizen benefits from the process.

The critics of fragmentation reject all these arguments. They contend that fragmentation itself is responsible for many of the problems found in urban areas in Texas. Specifically, they charge that fragmentation causes a disparity between needs and resources. Only the wealthy can afford to move to the suburbs. Therefore, as the city ages it increasingly becomes a "reservation" for the old, the poor, and racial minorities. These citizens have a greater need for government programs and services and therefore place heavy demands upon central city government. However, the resources necessary to solve problems and to finance programs have moved out to the suburbs. Moreover, the wealthy residents of the suburbs may continue to work in the city, using city services, but they pay no taxes.

The critics also charge that fragmentation encourages citizens to pursue narrow self-interest. If people do not like what the government is doing, they can solve the political problems (crime, taxes, bad schools) simply by moving to another jurisdiction. They have less incentive, as a result, to stay and work to make things better. But only wealthier citizens can afford to pick and choose among neighborhoods and governments. Therefore, intense class and racial segregation occurs within the metropolitan region. The most intense competition develops in the struggle to attract upper-class citizens. The needs of the poor are ignored in the process.

Some people believe that this competition to attract citizens has negative consequences. Rather than forcing governments to become more efficient and responsive in an effort to attract preferred customers, the competition produces a lack of cooperation among governments with respect to urban problems. Many if not most urban problems affect the entire region rather than just the central city. Crime, for example, may be disproportionately reported in the central city, but it has negative consequences for the entire urban area. High crime rates in the

218 *Chapter 10*

central city also make life more dangerous for the suburban resident who works downtown. More crime requires more courts, judges, jails, sheriffs, and prosecutors. Crime, in short, makes life unpleasant for everybody. The entire community pays for it in terms of declining social trust and greater expenditures.

According to the critics of fragmentation, governments have no incentive to work together to solve these area-wide problems. In a fragmented system things may even appear to get better for some governments as they get worse for others. As crime rates rise in the central city, for example, residents will have a greater incentive to move to a jurisdiction where crime is lower. And those governments will have a continued incentive to maintain low crime rates—by attempting to attract middle- and upper-class citizens and excluding the poor.

The critics of fragmentation argue that both individual citizens and governments are encouraged to pursue their own narrow self-interest in a fragmented system. In such an environment the prospects for cooperative problem solving are dim indeed. In fact, neither the supporters nor the critics of fragmentation would expect serious attempts by urban governments to work together to resolve major issues.

| Annexation |

Although the critics of governmental fragmentation point out a number of its negative features, the situation would be even worse if it were not for the broad annexation powers that state government grants to Texas cities. Before 1963 there were essentially no limits on the power of a home-rule city to annex unincorporated areas. Even with the new law, however, those powers are still significant. A city has what is known as **extraterritorial jurisdiction**. That jurisdiction extends from 0.5 to 5 miles (depending on the city's population) from the city's boundaries. The city may annex areas within its jurisdiction up to a total of 10 percent of its land area. It may even exceed the 10 percent limit if the landowners and citizens of an unincorporated area request it. If it does not use up the 10 percent allotment in a given year, it may carry over the unused portion up to a total of 30 percent of its total land area.

Cities such as Houston have used their annexation power to minimize the effects of suburbanization. When new middle- and upper-class suburban areas develop outside the central city, Houston annexes them. Some of those annexed areas, such as Alief and Clear Lake, have vigorously protested their annexation. They argue that they are required to pay city taxes but do not receive adequate municipal services (although the law requires that such services must be provided). Because the annexation law gives great power to the central city, these annexation disputes are seldom resolved in favor of the suburb.

Nevertheless, we can anticipate two consequences as suburbanization and so-called white flight continue. First, new suburban development may be pushed even a greater distance from the central city as communities seek to escape the extraterritorial jurisdiction of the central city. Second, as suburban representation continues to increase in the state legislature, the broad annexation powers currently exercised by central cities may be curtailed.

State–City Relations

The powerful forces of economic change and development on the one hand, and huge amounts of federal aid on the other, have combined to stimulate the dramatic growth of urban areas in Texas. A region cannot develop economically without freeways, bridges, roads, airports, and water, sewer, drainage, and flood control services. The federal role in urban development has been crucial because state government in Texas essentially ignores its urban areas. Although the county might be an appropriate governmental unit to deal with the problems of urban regions, county officials have neither the power nor the inclination to do so.

One study concluded that Texas was first among the fifty states in terms of the discretion it granted to its cities (Thomas, 1983). That means that state government in Texas leaves its home-rule cities alone. Within broad limits, large cities enjoy great flexibility with respect to taxing, gathering revenue, spending, programs and policies, and annexation. It also means that the state has typically ignored urban problems.

As the state becomes highly urbanized, however, this lack of concern for urban affairs has forced cities to improvise in an effort to manage rapid growth. Because municipalities can expect little help from the state or county, they have turned to the federal government for assistance. Moreover, special districts have been widely employed to deal with area-wide problems. We will discuss both county and special district governments and their roles in solving urban problems in Chapter 12.

The continued lack of state government concern for urban areas might initially be surprising, given the level of urban representation in the legislature. But urban areas contain wealthy suburbs as well as central cities—and those suburbs tend to be conservative. Their representatives in the state legislature are likely to have legislative priorities that differ from the agendas of representatives of inner-city districts.

The Policy Priorities of Texas Cities

We have observed that metropolitan areas have especially difficult social, economic, and environmental problems. Crime, pollution, transportation, public health, and

220   *Chapter 10*

sanitation are typical ones, but so are poverty and economic decline, especially in central city areas. One might be led to believe, therefore, that cities would give high priority to all these problems and have many programs to contend with them. Yet that is not the case. Cities must provide some essential services—like policing, garbage collection, street maintenance, and so on—at least at minimal levels. However, they choose largely to ignore some other problems—especially those related to poverty—in favor of economic development concerns.

Paul Peterson (1981) has offered an explanation for this phenomenon. According to Peterson, three elements are essential to the character of the city: labor, capital, and land. But of those three, the city exerts significant control only over land. Labor and much of the city's capital are highly mobile and free to move about within a fragmented metropolitan area. The city cannot prevent people, money, resources, and businesses from moving to another city or neighboring suburban jurisdiction. Yet the city is heavily dependent on business, industry, and its middle- and upper-class citizens. The business community provides jobs, while well-employed and better-off citizens pay taxes and make relatively few demands on government. But it is the wealthy who are especially able to leave the city for the suburbs to avoid the worst urban problems.

Thus the city's primary policy concern becomes keeping such individuals and businesses happy and in the city limits. That concern means that cities come to employ especially large resources to help ensure economic growth. Growth creates new jobs and new city revenues, and it helps keep taxes low. And growth ensures an attractive atmosphere that helps retain existing businesses and well-off residents.

Because cities have an overwhelming interest in economic growth, they are most concerned with **developmental policies**. Examples of developmental policies include the construction of a new sports stadium complex to attract a professional franchise, the development of a civic and convention center, the construction of a new airport and transportation network, and tax, land, and credit incentives to attract new industries. Because developmental policies stimulate economic growth, they are perceived to be in the best interests of all. As a result, the support for these policies is widespread on the part of both political and economic elites.

Redistributive policies, in contrast, will be strongly opposed. A **redistributive policy** is one that takes resources from the haves and gives them to the have-nots. Examples would include a new public housing project for the poor and increased city expenditures for social welfare programs. Cities resist redistributive programs because they harm economic growth. If a city invests significant resources in public housing, it will contribute nothing to economic development. No new jobs will be created. Funds for the project will have to come from tax revenues. Taxes may eventually have to be increased. The availability of public housing units will also attract more poor people to the city. They, in turn, will place further demands upon government. As a result, the city will become a less attractive location for both existing and prospective business and industry.

Peterson's argument appears to apply well to Texas cities. They spend only minuscule proportions of their budgets on redistributive programs, leaving those concerns to the states and the federal government. Instead, cities concentrate their efforts on two other kinds of activities. First, they attempt to provide sufficient levels of basic services (such as policing, street maintenance, garbage collection, and so on) to ensure an attractive general environment and to keep middle- and upper-class residents satisfied. Second, they aggressively pursue economic growth by luring new business and industry to the city. A Sea World in San Antonio, a Sematech computer research consortium in Austin, a General Motors automobile plant in Arlington—these are the prizes sought to add to a city's economic luster.

In sum, the dynamics of the process of metropolitan growth and the opportunities that wealthier residents and businesses have to be mobile in that environment work together to shape the policy priorities of cities. As a result, the needs of the relatively poor are assigned little importance while the interests of the better-off get considerable attention.

Conclusion

Cities in Texas reflect the profound changes that have taken place in the nation's economy. The compact industrial city has given way to the decentralized city. In fact, urban areas in Texas consist of several cities and suburbs and sometimes spread across several counties. Such decentralization is possible because the major elements of the economy—labor, management, capital, raw materials, markets—no longer have to be close to one another. Advances in technology and transportation make it possible for these various components to be in separate locations. As a result, the city's population and economic activities no longer have to be clustered around a central business district. Individuals and businesses have much greater freedom with respect to place of residence and location of economic activities in such a decentralized urban environment.

The political consequences of these trends have been significant. Coincident with the growth of large metropolitan areas has come the fragmentation of local governmental power. That fragmentation has produced a disparity between needs and resources, leaving problem-ridden central cities with relatively few resources while wealthier suburbs suffer fewer problems. Fragmentation also impedes co-

222 Chapter 10

operative efforts to solve common, metropolitan-area-wide problems such as crime, transportation needs, and pollution.

Perhaps of even more importance, the growth of large metropolitan areas and the different opportunities they provide different residents have affected the policy priorities of cities. The needs of the poor, in particular, get little attention. Cities are led, instead, to cater to the interests of the economically better-off. Thus the process of metropolitan growth has not been politically neutral. Besides shaping the way in which most Texans live, it has affected how they are governed and whose interests are best served by local governments.

References

Peterson, Paul E. 1981. *City Limits.* Chicago: University of Chicago Press.

Thomas, Robert D. 1983. "State-Urban Relations in Texas." Paper delivered at the annual meeting of the Southwestern Political Science Association.

U.S. Bureau of the Census. 1983. *1980 Census of Population, General Social and Economic Characteristics: Texas.* Washington, D.C.

_____ . 1988. *1987 Census of Governments: Government Organization.* Washington, D.C.

_____ . 1991. *1990 Census of Population and Housing, Summary Population and Housing Characteristics: Texas.* Washington, D.C.

Chapter 11

Government and Policy in Texas Cities

Cities, also known as municipalities or municipal corporations, are the most important of local governments. They have the greatest array of responsibilities and deliver the greatest number of services. In addition, city political affairs capture more public attention than do the affairs of other local government units. Thus we will discuss the character and activities of Texas cities in some detail in this chapter. To begin our discussion, we will consider the distinctive political and policy situation that cities occupy.

City and State Governments Compared

Citizens probably think that city government in Texas is just a smaller version of state government. Certainly the two governments have some similar functions. Both governments tax, write budgets, spend money, and pass laws. There are, however, some fundamental differences between them. Because of those differences, the job of governing Texas cities is more difficult and complex than that of governing the state. Local government officials find it more difficult to solve problems and respond to citizen demands (Yates, 1976).

One of the distinctive characteristics of Texas cities is that public services are delivered daily and frequently involve an encounter with a public employee. Garbage collectors pick up the trash, police officers respond to calls for service, and teachers interact with students. The citizens can see the service they are getting or not getting. They have a continuous opportunity to evaluate the quality of the service being delivered—and, therefore, the performance of local government. Thus citizens are likely to have opinions about local public services. That is less likely to be the case at the state level. Although citizens may see a state highway patrol officer now and then, the services delivered by state government are generally much less conspicuous.

Another characteristic of local government in Texas is the essential nature of

225

226   *Chapter 11*

the services provided. Society simply cannot do without police, fire, and education services. They are vital to the public safety, well-being, and hopes for the future. Issues of war and peace and the state of the economy may dominate the national political debate. At the local level, however, the crucial issue on a day-to-day basis is the quality of the public services provided. Many citizens are deeply concerned about those services and are therefore more inclined to make demands upon government in an effort to influence their delivery. Public services provided by the state are seldom as prominent and urgent.

Another distinctive characteristic of local government is the citizens' proximity to public officials. Government that is close to the people may not necessarily be the best government, but it is certainly the most accessible. If citizens have a complaint about local government, they can express their discontent directly to the appropriate officials. They may visit a council meeting or a government office, telephone a bureaucrat, engage in a conference with a teacher, or organize a march on city hall. It is much easier, therefore, to communicate with public officials at the local level than at the state level. Citizens who have a gripe about state government have to travel a considerable distance just to present a case, unless they live in Austin. State government is far removed and even alien territory. The typical citizen feels far more familiar with local government. Consequently, citizens are more inclined to try to influence local government activities.

Local government is also distinguished by its degree of bureaucratic discretion. For many local services, the bureaucrat is the service. The teacher in the classroom, the police officer on the street, and the building inspector investigating code violations are the heart of the public services being delivered. One problem for supervisors is how to keep an eye on these street-level bureaucrats (Lipsky, 1980). Much of the time, no doubt, such public employees are doing an adequate or even superior job. But how do supervisors know that? What are the teachers teaching and how well are they doing it? Which laws do the police officers enforce and which ones do they ignore? What if the department head wants employees to change their approach? How can the supervisor ensure that they respond? In recent years, some large cities in Texas have experienced problems with their police departments. Citizen complaints include charges of police brutality. But when a service such as police protection is delivered on the street by an employee far removed from control or even observation by supervisors, it is one thing for public officials to recognize a problem; it is another to resolve it. Because of the discretion of street-level bureaucrats, the job of local government officials is more difficult. When trying to change the behavior of public employees in response to citizen demands, supervisors may find that the solution is as difficult as the problem.

Another distinctive characteristic of local government is the frequency with which citizens express different demands for the same service. Some citizens may want the police to do one thing (have more neighborhood patrols, for example) while others want them to do another (place more emphasis on traffic problems). Different groups also have different expectations for the public schools. Although all groups want quality education, they may disagree on how to define it and how to achieve it. Because of such conflicting expectations and contradictory demands, the public official finds it impossible to satisfy all citizens.

Still another characteristic that distinguishes local government from state government is the extent to which cities are influenced and limited by other levels of government. The national government, for example, has intervened and forced changes in the electoral structure of Texas cities (from an at-large scheme to a district arrangement). In addition, the city often does not have authority or jurisdiction in certain matters, because they are the responsibility of the county or state. The state limits the power of the city in numerous ways—ranging from the types and levels of taxes that can be imposed to the training and control of public employees. Such limitations make it difficult if not impossible for local public officials to deal with many problems.

Because of these distinctive characteristics of local government, policy making at the local level is more complex than at the state level. The public services delivered at the local level are essential, so citizens are more likely to make demands upon government. Moreover, the immediacy of local government encourages citizen involvement. Public officials find it difficult to respond to those demands, however. Not only are the public's expectations often in conflict, but the behavior of street-level bureaucrats is also hard to control and, in many cases, the city lacks jurisdiction over major policy areas. Thus many problems remain unsolved.

Forms of City Government

The elected leadership and the management system of cities can assume various forms, several of which have been adopted by different Texas cities. The most common form by far is the **council–manager plan**. The system is also referred to as one of **reformed** government, because it was created by "good government" advocates around the beginning of the present century to eliminate political abuses associated with more-traditional governing systems. In its pure form the system has a city council elected on at-large, nonpartisan ballots; that is, all residents of the city can vote in all the council races, and candidates do not run under political party labels. In addition, a mayor is elected at large to preside over council meetings. The council sets broad city policy and hires a city manager. The manager appoints department heads and runs the city government on a day-to-day basis in a professional, rather than a political, fashion. The vast majority of Texas cities uses the council–manager form of government. However, many Texas cities, especially the larger ones, have mixed council election systems; that is, some council members are elected at large, and some are elected from specific districts, or wards.

228   *Chapter 11*

The **mayor–council plan** is the second most common form of city government in the state. It is at times referred to as the **unreformed** system of city government because it was associated with the political abuses that led to the creation of the council–manager plan. Typically, under the mayor–council system the mayor is elected at large and the city council is elected from individual geographic districts. Furthermore, the mayor is usually the chief administrative official and thus has powers equivalent to those of the city manager in the council–manager system. When the mayor assumes those powers, the city has the **strong-mayor** version of the mayor–council plan. In the **weak-mayor** version the mayor lacks administrative powers and can be overruled by a majority of the city council. The weak-mayor system is rare in Texas, however, as it is in the rest of the nation.

Only a handful of Texas cities use any form of the mayor–council plan, and Houston and El Paso are the only large cities that employ it (Table 11-1). On paper, both El Paso and Houston have the strong-mayor version of the system, but they, like many other cities, actually have a mixed version. Houston, for example, has a senior professional administrator, much like a city manager, who serves at the pleasure of the mayor and thus actually exercises many of the day-to-day management responsibilities. In addition, both Houston and El Paso elect some of their council members in at-large races and some in district races.

Finally, among cities with populations of at least 10,000, only Pharr and Texas City use the **commission** form of government. Under this system, which was invented in Galveston early in this century, voters elect several commissioners instead of a city council. Each commissioner then becomes the head of a single city department, and the city has no mayor or city manager. The commission form of government was popular for a time but has fallen into disfavor and is little used because it does not allow for a chief executive officer. Even Galveston, its innovator,

---

Table 11-1 ▌ **Texas cities with Mayor–Council Governments, 1987**

Balch Springs	Pasadena
Bay City	Pearland
Brenham	Richmond
Conroe	Robstown
Dumas	Rosenberg
El Paso	Seguin
Houston	South Houston
League City	Vidor
Missouri City	Watauga
North Richland Hills	

Note: Only cities with populations of at least 10,000 are included.

Source: Moulder (1987).

subsequently converted to a council–manager plan to provide for better administrative control.

Does the Form Really Matter?

What difference does it make whether a city has a mayor–council or a manager–council form of government? Does it make any difference to the citizen whether a mayor or an appointed manager is in charge? The evidence from national studies suggests that the form of government does make a difference. Unreformed governments (mayor–council) tend to spend more and tax more than reformed ones. There is also evidence that blacks and other minorities are better represented on city councils in unreformed cities because council members are elected by wards rather than at large. Unreformed cities are also thought to be somewhat more responsive and accessible to the variety of groups and interests that make up the city. Because political parties are active and organized, the demands of different groups are more likely to be articulated. Because the chief executive is elected rather than appointed, and because the members of the council are accountable to individual wards, municipal government is alleged to be more responsive to group needs and demands (Lineberry and Fowler, 1967).

Do these findings apply to Texas cities? It is not possible to answer that question with much certainty. For one thing, most of the larger cities have the manager–council form, whereas most of the small ones have the mayor–council form. Thus, because most cities of comparable size have the same form of government, it is not possible to make many comparisons on the basis of different forms.

One can, however, speculate about certain impacts. For example, mayor–council cities do not appear to spend and tax more than manager–council cities in Texas. In fact, if we look at the largest cities, we find that only one (Houston) of the four top spenders on a per capita basis has the mayor–council form. Similarly, the mayor–council cities (Houston and El Paso) generally have lower property tax rates than the manager–council cities.

The election system—ward versus at-large—does seem to make a difference. When San Antonio and Houston switched from at-large to district council systems, the level of minority representation on the city councils increased. But does greater minority representation make a difference in terms of the public policies that are produced? That is a much more difficult question to answer. One would certainly think that more minority representation on city councils would ensure additional programs designed to respond to minority needs. However, there is, as yet, insufficient evidence to reach that conclusion.

One major difference that is frequently alleged to exist between mayor–council and manager–council cities concerns efficiency. Because unreformed cities are run by popularly elected mayors whereas reformed cities are governed by professional

230   *Chapter 11*

city managers, reformed cities are generally thought to be more efficiently managed. It is often pointed out, for example, that Dallas has a more efficient municipal government than Houston. Stating that one government is more efficient than another, however, is much easier than demonstrating it. If we wanted to prove that the municipal government in Dallas is more efficient than the one in Houston, how would we go about the task? Frequently, alleged differences in efficiency are based more on personal impressions than on any systematic evidence. Moreover, even if one city government in Texas is shown to be more efficient than another, that does not necessarily mean that the form of government is the cause of that difference.

In any event, much of the political conflict in Texas cities continues to be a fight between reformers and those who would be willing to sacrifice some degree of efficiency in government for a more open and responsive government. One historian has argued that the original reform movement was dominated by powerful business interests. The goal of those interests was to wrest control from neighborhoods and place it in the hands of "professionals" who would govern the city in the "public interest." To those reformers, however, the public interest was business interests (Hays, 1964). Much of the political battle in Texas cities today is still a confrontation between citizens' groups on the one hand and, on the other, those who believe that the real business of city government is business.

Who Governs Texas Cities and Other Local Governments?

Just as we have done with major state institutions like the legislature and the governorship, we will describe the kinds of people who are typically elected as mayors and city council members in Texas cities. Unfortunately, only limited information is available on that subject. Casual observation and mass media reports often give the impression that there is a good deal of ethnic and gender diversity among local elected officials. Most big cities, for example, have at least some women, blacks, and Hispanics on their city councils, and most of the largest cities in the state have had women as mayors in recent years.

Yet such impressions are not accurate with respect to the entire population of local elected officials. Such systematic information as is available on the gender, ethnicity, and Hispanic origin of elected officials in all Texas local governments (that is, those in cities, counties, school districts, and other special districts) are provided in Table 11-2. Separate data are not available for cities alone, but one must suspect that the patterns for cities would not be remarkably different from the patterns suggested in Table 11-2. According to those figures, local Texas government is dominated by white males. Although almost 40 percent of the state's

Government and Policy in Texas Cities   231

Table 11-2 | Gender, ethnicity, and Hispanic origin of elected officials in local Texas governments, 1987

	Gender	
Ethnicity and Hispanic Origin	Male (%)	Female (%)
Anglo-American	82	15
Hispanic-origin[a]	6	1
Black	2	1
Native American	—[b]	—[b]
Asian	—[b]	0

Note: Elected officials are from all local Texas governments—cities, counties, school districts, and other special districts.

[a]Hispanic-origin individuals may be of any ethnicity.

[b]Less than 1 percent.

Source: U.S. Bureau of the Census (1990:18–19).

population is Hispanic or black, those ethnic groups are only modestly represented in the elected leadership of local governments. Women also are remarkably underrepresented there.

Participation in City Politics

One might well imagine that the proximity of Texans to their city government and the day-to-day importance of city services to their lives would provoke great interest and participation in city politics. Citizens have several ways of getting involved with or attempting to influence city government, and some of those avenues are, indeed, enthusiastically pursued—at least by some Texans. Yet the reasonable expectation of high public participation in general is not borne out by the facts.

Voter Participation

The most typical and best known means of public participation in the political process is by voting in elections. In the process, the individuals who will make policy decisions and govern the city are chosen. Citizens endorse the campaign promises of some candidates and reject those of others. And citizens often get to vote on proposed bond sales, city charter amendments, and selected policy resolutions. Voting is, then, a limited but still quite important way in which citizens can help shape city government policy. It is also the easiest means of participation, requiring little time or even premeditation.

232   *Chapter 11*

Nonetheless, public participation in city elections in Texas (and across the nation, for that matter) is embarrassingly low. Voter turnout estimates for a selection of recent Texas city elections are presented in Table 11-3. The election date of May 2, 1992, was chosen explicitly because only local election races and matters were on the ballot. Some cities hold their elections on dates when state government or even national government elections are also being decided. The latter elections may thus draw some voters to the polls who would not participate in city elections alone.

As one can see from Table 11-3, voter turnout ranges from poor to abysmal in city elections held alone. (The especially bad showing of Arlington and College Station may arise because of the large number of college students who reside in those cities and who may be especially uninterested in city politics.) Clearly, immediate relevance and importance are not enough to stimulate notable public interest in city elections.

Most of the cities in Table 11-3 are small to middle-sized, and it is fair to ask whether bigger cities achieve higher rates of participation. Our earlier remarks about the unusual policy problems that big cities face suggest that could be the case. Because the problems of big cities are more controversial and formidable, their residents might be especially concerned with city governance and, hence, local elections. Yet such does not appear to be true.

Dallas and Houston, for example, held mayoral and city council elections on November 5, 1991, when the additional items on the ballot were proposed state constitutional amendments. Included in the latter items was the proposal to create a state lottery. Because the lottery proposal had received so much media attention and was a controversial proposal, one could fairly speculate that it would draw many people to the polls who would otherwise not vote. Yet the turnout in that election

Table 11-3 | **Voter turnout in Texas city elections held May 2, 1992**

City	Estimated Percentage of the Voting-Age Population Voting[a]
Arlington	4
Brazoria	24
College Station	4
Grand Prairie	10
Kingsville	16
Laredo	10
Richland Hills	19
Richmond	12
Robstown	23
Tomball	18

[a]Estimates were calculated by the authors from U.S. Census data and media reports for the elections.

was only about 21 percent of the voting-age population in Dallas and 29 percent of that in Houston. Thus, even with the added drawing power of the lottery proposition—on top of an especially fierce three-way mayor's race in Houston—the turnout in those two big-city elections was not remarkably better than that in some of the smaller cities the following May.

Reasons for Low Turnout Why is voter turnout generally lower in local elections than in state elections? There are several reasons. First, state elections are thought to be more important. They involve the selection of the governor, lieutenant governor, attorney general, and other major statewide officials. Second, state elections are more prominent, largely because of media coverage. Major newspapers and television stations give state elections considerable coverage and thus stimulate citizen interest in the campaign. Another factor is the role of the political parties. Increasingly the Republicans are challenging the Democrats for state offices. The party organizations raise and spend money, contact voters, and stimulate debate and interest in issues and candidates. These various activities raise the level of voter turnout.

A final factor is the role of interest groups such as labor unions and business organizations. Their political action committees are more likely to be highly active in state elections than in local ones. Interest groups generally perceive that their interests are more directly affected by state government than by local government. Public employee unions such as the Texas State Teachers Association are very active in state elections, for example, but play no role in city elections. When interest groups do not support candidates and encourage their members to vote, turnout declines.

The average citizen simply does not believe that local elections are as important as the election for governor and other state officials. Moreover, the reduced level of television and newspaper coverage, the limited activity of interest groups, and the absence of political parties all combine to depress voter turnout in city elections. With regard to the last point, national studies have indicated that the level of voting is higher in city elections where political parties are active than in those where they are not (Alford and Lee, 1968). Most Texas cities do not have active political party organizations.

Consequences of Low Turnout What difference does it make if only a small percentage of citizens bother to cast ballots in major local elections? Above all, public policy is probably much more conservative than it would be if more citizens decided to participate. Although we have been focusing on the factors that account for low overall turnout in city elections, it is also important to analyze the composition of those who do vote. Research indicates that conservative voters dominate the local electorate (Hamilton, 1971). Liberal voters are much less likely to participate. Because government officials respond to those

234 *Chapter 11*

who participate actively, local public policy tends to be conservative (Verba and Nie, 1972).

Furthermore, political participation in general is class-biased. The higher a citizen's income, education, and social status—recalling the discussion of elections and parties in Chapter 5—the more likely it is that the citizen will participate. In turn, the elements that account for higher turnout in state elections—media coverage, party activity, and interest group activity—have the greatest effect upon low-income voters. When those factors are not at work, the people most likely to vote for the more liberal candidates drop out of the electorate. The absence of political parties in local campaigns is particularly detrimental, for example, to working-class citizens, who rely upon the parties for information about issues and candidates. In nonpartisan elections in which candidates are not identified by party label, such information is not available. Wealthier and better-educated citizens do not rely as heavily upon party affiliation as a cue to voting. They have access to alternative sources of information. As a result, the electorate tends to be dominated by conservative voters.

In Chapter 10 we also explained how the public policies of Texas cities are conservative, focusing on developmental goals and ignoring redistributive goals. (We will expand that discussion later in this chapter.) Municipal governments spend little on health and social welfare programs. Moreover, they rely upon regressive sources of revenue (taxes that take a larger share of the income of poorer persons such as sales taxes, property taxes, and user fees). Given the low turnout in local elections and the domination of the electorate by conservative voters, the conservative nature of urban public policy is not surprising.

Interest Groups

Another important avenue for citizen participation is through interest groups. In earlier chapters we considered the roles of interest groups in state politics in general, in state elections, and in influencing the state legislature. Hundreds of interest groups are involved in Texas urban government too. Some of them, such as chambers of commerce, are well financed and influential. Others, such as associations of police officers, represent municipal public employees. Still others are branch chapters of national organizations (the NAACP, for example) and represent racial minorities. But most interest groups at the local level are not as well organized and prominent as these. Instead they represent loose-knit collections of citizens who are organized around neighborhood concerns. These neighborhood protective or improvement associations are primarily concerned with ensuring that zoning and deed restrictions in their subdivisions are enforced. They are also interested in the level of public services they receive. When they have a complaint about police protection or trash in the neighborhood, they report it to the mayor's office or a city department. Such organizations serve as watchdogs for their neighborhoods and are the most prevalent type of interest group in the city.

Other than mentioning the various types of interest groups that exist in the state's cities, there is not much that one can say about them. The necessary research has not been conducted. One might fairly assume, however, that business interests are the most effective political organizations at the local level. Certainly such groups have the most money, which allows them to establish and maintain an organizational structure. They can afford office space, clerical and research support, and lobbyists. Their access to vast resources also allows business groups to press their claims upon government effectively. They can provide financial support to candidates in political campaigns, they can mold opinion through media advertisements—and they can supply politically relevant information. Public officials need information in order to make decisions. Because of the expense involved in gathering, packaging, and presenting information, business groups such as a city's chamber of commerce are often in a preferred position. Certainly such organizations have recognized that information can influence local decisions, and therefore they devote a significant share of their resources to research and analysis of major issues affecting local government.

There is another reason why organizations that represent business interests are generally the most effective: They enjoy status and legitimacy. Business groups are identified with stability, prosperity, fiscal conservatism, jobs, and economic growth. The business of the city, to many, is business. Public officials also find much common ground with representatives of business organizations. Both are well educated and upper-class. Both are in favor of low taxes and economic growth. Because of those common goals and backgrounds, business interests enjoy a special relationship with public officials.

One example of a powerful nonbusiness interest group at the local level is San Antonio's Communities Organized for Public Service (COPS), which represents the Hispanic neighborhoods in the city and was founded in the 1970s to protest the inadequacy of basic essential services such as flood control. From the beginning, COPS relied upon a strategy of confronting public officials and demanding action. Group members held rallies, marched on city hall, and shouted down their opponents.

Such behavior is not unexpected from an organization that seeks change and yet represents a group that lacks significant resources. Well-established and wealthy organizations do not need to rely upon parades, demonstrations, pickets, and other forms of protest to influence government effectively. Instead, they depend upon more conventional tactics such as lobbying to achieve their goals.

The protest strategy employed by COPS was successful. By most accounts, city services have improved in Hispanic areas. Ironically, that success has entailed certain costs to the group. With its growing reputation as a major force in city politics has come a recognition that a failure to modify its previous behavior may antagonize other influential groups. COPS is now accepted by the business com-

236   *Chapter 11*

munity and public officials as an influential group in the policy process. Its position on major issues is heeded in policy deliberations. If it continues to behave as an outsider group, it runs the risk of losing some of its influence in establishment circles.

The structure of groups in Texas cities has changed considerably over the past twenty-five years. Although traditionally powerful business groups such as builders, developers, and chambers of commerce continue to play a major role, they now share the local political stage with groups that were either ignored or unheard of two decades ago. Black and Hispanic organizations are much more active and influential in city politics. Municipal employee unions are also a relatively new and powerful group. In particular, police and fire fighter associations are active and organized. Their political activities include support of candidates for public office. In addition, they sometimes conduct advertising campaigns in newspapers and on television to mobilize public support on behalf of demands for improvements in pay and working conditions.

Finally, the structure of the business community itself has also changed. Increasingly, the executives of major corporations are relative newcomers to the state. They generally have little interest in local politics. Their political attitudes are more tolerant and cosmopolitan than those of the old-guard bankers and oil producers. This new breed of corporate managers has a greater stake in national and international politics than in city and county affairs. Therefore, they are not very active in local politics.

Sometimes ethnic minority groups and the business community form temporary alliances in support of certain issues. In 1986, for example, San Antonio voters defeated a proposition that would have limited the growth of city spending to an amount equal to the inflation and population growth rates. The measure was supported by military retirees and middle-aged, middle-class citizens. It was opposed by the Hispanic community and business leaders. The business community feared that the ceiling on spending would retard economic growth, whereas Hispanic opposition focused on the almost certain cuts in service that would occur as a result.

Protest as Participation

Another form of political participation in the city is protest. There are two types of protest. In a nonviolent protest, citizens join together and demonstrate, parade, sit in, picket, or strike on behalf of a political goal. Such events are peaceful and frequently rely on television coverage to dramatize an appeal for the sympathy and support of other citizens who are unaware of the protestors' grievances. A variety of issues may generate a protest—from inadequate municipal services in a neighborhood to alleged racial discrimination or police brutality. Generally, citizens resort to protest only after conventional forms of political participation such as voting, contacting bureaucrats, and group activity have proved ineffective.

In a violent protest, citizens deliberately employ violence to achieve a political goal. Such protests are highly unconventional and are seldom seen in Texas cities. Riots have occurred in Texas cities in the past, however, and the Los Angeles riots of 1992 after the decision in Rodney King's police brutality court case remind us of how influential such events can be. Yet political violence is a rare and highly unorthodox form of political participation. It typically arises almost spontaneously, with little or no deliberation among participants about what political consequences it might have. Thus the results are not always what the participants might have sought.

Exiting as Participation

One widespread but seldom noted form of political participation is exit from the city. When citizens are upset with what their government is doing or failing to do, they can respond in one of three ways. First, they might do nothing. In fact, that response is the typical reaction of most citizens faced with a political problem— either because they are apathetic or because they do not believe that taking action would do any good. Another choice is to engage in the types of political activities we have already discussed—voting, joining an interest group, protesting.

A third option open to citizens has proved to be popular with many Texans. They can solve their political problems by moving away from them. That phenomenon has aggravated another major problem of Texas cities—fragmentation, which was discussed in Chapter 10. Central cities in Texas are surrounded by both incorporated and unincorporated jurisdictions. Therefore, if residents of the central city are displeased with taxes, crime, or the quality of public services, they can simply move to another jurisdiction. For citizens who can afford it, this form of political participation is highly effective.

The Effectiveness of Participation

Some types of political activity are more effective than others. We should be clear, however, whether we are talking about effectiveness for an individual or for a group. The vote, for example, is not an effective form of political participation for the individual. The citizen's vote is only one vote of many. The vote can be successful for a group, however, if that group votes as a bloc and supports a victorious set of candidates. Yet even then the group may not get what it wants. Other groups will also make demands upon public officials, and resources or the power to use them may not be available to achieve campaign promises. If individual citizens want prompt and effective action from government, they should not expect the vote to provide it. The vote, if it works at all, works slowly.

Interest groups, in contrast, can be highly effective. As we have noted, however,

238 *Chapter 11*

their success is directly dependent upon the groups' control over resources. Therefore, business groups are the most influential at the local level.

Neither violent nor nonviolent protest is likely in most cases to elicit a positive response from government. Given that protest is used only after conventional forms of participation have proved ineffective, the protesters tend to be politically powerless. The protest is an attempt to gain public support and sympathy as well as an ally with clout who will champion their claims upon government. As an effort whose success depends upon establishing a coalition with others, protest is seldom successful.

Exiting is perhaps the most effective form of participation for the individual. By simply moving away from their problems, individuals manifest a great degree of control over the situation, because they are not dependent upon government to respond to their demands for action. Such mobility within an urban area is closely tied to the individuals' wealth and income, however. Poor citizens do not enjoy the exit option.

| City Budgets |

It is useful to consider some of the specifics of city government activities and policy priorities. We discussed certain aspects of those priorities in Chapter 10, emphasizing the great interest that city governments have in developmental as opposed to redistributive policies. We can amplify that discussion by examining the data in Table 11-4 on the expenditure priorities of the state's ten largest cities.

Total spending per city resident and spending per resident on selected major policy functions are presented in the table. Per capita spending provides a useful common comparison, whereby each city's spending level is related to the size of the population intended to be served by the particular activity. There is a good deal of variation among the cities in the aggregate size (in per capita terms) of their budgeted activities and in the relative priorities they assign to particular policy functions. Yet we still get a good general portrait of their common functions, as well.

In these terms, roads and highways, sewerage and solid waste management, and policing are typically sources of major expenditures in all of these cities. Alternatively, and in keeping with our discussion in Chapter 10, welfare spending per se is essentially nonexistent. Even related policy functions like health care and housing typically receive modest attention in these spending terms. The generally greater variability with respect to spending on the remaining categories is likely explainable by unique policy problems or commitments of individual cities. At the same time, bigger cities generally spend more per resident on most of the primary policy functions like roads, sewerage, policing, and fire protection, as we would

Table 11-4 | **Per capita expenditures on selected policy activities in Texas's ten largest cities, 1989–1990**

City	Total	Roads and Highways	Sewerage and Solid Waste Management	Police Protection	Fire Protection	Parks and Recreation	Welfare	Hospitals and Health Care	Housing and Community Development	General Administration
						Per Capita Expenditures ($)				
Amarillo	614	50	65	88	45	41	—	10	26	35
Arlington	682	89	69	84	58	38	—	5	47	42
Austin	2,178	154	163	97	66	50	4	234	12	75
Corpus Christi	676	66	81	81	43	53	—	20	2	42
Dallas	1,002	88	141	143	73	96	—	16	12	48
El Paso	567	24	113	82	37	28	—	23	9	25
Fort Worth	1,174	88	181	114	73	61	—	20	15	76
Garland	1,261	111	92	73	49	38	—	6	20	33
Houston	977	54	183	140	78	33	—	29	11	35
Lubbock	800	59	51	75	56	46	—	11	14	38

Source: U.S. Bureau of the Census (1992:81–83).

240   *Chapter 11*

expect from our earlier observations about the policy problems of large metropolitan areas.

Budget data do not, of course, tell us everything we might want to know about city policies and priorities. How much a city spends on a particular activity gives us some information in that regard, but it is inevitably incomplete. We do not learn from such information how or how effectively that money is spent, and we do not learn how the activities supported by those expenditures are provided throughout the city. Do some neighborhoods get superior police service, for example, while others get mediocre service? Despite these limitations, budget data are useful for providing an initial, general characterization of the major policy activities of government. As can be seen from the data in Table 11-4, major Texas cities concentrate their spending on routine, essential public services, spending little on frills or redistributive efforts.

Conclusion

Cities are the most important of local governments, and they should be of special concern to the average citizen, even relative to the state government. Cities provide the government services and programs that affect citizens' lives most immediately on a day-to-day basis. In large metropolitan areas in particular—but even in smaller cities and towns, as well—city government policies are the principal buffer between the citizen and the harsh realities of modern urban life. To the extent that city governments are successful, they allow citizens to enjoy the social and economic promises of the metropolis while minimizing the negative aspects.

Texas cities are, however, remarkably conservative governments. They emphasize developmental policies and the delivery of the most essential public services. Cities with larger populations must spend more to implement such policies and services, but their focus is otherwise little different from that of smaller cities. In part, this conservative posture arises from a concern with the economic growth of the city and beliefs about what policies will and will not facilitate growth, as we explained in Chapter 10. In part, too, this conservative posture simply represents the dominant political ideology in the state. It may be the responsibility of cities to moderate the harsh realities of urban life, but only the roughest edges will be polished. Individuals still must fend for themselves to a notable degree in dealing with the many difficulties of modern urban life.

We should probably not be surprised that Texas cities take a conservative posture. Mass public participation in city government is quite limited, especially participation of the poor. Voter participation in elections is low and is concentrated among the better-off, more conservative residents. Regular, consistent pressure from interest groups is most likely to come from conservative elements too, especially from the business community. Other groups can be influential, but they are far less likely to be well organized and persistent in their efforts to shape government policy. Finally, the active leadership of Texas cities is likely dominated by political conservatives. Most elected officials are white males, and women and ethnic minorities are remarkably underrepresented.

References

Alford, Robert R., and Lee, Eugene C. 1968. "Voting Turnout in American Cities." *American Political Science Review* 62 (September): 796–813.

Hamilton, Howard D. 1971. "The Municipal Voter: Voting and Nonvoting in City Elections." *American Political Science Review* 65 (December): 1135–1140.

Hays, Samuel P. 1964. "The Politics of Reform in Municipal Government in the Progressive Era." *Pacific Northwest Quarterly* 55 (October): 157–189.

Lineberry, Robert L., and Fowler, Edmund P. 1967. "Reformism and Public Policies in American Cities." *American Political Science Review* 61 (September): 701–716.

Lipsky, Michael. 1980. *Street Level Bureaucracy: Dilemmas of the Individual in Public Services.* New York: Russell Sage.

Moulder, Evelina R. 1987. "Profiles of Individual Cities and Counties." *The Municipal Year Book, 1987.* Washington, D.C.: International City Management Association.

U.S. Bureau of the Census. 1990. *1987 Census of Governments: Government Organization— Popularly Elected Officials.* Washington, D.C.

———. 1992. *City Government Finances: 1989–1990.* Washington, D.C.

Verba, Sidney, and Nie, Norman H. 1972. *Participation in America.* New York: Harper & Row.

Yates, Douglas. 1976. "Urban Government as a Policy-Making System." In Louis Masotti and Robert Lineberry (eds.), *The New Urban Politics.* Cambridge, Mass.: Ballinger.

Chapter 12

Counties and Special Districts

We noted earlier the large number and variety of local governments, and we have discussed some of the consequences of their existence. Chapter 10, in particular, explored the fragmentation of political authority and policy effort, especially in large metropolitan areas, that results from having many forms of local government. Cities are doubtless the most important of local government units. They provide the greatest number of public services, have the greatest responsibilities for resolving local problems, and are the most visible of all local government entities. For that reason we discussed the character and activities of cities at length in Chapters 10 and 11. But a good understanding of Texas politics and public policy also requires some knowledge of the other forms of local government. Thus we will consider the most important attributes of counties, special districts generally, and school districts in this chapter.

Legal Responsibilities of County Government

In principle, the county is simply an administrative arm of the state that exists to collect taxes and carry out state laws and policies. Counties also exercise broad discretion, however. Although tax rate ceilings are set by the state, counties enjoy considerable flexibility within those limits. They can impose the maximum property tax rate or one that is substantially below the legal ceiling. Moreover, they can spend a great deal of money or very little. They can emphasize some programs and services and ignore others. Counties, therefore, are much more than simple administrative appendages of state government.

In fact, the state does not pay much attention to its counties. It does not insist upon uniform and standardized personnel or financial procedures. It does not require a minimum level of services. It does not provide any financial assistance. In short, the county in Texas is essentially an autonomous unit of government,

244   *Chapter 12*

free to chart its own course within the broad limits established by the constitution and state laws.

Constitutional Provisions

The Texas Constitution does not provide counties with many significant powers. It does, however, carefully prescribe the structure and functions of the various governmental offices. Few departures from the system of offices as specified in the constitution are allowed. Counties, unlike Texas cities, do not have the option of home rule. The least heavily populated county has the same form of government as the largest county. That lack of flexibility with respect to structure reflects a governmental form that was adopted to serve the needs of a rural state. No modification has been made in response to rapid urbanization, and the constitution makes no provision for adaptation in response to changing conditions.

An amendment added to the state constitution in 1933 did provide for home rule. Because of its ambiguity, however, it could not provide a workable solution to the home-rule problem, and the amendment was deleted from the constitution in 1969. Only three counties ever reached the stage of actually writing charters for home rule under the amendment, and only one proposed charter (in El Paso County) was presented to the voters for approval. It was defeated.

Nevertheless, home rule is not a dead issue. The growing complexity of government in urban areas increases the possibility that residents of urban counties will eventually demand that county governments be given the power to deal with metropolitan-wide problems. A single urban county in Texas may encompass millions of people and hundreds of separate units of government. Only the county has jurisdiction over the entire area. It is the logical choice, then, to assume responsibility for problems that do not respect municipal boundaries. Yet significant changes are required in both law and custom before county governments can play a larger role. Although the growing complexity of local government increases the possibility that such an expanded role may eventually come about, it certainly does not guarantee it.

One major barrier to change in the structure and powers of county government is a lack of flexibility. Counties require a specific grant of authority as provided in the constitution or state statute before they can undertake various programs. Although the responsibilities of urban counties in Texas have significantly increased in recent years, that growth can be attributed to factors other than expanded powers. For example, county governments spend much more money on the criminal justice system than previously because of revenue-sharing funds and specific federal grants (such as the Law Enforcement Assistance Administration). Moreover, the federal courts have forced change. The new jail complex in Harris

Counties and Special Districts　　　245

County (Houston) was built under a federal court order. It remains to be seen whether cutbacks in federal funds will be compensated for by increases in locally generated revenues. Most of the innovations in county government in recent years in areas such as law enforcement, the courts, corrections, and prosecution can be directly traced to federal funds and court orders.

Offices of County Government

The Commissioners' Court

The commissioners' court is the closest thing that county government has to a central policy-making body. The court consists of four commissioners (each elected from precincts of approximately equal population) and a county judge who serves as the presiding officer. Each commissioner has responsibility for the county road and bridge construction and maintenance program in his or her precinct. The commissioners' court performs the following functions and duties:

1. Setting the property tax rate within the limits established by the state
2. Setting service charges and fees
3. Approving the county budget
4. Appointing various officers
5. Filling vacancies in office
6. Letting contracts for supplies and equipment
7. Drawing the boundaries for justice of the peace precincts
8. Deciding which of the optional programs provided by the state will be adopted and funded
9. Submitting to the voters proposals to levy certain special taxes as provided by law

The powers of the commissioners' court are significant but limited. One of its most significant powers is exerted through its control over the budget. It has a great deal to say about which services will be provided and at what level. Through its control over the property tax rate (within the limits established by the state constitution) and its power to set service charges and fees, it strongly influences the amount of revenues available to county government. Through its control over how much money will be spent for each service, it also influences the level and quality of services. In addition, the commissioners' court exercises significant power when it decides upon various optional programs and facilities. It may, for example, choose to build an airport, a county hospital, or a network of park and recreational sites.

The court's powers are also limited, however. One major limitation concerns revenue generation. The only tax the county can levy is the property tax. Further, the rate at which the property tax can be assessed is fixed by the state. And though the court controls how much money is spent for various programs and purposes, elected officials decide how county funds will be spent in various areas. Because the court does not appoint department heads and direct their performance, its ability to influence how county dollars are actually spent is very limited.

Another limitation is that the court has few powers beyond those expressly granted by the state. An active county government would find it difficult to assume responsibilities beyond those specifically authorized by state government.

The power of the commissioners' court is also limited by a factor that has nothing to do with legal and constitutional restrictions. Instead, this limitation is self-imposed. Traditionally, county government has been concerned with providing as few services as possible. Limited responsibility, low taxes, low spending, and minimal service levels have long been the norm for county governments. Commissioners are more concerned with the road and bridge program in their precinct than with setting policy for the county as a whole. County officials have generally found little to complain about in a political system where responsibility is limited and power is fragmented. Such a system insulates public officials from the public's demands and significantly reduces the level of pressure under which most politicians must operate. For example, citizen demands for more and better government services can be dismissed with the response that the state constitution or laws do not allow them.

The County Judge

The county judge is elected by the voters in the county and presides over the commissioners' court. The county judge's functions include the following:

1. Preparing the county budget
2. Performing certain duties with respect to elections (posting notices and forwarding election results to the state)
3. Serving as judge of the county court, where judicial responsibilities include probate jurisdiction
4. Issuing licenses for the sale of wine and beer in counties that permit such sales

The county judge can, however, be either more or less influential than these specified powers would imply. For example, the county judge has few or no judicial responsibilities in counties where county courts at law have been provided to assume the judicial functions. That loss of judicial power has not diminished the county judge's work load, however. Instead, the judge's informal responsibilities have increased—particularly in counties that have experienced dramatic population growth. The county judge is frequently the dominant political leader in the county, for example. Given the county judge's prominence in both the government and the politics of the county, he or she is often called upon to resolve disputes and respond to complaints about services and programs.

Although the county judges are the chief executives in county government, they are chief executives in name only. They cannot appoint the major department heads or remove them. They cannot control how county funds are spent in such major areas as law enforcement and roads. They certainly are not the chief executive of county government in the sense that a city manager in a reformed city and a mayor in an unreformed city are chief executives. The county judge coordinates rather than controls.

Other Elected Officials

The **sheriff** is the chief law enforcement officer in the county. In addition, the sheriff operates the jails, and in counties of fewer than 10,000 people, the sheriff serves as tax assessor and collector.

A **justice of the peace** (JP) is elected from each precinct. (In Texas each county is divided into four to eight precincts.) The JP presides over a court that has jurisdiction over misdemeanors involving no confinement and over some civil issues. The JP also functions as county coroner except in large counties where the coroner is appointed by the commissioners' court.

A **constable** is elected from each JP precinct. The constable is a process server and serves writs and warrants, as well.

The **county clerk** provides clerical services for both the county court and the commissioners' court. The clerk maintains records pertaining to contracts, voting, deeds, marriages, and mortgages. In counties without an auditor, the clerk also maintains certain financial records.

An **assessor and collector of taxes** is elected in counties with a population of 10,000 and more. The chief function of this office is to assess and collect the county property tax. Other duties include the registration of voters and the sale of automobile license plates and certificates of title.

The **treasurer** has control over the receipt and payment of county funds as authorized by the commissioners' court. The treasurer also periodically examines the financial records of county offices.

The **county attorney** has different duties and functions, depending upon the county. In counties that have no **district attorney**, the county attorney serves as a legal adviser and prosecutes criminal and civil cases in both the county and district courts. In counties that have a district attorney, the county attorney is the prosecutor for the county and justice of the peace courts, and the district attorney prosecutes cases in the district (state) courts.

Appointed Officials

Other county offices are also provided for by state law. A **county auditor** is required in counties with populations of more than 35,000 or with taxable property valued at more than $15 million. Appointed by the district judge or judges in the county, the auditor inspects financial records and evaluates claims against the county. A **health officer** is appointed by the commissioners' court to provide medical care to prisoners, to supervise general health services and facilities, and to undertake programs of sanitation and disease prevention and control. Other appointed county officials include agricultural and home demonstration agents, a county engineer, and a county juvenile officer.

The Problems with County Government

Because most county officials are elected by the voters, executive authority is fragmented. Department heads are elected rather than appointed, and there is essentially no centralized supervision of either personnel or finances. Individual offices and officials are free to chart their own course. Because of the large number of elected officials, all but the best-informed voters are probably ignorant of the various candidates' positions on the issues. The county does not have a chief executive with sufficient powers to implement policies, enforce compliance, or supervise the various departmental programs. Instead county government is fragmented into several separate fiefdoms. Even individual programs reveal divided responsibility. The authority for the county road and bridge program, for example, is parceled out to four different commissioners. Although the county is the logical jurisdiction to assume responsibility for metropolitan-wide problems, it is unlikely that such a development will soon take place. Certainly such an expansion of authority would require changes in the constitution and state law. Because of tradition, apathy, and the power of entrenched interests, it will be exceedingly difficult to bring about such change.

The Policy Priorities of Texas Counties

We have alluded to, but have not fully explained, the character of county policy efforts. The average county, as we suggested earlier, mounts a modest program effort that centers around a few key priorities. Road and highway maintenance, the policing activities of the sheriff's office, the activities of the county courts and the county jail, and the central record-keeping functions given the county by the state are the major activities. And, to reiterate, the levels of service provided are generally modest.

At the same time, some counties face an array of not-so-modest policy problems and public demands for service, especially in heavily populated metropolitan areas. For that reason such counties have sizable budgets and mount programs of some magnitude to grapple with selected problems. They have to handle the same basic responsibilities as the average county, but they face other, more challenging problems as well.

An appreciation of the distinctive policy efforts of urban counties can be gained by studying Tables 12-1 and 12-2. Selected information on the per capita expenditures of the six most populous counties in the state is presented in Table 12-1, and comparable information on six medium-sized counties is given in Table 12-2. Ideally we would contrast the most populous counties with small-town and rural ones, but comparable data are not available for the latter counties.

In general, counties in large metropolitan areas must provide a more extensive and intensive variety of public services, as witnessed by their generally high total per capita expenditures. Two of the most notable, specific responsibilities of metropolitan counties are also indicated by high per capita spending—for hospitals and health care and for corrections. The medium-sized counties have far more modest responsibilities in those two areas, and we could expect that smaller counties would have even more limited health care and corrections efforts.

Additional evidence on the policy and service activities of these differently situated counties can be seen in their employment statistics. Quite simply, a metropolitan county must have an unusually large work force to implement its unusually expansive mission. In 1990, for example, Bexar County employed almost 7,000 people, Dallas County almost 11,000, El Paso County more than 3,000, Tarrant County almost 5,000, Travis County more than 2,000, and Harris County more than 16,000. In contrast, medium-sized Taylor and Wichita counties each employed fewer than 400 people (U.S. Bureau of the Census, 1991a:14).

From Tables 12-1 and 12-2 we can make additional observations on the essential services that all counties provide and that we listed earlier. Roads and highways, corrections, policing, and general administration—in good part to serve state-mandated record-keeping functions—are prominent expenditure categories in all these counties. We can also observe that counties have very modest public welfare functions. In that respect they are much like Texas cities (see Chapters 10 and 11). Like cities, as well, counties concentrate their expenditures on what one might call nuts-and-bolts local services.

Table 12-1 | **Selected per capita expenditures of Texas's most populous counties, 1988–1989**

County	1988 Population	Per Capita Expenditures ($)						
		Total	Corrections	General Administration	Hospitals and Health Care	Police	Public Welfare	Roads and Highways
Bexar	1,211,700	309	31	54	112	8	3	16
Dallas	1,854,700	296	36	64	121	10	5	19
El Paso	585,900	219	30	38	105	12	3	4
Harris	2,786,700	505	37	68	124	14	5	90
Tarrant	1,128,600	254	23	46	91	6	4	12
Travis	556,300	318	50	58	31	17	10	48

Source: U.S. Bureau of the Census (1991b:102–105).

Table 12-2 | **Selected per capita expenditures of medium-sized Texas counties, 1988–1989**

County	1988 Population	Per Capita Expenditures ($)						
		Total	Corrections	General Administration	Hospitals and Health Care	Police	Public Welfare	Roads and Highways
Brazos	116,600	252	17	27	2	31	6	36
Gregg	109,100	203	7	57	4	20	3	21
Midland	107,300	181	21	55	—	25	1	14
Potter	102,800	184	12	87	2	43	4	7
Taylor	121,800	127	23	49	1	12	7	11
Wichita	124,600	140	20	51	2	12	5	12

Source: U.S. Bureau of the Census (1991b:102–105).

252   *Chapter 12*

Special Districts

The most numerous form of government in Texas is the special district. The U.S. federal government's 1987 census of governments recorded 254 counties, just over 1,000 cities, just over 1,000 school districts—and 1,859 special districts in the state. By the federal government's classification system, the most numerous of the special districts were those with sewerage and water supply functions, followed by housing and community development districts, utility districts, and soil conservation districts (Table 12-3).

Special districts have grown notably in number over the last several decades. In 1962 there were 733, and in 1982 there were 1,691. Further testimony to the importance of these entities, beyond their simple numbers, is indicated by their finances. In 1987, special districts in Texas collected over $4 billion in revenues and carried almost $16 billion of outstanding debt at the end of the year.

The state of Texas labels its special districts somewhat distinctively, in accordance with state constitutional and statutory law. In Texas nomenclature the most numerous special districts are the ones with water and sewerage functions of some kind. They include municipal utility districts (MUDs), water control and

Table 12-3 | **Special district governments in Texas, 1987**

Type of District	Number
Airport	3
Drainage	44
Fire protection	69
Flood control	67
Health	6
Hospital	135
Housing and community development	390
Irrigation and water conservation	69
Natural resources and water supply[a]	13
Parks and recreation	3
Sanitation or sewerage	9
Sewerage and water supply[a]	469
Soil conservation	208
Utilities	212
Water transportation and terminals[a]	23
Other	139
Total	1,859

[a]Multiple-function districts.

Source: U.S. Bureau of the Census (1990:124–126).

improvement districts (WCIDs), drainage districts, navigation districts, and river authorities.

Water districts enjoy significant powers. The state constitution gives MUDs the authority to provide water and hydroelectric power, to conserve natural resources, to combat water pollution, to provide park and recreational facilities, to dispose of sewage, and to collect solid waste. Water control and improvement districts have similar powers. If created according to one article of the constitution, WCIDs have all the powers of MUDs with the exception of the authority to provide park and recreation facilities. If established under still another article, WCIDs can undertake flood control, irrigation, navigation, and drainage programs. Water districts perform several governmental functions. Other types of special districts tend to limit their activities to a single function.

Reasons for the Growth of Special Districts

The proliferation of special districts in Texas did not occur by chance. The rapid spread of these governments can be traced to several factors. First is the inability of existing governments to deal with problems. As we indicated in earlier chapters, municipal and county governments do not have sufficient powers to deal with many problems. Frequently their problems do not stop at jurisdictional boundaries. Flooding and an inadequate supply of fresh water, for example, are major problems that generally extend across several jurisdictions within a county or metropolitan area. Yet no single government has either the authority or the resources to deal with the problem. Special districts provide a way whereby the fragmented power that characterizes local government in Texas can be overcome. They permit government to deal with issues that are area-wide and extend across several jurisdictions.

Another reason for the spread of special districts is the unwillingness of existing governments to deal with problems. Traditionally, local government in Texas has been very limited government. Local public officials emphasize minimum service levels and low taxes. They seldom champion an aggressive expansion of government spending and programs. That attitude toward the appropriate scope of government is deeply rooted in the political culture of the state. The emphasis upon a narrow role for government collides head-on, however, with another fact of political life: Texas is no longer a rural state where very limited government will suffice. The demands of dramatic population growth and rapid urbanization require that government undertake certain programs and activities. Drainage, flood control, water, and health care have to be provided. The special district provides a mechanism whereby government services can be delivered without existing governments assuming responsibility for them. Thus the myth of limited government can be preserved. Moreover, public officials are insulated from citizen complaints about inadequate performance. The most effective way for a local

254   *Chapter 12*

government official to deal with outraged citizens is simply to maintain that the problem is the responsibility of another jurisdiction.

The unwillingness of existing governments to cooperate with respect to area-wide problems is yet another reason for the proliferation of special districts. Although cooperation alone would not solve common problems, it would provide a partial solution. Much could be done to address jointly the problems that are now frequently handled by special districts. Instead, individual municipalities and counties show little interest in cooperation. They jealously guard their separateness and appear to be little concerned with working together to solve common problems. In the absence of cooperation, the special district is necessary if action is to be taken to solve problems.

Taxing and debt ceilings favor the spread of special districts, as well. Cities and counties are restricted in terms of how much revenue they can generate. State law limits the rate at which the property tax can be assessed. When tax and debt constraints prohibit an existing government from undertaking a new service, the special district provides a convenient alternative. A new unit of government is simply created to deliver the service. The new government generates the necessary revenue through the assessment of taxes or the sale of bonds.

Certainly there are few barriers to the creation of special districts. Special district governments are relatively easy to establish. As a result, they are more likely to be created to deal with service problems than they would be if the creation process were intricate and scrutinized carefully by various agencies and groups.

Moreover, special districts offer certain advantages to builders and developers. Thus municipal utility districts (MUDs) have been exploited by some residential builders. Because new developments require a variety of services, the MUD has been used to provide them and shift the cost burden to those who eventually buy homes in the subdivision. The MUD has the power to tax and raise revenues. The developers use those revenues to construct essential service facilities. The new homeowners are generally unaware that their purchase of a home in the MUD makes them responsible for retiring the debt incurred. Hundreds of such MUDs have been created in the Houston area alone to finance the service infrastructure in new housing developments. Many more MUDs would be in operation if they had not been annexed by various cities. When a city annexes a MUD, it assumes responsibility for all debt incurred as well as for provision of services.

Finally, special districts are sometimes used to obtain federal aid. For example, soil conservation districts and public housing authorities cannot levy taxes. (Housing authorities can, however, sell revenue bonds.) Thus they rely heavily upon federal dollars to fund their operations. By the creation of such districts, an area can take advantage of federal aid without involving an existing government in a controversial program.

Problems with Special Districts

The criticisms of special district government are numerous. First, special districts are subject to little or no supervision by the state. Consequently, administrative, personnel, and financial practices are inefficient if not primitive. Second, special district government is neither responsive nor accountable. Public knowledge of these governments is essentially nonexistent. They are shielded from public scrutiny. There are so many of them and their functions are so narrow and technical that they are effectively removed from citizen control. Thus they are antidemocratic. Third, special districts compound local problems rather than solve them. Special district government is a stopgap effort. Special districts will never be able to deal adequately with the issues of water supply, flooding, and housing. Instead they simply delay cooperative action by city and county governments. Special districts prevent effective, long-term solutions such as city–county consolidation or a significant expansion of the powers and functions of county government. Local government has little incentive to change its approach to area-wide problems so long as the special district remains a stopgap option. Fourth, special districts impose yet another layer of government on local areas that already may have dozens and even hundreds of governments. The increased complexity not only contributes to confusion in government but also is inefficient. Because special district government is small government, it cannot take advantage of economies of scale.

Despite all the criticisms of special districts, it is unlikely that these governments will diminish in number or significance in the near future. They are symptomatic of an unfulfilled need in local government. That need is for a unit of government with sufficient powers to deal with the problems that counties or cities cannot or will not confront. That the special district has been less than effective in filling that void suggests that fundamental change is required.

School Districts

One of the most important kinds of special district is the local school district. Because of their importance and their distinctiveness, we will consider school districts separately from other special districts. These entities provide public elementary and secondary education in particular geographic areas. We seldom think of school districts or their policies for delivering education services as being politically controversial, but that is precisely the case today—for reasons explained below. Before considering the current politics of public education and school districts, however, we should briefly describe their governance and the policy setting in which they function.

School District Governance

School districts are, indeed, local special districts. Each has a locally elected governing board—the school board—whose members run for office in non-partisan elections for three-year terms. The school board appoints the super-intendent, who is a professional manager for the district, much like a city man-ager is for a city. The board also establishes broad policy for the conduct and administration of the school system, sets the property tax rate to raise local revenues, approves the budget, and controls a number of other major district policy decisions.

At the same time, school districts share the power to control local education policy with the state government. The state government has the power to establish uniform, statewide education policies through constitutional law and through statutory law adopted by the legislature and the governor. The Texas Education Agency implements the relevant constitutional and statutory laws, under the guidance of the State Board of Education. Composed of fifteen elected members from different regions of the state, the State Board of Education establishes particular state education policies and practices within the guidelines of the preceding laws. Then the Texas Education Agency implements that state policy. The Texas Education Agency accredits local districts in accordance with state standards, distributes state and federal funds to school districts, monitors com-pliance with various state and federal laws, and provides technical and information assistance to school districts.

The Politics of Public Education

Most Americans would probably like to think of education policy as being nonpolitical, but that ideal situation is not realized in Texas or in the United States generally today. For several reasons the goals and character of public education, and the institutional mechanisms by which it is provided, have become matters of intense political controversy.

Since the early 1980s there has been considerable debate in Texas about the quality of Texas public schools and their ability to prepare students for careers in the evolving economy and uncertain socioeconomic times described in Chapters 1 and 2. That debate has been fueled by national concern over the problem, but it has been aggravated in Texas because of some notable problems in Texas schools. To cite only a few of those problems, dropout rates are especially high among Texas high school students; Texas scores on standardized achievement tests, such as the Scholastic Aptitude Test (SAT) and the American College Test (ACT), are below the national averages; and public funding for education in Texas is below the national average.

The Texas Legislature made a first attack on these problems in 1981 when it mandated a core curriculum for students, with "essential elements" defined for the curriculum in thirteen different subject areas. To remain accredited, each local school district has to provide instruction in those essential elements. A far more comprehensive set of reforms was adopted by the legislature in 1984 with the famous House Bill 72. Extensive changes in curricula, financing, teacher education and performance, and student performance were included in that law.

The legislature has continued to tinker with public education requirements in every subsequent legislative session. The direction of state policy is also quite evident—greater state control and less local school district autonomy, with the hope, at least, of providing as many students as possible with an education suited for the twenty-first century. But that goal is itself a controversial one, and even educational experts disagree about how it best can be achieved. Thus the policy debate will continue, and it will inevitably divide candidates for public office and their political parties.

The goal of educating for the twenty-first century does, however, elicit one point of wide agreement—which itself leads to more controversy about education policy. Achieving that goal for a large proportion of Texas schoolchildren will inevitably be quite expensive. The reforms adopted already have added many new costs, and many more will be required if the state is to be successful in this effort. Yet these are difficult times in which to propose extensive new spending in any area of state or local government. Both the state government and all local governments face tight budget prospects. Federal aid has declined since the early 1980s, and local property tax values, the key revenue base for school districts, have generally declined since the oil bust of the mid-1980s. For those reasons most school districts, like all local governments, have had to consider tax increases nearly every year. But taxpayer resistance to such increases has been great—in part because so many local governments have so regularly enacted them and in part because of the general concern over the quality of education policy that tax revenues are buying. Thus the financial climate of the times complicates the effort to reform education policy, and it increases the debate over any reform that will increase the cost of public education.

If the preceding problems were not enough, another complication was added in 1987 when the state's system for funding public education was found unconstitutional in a state district court. The lawsuit that led to the ruling was filed by a group of poor school districts and the Mexican-American Legal Defense and Education Fund, and it charged that the funding system discriminated against students in poor districts. Wealthier districts were able to supplement state-provided funding with additional revenues that allowed them to provide vastly superior education to their students.

The district court ruling was appealed to the Texas Supreme Court, which agreed with the district judge's decision and ordered the state to create a constitutional funding system by May 1, 1990. After struggling with that task through four special sessions, the legislature created a new system of state funding. But in

258 *Chapter 12*

January 1991 the Supreme Court found that plan unconstitutional, as well, and ordered that a new plan be adopted into law by April 1 of that year. The legislature rose to the latter task and produced yet another funding scheme. But the Supreme Court rejected that third scheme in January 1992 and required that a new one be adopted by June 1993. This brief chronology of the state government's efforts to create an education funding system in accord with the Texas Constitution is doubtless sufficient testimony for how this new problem has complicated efforts to make education policy.

One additional complicating element must be mentioned. Many of the poor school districts in the state—and the most noted of those that filed the lawsuit discussed above—are ones with largely Hispanic and black populations. Many of them are poor central-city districts, and others are in poor rural areas. Most of the state's wealthy districts, in contrast, have largely Anglo populations. In light of these facts many critics of the state's funding system believe that the state's inability to craft a constitutional plan arises because of ethnic prejudice and a general lack of interest in the poor. Thus ethnic tensions are heightened, and charges of ethnic bias have been added to the debate.

For all the preceding reasons, school districts and their programs have become major political concerns and are likely to remain so for some time. The governor and the legislature have grappled with education issues in every recent legislative session. The Texas Education Agency and virtually every local school board have done so, as well. Education policy has thus become one of the most important topics for election and partisan politics.

The Number and Variety of School Districts

Establishing a comprehensive education policy for the twenty-first century is made more difficult by the character of local school districts. There were 1,058 public school districts in 1989–1990, ranging in size from tiny Allamoore Independent School District in Hudspeth County with 3 students to Houston Independent School District in Harris County with 174,340 students. As can be seen in Figure 12-1, 412 school districts, or 39 percent of the total, have fewer than 500 students. At the other extreme, 65 districts, or 6 percent of the total, have more than 10,000 students. Thus Texas has considerable numbers of large and small districts, and it is certain that the governance and administrative problems of large and small districts are vastly different. Thus any general education policy must be modified to accommodate to the practical realities and differences among districts.

The local financial resources of school districts are equally variable. The principal funding of public schools comes from local property taxes, but the taxable property base in individual districts ranges from the minuscule to the magnificent. In 1989–1990 the poorest district was Edcouch-Elsa in Hidalgo County, with a mere

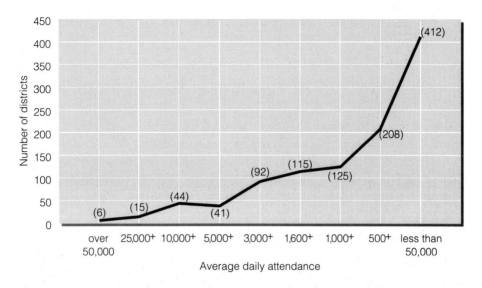

Figure 12-1 | **Average daily attendance in Texas school districts, 1989–1990**
Source: Texas Education Agency (1991:4)

$20,404 in taxable property for each pupil in the district. At the other extreme, Laureles Independent School District in Kleberg County had $9,266,470 in taxable property per student (Texas Education Agency, 1991). Even if Edcouch-Elsa set the maximum tax rate allowable, it could never collect the funds that Laureles can extract with a modest tax rate. Thus the students in some districts are consigned to a second- or third-rate education by the accident of where they were born or where they now live.

Having a large number of local school districts greatly enhances the possibility of close local control of schools, which is highly desired by most Texans, but it creates many problems and inequities as well. Doubtless, the overall efficiency of the public school system is highly compromised by having a separate governance system and administrative apparatus for each school district. Texans pay far more to administer such a system than they otherwise would, and those excess administrative expenditures could be more productively spent on education per se.

In addition, the efforts of the governor, the legislature, and the Texas Education Agency to provide central direction and coordination in education policy are constrained by the large number and disparate capabilities of individual districts. Most important, however, the financial circumstances of many school districts make the promise of local control a virtual fraud. School districts with modest financial resources, which currently gain little assistance from the state's supplementary funding, have insufficient capabilities to exercise that local control and to implement desired education programs.

Conclusion

Counties, special districts, and school districts could be considered minor administrative units on the local government scene in Texas. They have especially limited powers and responsibilities, and thus their activities are far more restricted than are those of cities. Yet a knowledge of these more specialized units of government is important to an appreciation of the full scope of governmental responsibilities and administrative forms in Texas. Knowledge of these units of government also provides further evidence for a number of general observations we made earlier.

All units of local government are in some respects sharply limited in their powers by state law. All of them concentrate their efforts on selected programs or policy priorities. All of them have been substantially affected by the processes of urbanization and suburbanization. And a number of them have been touched by the politics of ethnic conflict and discrimination against minorities.

A survey of the entire range of local government units also reinforces the discussion in Chapter 10 of the fragmentation of governmental effort at the local level, especially in large metropolitan areas. The great number and variety of local governments lead, first, to several kinds of inefficiencies—in part so that local control and autonomy can be advanced. Thus those who desire local autonomy should understand the costs of that goal. Yet at times this fragmentation means that those in control locally are unable to effectively tackle the policy problems for which they are responsible, because of the limited powers and resources of their governmental unit. School districts probably offer the best example of this problem, as we noted in this chapter, but much the same can be said for cities, counties, and many special districts.

Fragmentation of local government units makes coordination of public policy by the central state government far more difficult, too. We may hope that the governor and the legislature will successfully craft policies to reduce the problems of urban areas, to provide education suitable for the twenty-first century, and so on, but their ability to do so is often hampered by the complex of local governmental units, with differing capabilities and interests, that must actually implement such policies.

Finally, a multiplicity of local governments in a particular geographic area makes cooperation among those entities far harder to attain. Individual cities, counties, and special districts often fear cooperation, believing that it will reduce their own power and independence. Smaller governmental units, in particular, fear the clout of larger cities and counties. And some local public officials probably fear that their personal political power will be diminished by cooperative efforts, as well.

References

Texas Education Agency. 1991. *Snapshot '90: 1989–1990 School District Profiles*. Austin.
U.S. Bureau of the Census. 1990. *1987 Census of Governments: Finances of Special Districts*. Washington, D.C.
———. 1991a. *County Government Employment, 1990*. Washington, D.C.
———. 1991b. *County Government Finances, 1988–1989*. Washington, D.C.

Lottery

TEXAS LOTTERY
LOTTO TEXAS DRAWING

Leo

Two Hundred Seven

Void

Chapter 13

Taxation and Spending

This is the first of two chapters in which we will examine the products of the governmental system of Texas—in other words, the public policies adopted by the state government and its local subdivisions. Such matters have been discussed at several earlier points, but these two chapters present a more comprehensive treatment and draw together a number of themes and conclusions from prior discussions in the book.

This chapter begins with a description of the structure of taxation and public spending in Texas—that is, the kinds of tax instruments and the kinds of spending priorities. Next, the level of taxation and the distribution of public spending across different policy priorities will be considered. Thus we will examine where the state puts its emphasis in allocating both the burdens and the benefits of its policies. An important component, as well, will be comparisons with policies in other states. We will then be able to offer some conclusions about the policy goals implicit in the state's taxing and spending systems and about the social effects of those systems.

In earlier chapters, we examined city and county government spending separately, but in the present chapter we will analyze combined state and local taxation and spending information. This approach is necessary to summarize the overall character of the state's governmental priorities. It is also necessary if we wish our comparisons with other states to be fair—because the states differ to some degree in the ways they divide responsibilities between the central state government and their local governmental units.

The Level of State and Local Taxes

The first question that probably occurs to the average citizen when the broad topic of taxes is raised is, Just how high are my taxes? To calculate average taxes, one can simply divide the total amount of tax revenues raised in a given year by the population of the state in the same year. Although each citizen did not pay that

264   *Chapter 13*

exact amount of taxes, the method provides a general indication of the tax level and is useful for making state-by-state comparisons.

In 1989, total state and local per capita taxes in Texas were $1,563; the fifty-state average was $1,888. Most of the other large, highly industrialized, and urbanized states like Texas had per capita tax burdens in the range of $2,000 to $2,300. The conclusion from these figures is obvious: Texas is a low-tax state, especially relative to other states with comparable public policy problems, but even relative to the average state.[1] Other research has indicated that relatively low taxes have been a traditional feature of twentieth-century Texas government (Anderson and Mc-Millan, 1953:63–70; Penniman, 1965:313–315). All Texans have reason to be pleased by this circumstance. Why, one might ask, would they pay more taxes than they already do?

Sources of Tax Revenues

Just as it is important to examine the level of taxes, it is essential to consider from what sources taxes are derived. The several tax instruments that states may use to distribute the total tax load do not fall equally on all citizens. Thus the selection of tax instruments can have a substantial impact on which individuals or groups bear relatively high or low tax burdens.

The Major Tax Instruments

The most important tax instruments are property taxes, general sales taxes, selective sales taxes, income taxes, corporation income taxes, licensing fees, severance taxes, and lotteries.

Property Taxes The ad valorem property tax—assessed as a percentage of the assessed market value of certain property—has been the traditional mainstay of state and local government revenues. Typically it is collected on the value of land, residences, and commercial and industrial plants and equipment. Perhaps the greatest advantage of this tax is that such items are both highly visible and not easily movable. The administration of the tax is facilitated in some respects by those attributes, just as tax avoidance is made less of a problem.

The property tax does, however, suffer from some major problems. The main problem is that of maintaining equitable tax rates for all the items of property in the taxing jurisdiction. The fair market value of some items of property may be difficult to assess, the value of others may be subject to considerable disagreement, and the values of all the items on the tax rolls may be changing at differing rates and even in different directions. In consequence, fair and equitable assessment is a complex and often controversial task. Some of these same difficulties in Texas led to the creation in 1982 of single, countywide tax appraisal districts whose job is to maintain the property tax roll for each county. The property valuations on the roll are then to be used by all the separate taxing entities in the county. Although this system has made the valuation process more efficient and uniform, it has also made it more conspicuous and politically controversial in many counties.

In Texas the property tax is employed principally by cities, counties, and school districts. Each jurisdiction sets its own rate and then applies it to the values of items of taxable property that have been determined by the countywide appraisal district.

General Sales Taxes General or retail sales taxes are employed in forty-six of the fifty states in order to tax consumption spending. These taxes are relatively inexpensive to administer because private commercial establishments do the initial collecting of the tax at the point of sale. The sales tax is widely criticized, however, because it is particularly **regressive** with respect to income. That is, it typically extracts a higher percentage of total income from low-income rather than high-income earners. Thus it runs counter to the ability-to-pay philosophy of **progressive** taxation (in which high-income earners pay the higher percentage of income in taxes), which underlies much of American taxation. Retail sales taxes can be made less regressive by the exclusion of mass consumption items such as food, but even then the tax remains regressive.

The state government levies a 6.25 percent sales tax on retail sales and some services with the exclusion of food, prescription medicine, and farm equipment and supplies. Many cities and other local governments can add an additional 1 percent tax to that base rate. The total tax is collected by retail sales establishments and remitted to the state. The state then returns to any local entity that has an additional tax its proportionate share of the total revenue raised within its borders.

Selective Sales Taxes Selective sales taxes are imposed on the sale of certain goods. For example, Texas, like most states, has selective sales taxes on liquor and cigarettes. Some people have referred to these taxes as sin taxes on the consumption of harmful goods, but the tax level on such products is typically set for its revenue-generating potential and not as a significant barrier to reduce the consumption of such items. All the states impose a sales tax on gasoline but with a different rationale. The proceeds of the gasoline tax are often dedicated to highway construction and maintenance with the rationale that it is the users of highway services who pay the tax.

266   *Chapter 13*

Individual Income Taxes Most states have a progressive individual income tax with rates in the range of 2 to 10 percent applied to an adjusted income figure taken from the individual's federal income tax calculations. These taxes are typically quite progressive with respect to income—in other words, high-income earners pay a higher percentage of their income to this tax. Progressive income taxes are held in high technical repute by most scholarly students of taxation for that feature and for several others. As Musgrave and Musgrave (1980:392) observe:

> *The income tax has the great advantage of relating tax liability to a comprehensive measure of ability to pay and of permitting adaptation to the personal circumstances of the taxpayer [by means of exclusions, exemptions, and similar devices]. Among existing taxes, it is the personal tax par excellence, and, at its best, it is superior to all other taxes . . . in implementing horizontal and vertical equity.*

Texas is one of only six states that do not have an individual income tax.

Corporation Income Taxes Most states also impose a tax on the net income of corporations to generate at least a modest amount of revenue. Once again, the rates are typically set at low levels. Moreover, states exercise considerable caution so that their corporate tax rate will not be far higher than that of most other states (and thus drive businesses to lower-tax states). Texas is one of only three states that have no corporation income tax.

Since 1992, however, Texas has had a tax on businesses that many people allege is a corporate income tax in disguise. The state has long had a so-called **corporate franchise tax**, whereby corporations in 1991 paid a tax of $5.25 per $1,000 of their net worth (assets minus long-term debt). (Sole proprietorships and partnerships were exempt from the franchise tax.) The franchise tax had been long criticized because it placed a relatively high tax burden on capital-intensive companies—that is, those that own extensive buildings, equipment, and other capital assets. Many service industries and especially professional service firms require few such assets and, hence, paid little in the way of franchise taxes. In that sense, then, the tax was inequitable in the way it affected different kinds of businesses.

The state legislature revised the tax in 1991, changing the method for calculating the tax on capital assets and adding a surtax based on "earned surplus." Many argue that the latter provision of the tax amounts to a tax on net income, the base to which state corporate income taxes are characteristically applied. The new franchise tax is now much higher for many firms that had paid little under the old system. It is, then, more equitable in the eyes of some businesses but certainly more controversial and criticized by those now having to pay more.

Taxation and Spending 267

Licensing Fees Licensing fees are a catchall category that includes fees required of various businesses as a condition of doing business in the state, similar fees required of some professionals as a condition of practicing in the state, automobile licensing fees, fees for taking state professional licensing examinations, hunting and fishing license fees, and so on. Texas, like all states, employs a variety of these fees in an effort to tax directly certain activities or the beneficiaries of certain privileges or users of state services or resources.

Severance Taxes Severance taxes are duties imposed on the value of certain natural resources when they are extracted from the ground. Such taxes are motivated by the idea that the resources are exhaustible physical assets of the state. Thus those who extract such resources for business purposes should recompense the state to some degree for the loss of such assets. Only a few states in the nation, including Texas, draw a notable portion of their tax revenues from this source. Texas imposes severance taxes on petroleum, natural gas, and sulfur, and the bulk of severance revenues comes from the first two of these products.

Lotteries After being approved by constitutional amendment in 1991, the Texas Lottery began operations in 1992. The lottery is, in fact, a variety of gambling games operated by the state with ticket and game sales made by private vendors such as convenience stores and supermarkets. A portion of the gross proceeds of lottery sales is devoted to prizes, a portion goes to administrative costs, and the remainder becomes revenue to the state. The state comptroller estimated that the Texas Lottery would generate $461 million in net revenues (on $1.2 billion in gross sales) in its first fiscal year of operations. At that level of annual income the lottery would provide about 3 percent of the state government's projected fiscal year 1992 revenues.

The Texas Lottery—Playing "The Game of Texas"

On opening day of the Texas Lottery in May 1992, Governor Ann Richards purchased the first lottery ticket at an Austin feed and western-wear store—and lost. But the state's first-day lottery sales of $23.2 million and its first-week sales of $102.4 million set national records. During the first week the lottery was in operation, however, the state also received a record number of calls to its telephone hot line for counseling compulsive gamblers addicted to playing the game.

Earlier in the year State Comptroller John Sharp had labeled as "slime" the people who work in the private industries that sell services to and contract with state lotteries. Yet less than two weeks after the Texas Lottery began, the manager of the state's lottery claim center in Houston—an employee of Sharp's agency—was caught trying to cash a winning $50 lottery ticket, one of 2,000 tickets he had stolen. So began what was advertised as "The Game of Texas" and one of the state's most controversial revenue schemes.

And the lottery will likely remain controversial. Its proponents argued it would provide badly needed revenue to the state at the same time that residents derived considerable entertainment from playing the game. Some players would win big, too, with the possibility of instantly winning up to $10,000 with one of the initial $1 "scratch-off" tickets. Other players would qualify for weekly drawings for a grand prize of $1 million. However, the odds of winning $10,000 were estimated as 1 in 600,000, and the odds of winning $1 million as one in 41.6 million.

Opponents, on the other hand, charged that the lottery was yet another highly regressive means of generating state revenues—by which the poor paid far more than the well-off. That fact about lotteries has been demonstrated in other states, and an early analysis by the *Houston Post* indicated that many of Texas's poorer areas would have disproportionate numbers of licensed lottery sales outlets. Opponents also feared that the lottery would encourage other forms of gambling and the organized crime that is often associated with gambling. And owners of pari-mutuel horse and dog racing tracks worried they would lose business to the lottery.

Rating the Texas Tax System

The overall character of the Texas tax system can be represented by a breakdown of the sources of total state and local taxes in Texas and in the average state (Table 13-1). Several comparisons are striking. First, Texas depends heavily on sales taxes. Texas draws 31 percent of its total indigenous revenues from the general sales tax alone, whereas the average across all the states is only 24 percent. Thus the Texas system is unusually dependent on this regressive tax instrument.

Second, and equally important for its effect on who pays the bulk of taxes, is the absence of income taxes in the Texas system. That absence means that the Texas tax system does not have any revenue source that is clearly progressive in its impact and that, hence, is based on the ability-to-pay criterion of progressive

Table 13-1 | Sources of state and local tax revenues, 1988–1989

Source of Revenue	Texas (%)	Average Among All States (%)
Property taxes	39	30
General sales taxes	31	24
Motor fuel taxes	6	4
Motor vehicle licensing fees	3	2
Individual and corporate income taxes	—	26
Other sources	21	13

Source: U.S. Bureau of the Census (1991a).

taxation. Thus, although the average state draws a quarter of its total income from this kind of taxation, Texas takes none.

Current Controversies About the Texas Tax System

Since the early 1980s, Texas state and local governments have had especially difficult times raising adequate operating revenues, and considerable debate has arisen about how they might more easily raise such revenues. The problem arose, first, because of the unfortunate coincidence of several events. The U.S. federal government, in good part because of its own budget problems, began in the early 1980s to reduce the amount of money it gave state and local governments to run shared or federally required programs. At the same time, the federal government also began to yield to states the control of many previously jointly run programs. The latter development meant that the states had to assume more of the financial burden of those programs too. So the states' financial responsibilities increased while their resources declined.

To make matters worse for Texas, the market prices of natural gas and crude oil declined dramatically at almost the same time. The price of crude oil fell by two-thirds in the mid-1980s, for example, and has never fully recovered. The declining prices reduced the economic feasibility of exploiting many oil and gas fields, because the market price would not cover the cost of production. Thus the total volume of production was smaller than it otherwise would be, and the resources extracted were sold at a lower market price. For those reasons, state severance tax revenues plummeted. The severance tax, as we mentioned earlier, is a percentage of the market price of oil and gas produced in the state.

While these revenue sources have been declining, demands for government services have been growing. In Chapter 1 we discussed a number of challenges that Texas state and local governments face. In a wide variety of policy areas—education, criminal justice, economic development, environmental preservation, health care, and so on—Texans are expecting more from their governments than they did even a few years ago. The result of these several changes is that governments in Texas face extreme difficulties in finding the revenues to pay for all the public programs Texans want.

This problem has been widely discussed by government leaders. Governor Bill Clements appointed a Select Committee on Tax Equity, which studied the problem and in its final report, issued in 1989, reached many of the same conclusions mentioned above. The committee also noted several other problems in the Texas tax system, some of which we will take up later in this chapter. In 1991, Governor Ann Richards appointed another tax revenue committee, and State Comptroller John Sharp offered his analysis of the problems in his Texas Performance Review,

270   *Chapter 13*

a comprehensive review of state government requested by the legislature. Both of those studies echoed most of the conclusions of Clements's original select committee. Yet none of these groups or any other state official has found a solution that has achieved wide support. For the near term it appears that Texans will have to endure incremental increases in most of their existing—and often inefficient or inequitable—taxes, along with a large number of government programs that are underfunded and thus operating below their potential.

The Level of State and Local Spending

If Texas is a relatively low-tax state, it inevitably must be a low-spending state. The state government is restricted by the constitution to a balanced budget, and local government units are similarly restricted by the state (except for money they are allowed to raise through the sale of bonds).

More interesting than the overall level of spending, however, are the distribution of spending across policy areas and the level of spending within each area. Relevant to the first point, the distribution of state and local spending across major functional categories is given for Texas and the average state in Table 13-2. In these figures Texas does not appear extraordinarily different from the average state. Education and transportation take somewhat larger shares of the total Texas budget, and public welfare gets a notably smaller share. For none of the other categories, however, is there a remarkable difference between Texas expenditures and the averages for all the states.

Table 13-2 | **Distribution of state and local expenditures, 1988–1989**

Service	Texas (%)	Average Among All States (%)
Higher education	11	9
Elementary and secondary education	29	24
Public welfare and social services	8	12
Hospitals and health	8	9
Transportation[a]	11	9
Public safety[b]	8	9
Environment and recreation	7	7
Government administration	5	5
Interest on debt	8	6
Other	5	10

[a]Principally highways.   [b]Principally police, fire, and corrections.

Source: U.S. Bureau of the Census (1991a).

The preceding figures describe only how the whole budget pie, so to speak, is divided up. They do not take account of the size of the pie. To do that, we can compare the actual levels of spending provided Texans in different policy areas. Such comparisons also indicate some of the relative priorities of Texas government. They begin to address, as well, a second question that a sophisticated citizen might have in mind: What do I get in return for the taxes I pay?

Again we must emphasize that one cannot infer the quality of public service simply from the amount of state spending in a certain category. At the same time, the level of spending is obviously closely related to the possible level of actual service. Low spending puts significant constraints on the potential quality of public services, whereas high spending makes high-quality service at least possible. Keeping that caveat in mind, we will look at several kinds of spending comparisons that might help us assess relative state priorities and services. For some policy areas, we can fairly compare the level of spending by government relative to the size of the state's population. Such per capita spending data are appropriate when the entire population is at least the theoretical client group that might use the public services under consideration. Police protection, for example, is extended in principle to all citizens equally. Hence per capita spending on police service—when compared across the states—is a fair estimate of the relative levels of service provided by the different states.

Per capita spending figures for several services for which the entire population might be thought of as the client population are provided in Table 13-3. A consistent pattern is evident across all these areas: Texas state and local governments spend less or even far less than the average state. Keep in mind, as well, that these comparisons are with the average state, not with the most generous and high-spending ones. Public spending levels in Texas would fall considerably farther below those of the most generous states in these terms. Thus we can conclude that, for the policy areas in Table 13-3, it is unlikely that Texans get public services any

Table 13-3 | **Per capita state and local government spending on selected services, 1988–1989**

Service	Texas ($)	Average Among All States ($)
Libraries	9	15
Hospitals	172	190
Police protection	89	112
Fire protection	38	48
Parks and recreation	36	52
Government administration	121	165

Source: U.S. Bureau of the Census (1991a).

272   *Chapter 13*

better than those provided by the average state—and they might well get services of considerably below-average quality. In other words, Texans get what they pay for. Their taxes are low, but in return they are provided with low levels of public service.

There are also policy areas in which the clients can more appropriately be defined as only a portion of the entire population. In education, for example, the client population consists of students in public schools; in public welfare it is the poor of the state who are served by government welfare programs. In policy areas like these, strictly per capita comparisons do not make as much sense as they do for the areas considered previously. Instead, we should compare spending per client.

Comparative public expenditure data for some specific client populations are given in Table 13-4. The first two comparisons are for what we might call high-status clients: students in public schools and colleges. Education, in other words, has traditionally been considered a high-priority service in all states, and many Texans would surely share that concern for the importance of public education and its clients. Evidence for that concern is that Texas state and local

Table 13-4 | State and local government spending per client on selected services, 1988–1989

Service	Texas ($)	Average Among All States ($)
Elementary and Secondary Education Total public spending per pupil, 1988–1989	4,131	4,813
Higher Education State and local government appropriations per full-time-equivalent student, 1989	2,953	4,234
Public Welfare Average monthly payment per qualifying recipient under the Aid to Families with Dependent Children program, 1988	57	128
Corrections State and local government general expenditures on corrections per jail or prison inmate, 1988	15,009	20,926

Sources: U.S. Bureau of the Census (1990, 1991b, 1991c); U.S. Social Security Administration (1990); U.S. Department of Justice (1991).

governments together spend 40 percent of their budgets on education (Table 13-2). That amount is considerably larger than what the average state spends. Yet when we consider how much is spent per education client, as shown in Table 13-4, Texas spending falls below the average spending level among the states. (Education in Texas merely gets a larger slice of a much smaller pie.)

Many college students in Texas will recall the controversies in 1985 and 1989 over whether tuition fees would be raised substantially—which they were—and those students might find the figures in Table 13-4 puzzling at first glance. Was not part of the controversy, a student might ask, over whether the state was spending too much instead of too little in supporting college students? The controversy was actually over the portion of the cost of their education that college students were to bear directly through tuition fees. The fees were raised so that students would bear a larger proportion of the total cost, but that total cost was below the average among all the states. The astute student may recall, as well, that college and university budgets were cut at the same time. After those cuts, state spending per student fell farther below the average among the states. Thus, some people might conclude, college students were paying more but getting less after these tuition and budget changes.

Information on services provided to what one could call low-status clients—the poor and people incarcerated in the state's prisons—is also included in Table 13-4. The welfare program included under "public welfare" is one that is initiated by the federal government but implemented by the states. The states are allowed to determine their monthly support payments to qualified recipients. Not only is the monthly payment in Texas strikingly below the states' average, but it is also the fourth lowest in the nation.[2]

The comparison figure for corrections spending indicates, as well, that Texas spending fell well below the national average. Although most Texans would probably say they did not want the state to be generous with convicted felons, the figures in Table 13-4 might help them understand why in 1981 the federal courts found that Texas prisons were outdated and overcrowded and often allowed abusive or inhumane treatment of prisoners because of those conditions and the limited staff. The outcome of the trial that led to those findings was a federal mandate that the state significantly upgrade its prison facilities. In other words, the state was required by the federal government to spend more to improve the quality of its prison system.

Federal Aid in Texas

Until now we have considered only the money raised in Texas by indigenous taxes—that is, taxes of the state and local governments alone. Yet Texas governments, like those of all states, derive a notable portion of their total revenues from

274   *Chapter 13*

federal aid. In Chapter 10 we pointed out how important that aid has been to urban development in the state. Most federal aid is restricted in the sense that it must be spent on certain programs and under specific federal guidelines. What is most important about such aid for the present chapter, however, is that it raises public services above the levels the states themselves can afford. Thus, by using supplementary federal funds, a low-spending state like Texas could theoretically provide public services far better than its indigenous tax levels might allow.[3] Moreover, Texans would presumably desire that their state and local governments get their fair share of federal aid, because individual Texans pay for such aid through their federal tax payments. Texans might then wish to know how their state fares in getting its share of such aid.

Table 13-5 provides informative data on that question. It shows that, first, Texas governments derive a low percentage of their total revenues from federal aid. The amounts received per capita provide an even better way of looking at the level of federal aid. Texas ranked forty-fifth among the states in per capita federal aid received.

Federal aid is not intended to be distributed among the states on a strict per capita basis; different federal programs have different eligibility criteria and distribution formulas. The variety and complexity of those formulas make it difficult to predict what each state should receive or what might be its fair share of such aid. Yet many federal support programs are intended to alleviate the problems of urban areas—and in Chapter 2 we pointed out how highly urbanized Texas has become in recent times. A number of other federal programs are intended to improve the social and economic circumstances of the poor—and we have noted that there are many poor Texans. Some programs also use the total population as one factor in determining the aid a state or local government agency will receive— and we have seen that Texas is one of the largest states by population today. With these attributes apparently in Texas's favor, one might be especially puzzled by the low level of federal assistance that Texas enjoys.

Research on the distribution of federal aid among the states cannot offer a single explanation of this puzzle, precisely because the allocation formulas for the myriad of federal programs differ so much among themselves. Yet the research

Table 13-5 | **Federal aid for state and local governments, 1988–1989**

	Texas	Average Among All States
Federal aid as percentage of state and local government revenues	14%	16%
Federal aid to state and local governments per state resident	$376	$507

Source: U.S. Bureau of the Census (1991a).

Two recent examples illustrate some of the ways low professionalism and lack

clearly indicates three explanations, all of which are important to some degree. First, some state and local government officials are simply not as sophisticated as others in securing federal aid (Stein, 1981). The grantsmanship process is highly complex and requires an investment of time, resources, and intellect that many public officials do not have or are not willing to commit. Earlier we discussed the relatively low professionalism of many public officials in Texas. Thus one must suspect that lack of expertise is an important reason for the meager aid received by this state.

Second, research has also indicated that some state and local officials do not want to participate in all the available aid programs. Some do not want to accept the federal strings attached to their use of such aid. Some do not judge the aid provided by some federal programs to be worth either the effort of getting it or the costs of submitting to at least some federal controls in the process. One might suspect that the traditionalistic and individualistic political cultures still influence the way in which such officials judge the relative costs and benefits of such aid. Because those two political cultures are of considerable influence in Texas today (see Chapter 3), this factor should also be an important one in explaining the state's low federal assistance level.

Two recent examples illustrate some of the ways low professionalism and lack of interest in federal funds have hurt Texas. In 1986, because Houston was not spending the money fast enough, the city lost almost $3 million in federal community development aid it had previously been granted. The city even received a warning from the U.S. Department of Housing and Urban Development in 1987 that it was, once again, behind in its spending and could lose more of those funds. Given that most citizens associate bureaucratic inefficiency with spending money too rapidly and foolishly, this appears a remarkable and distinctive case of low professionalism.

An instance of lack of interest in federal aid comes from the city of Bryan. The city council there chose not even to apply for federal housing renovation aid when it initially became available in the 1960s. As late as 1987 Bryan was still turning down federal housing aid it could have had simply by asking (Skove, 1987). Yet a housing survey by the city administration that same year indicated that the bulk of the houses in one-third of the city's area were substandard or dilapidated and, hence, appropriate targets for federal housing aid.

Finally, some federal aid programs, especially the revenue-sharing program, employ a distribution formula that takes account of the indigenous tax and spending levels already used by the state and local governments. In other words, the formula assumes that states that have already imposed high tax burdens on their citizens need more federal assistance. Such states, it would be argued further, are already using their own tax resources to a relatively great degree. Obviously, given that Texas was shown to be a low-tax state earlier in this chapter, Texas is disadvantaged under such aid distribution formulas.

276 *Chapter 13*

Taken together, these three explanations suggest why the state of Texas does not fare well in competing for federal aid. The relatively parochial and insufficiently professional character of much of Texas government, the political culture that values independence over outside aid, and the low indigenous tax and spending levels explain why Texans receive relatively little return of their federal tax dollars.

Finally, it is worth noting some recent trends in federal aid to the states and their implications for Texas. Beginning in 1978 such aid began to level off, and sharp reductions were enacted under the Reagan and Bush administrations in efforts to reduce the federal deficit. Of particular note for Texas, however, is that considerable portions of those aid cuts were for social service programs and programs meant to address the special problems of big cities: welfare programs and health and education programs, for example (Fossett, 1984:156). Earlier in this chapter we suggested that many of these policy areas have traditionally been ones where state and local spending and services in Texas were especially low. Thus recent reductions in federal aid have come in areas where service levels were already low in the state and to which, one must assume, state political leaders have not assigned high priorities. If the priorities accorded such policy areas by local political leaders do not rise in the near future, then—because of the reductions in federal aid—Texans can anticipate even lower levels of such services in comparison with those provided in other states.

Distribution of Benefits and Burdens

Up to this point, we have examined public spending and taxing separately. Our survey has dealt only generally with the distribution of benefits and burdens arising from the Texas system. Yet several pieces of information have already suggested some conclusions about that issue. The relatively high reliance on regressive taxation, the virtual absence of progressive tax instruments, and the low levels of public assistance to the poor in Texas all point to a common pattern of benefits and burdens.

It is possible, however, to assess the distribution of public sector benefits and burdens more precisely. One part of such an assessment should be based on the incidence of tax burdens across income levels—addressing the degree of progressivity or regressivity in the entire state tax system. A number of research studies have produced comparative rankings of the fifty states in terms of the progressivity or regressivity of their state and local tax systems. The consistent finding of such studies is that Texas has one of the most regressive tax systems in the United States.

To illustrate that characteristic of the state's tax system, 1984 state and local tax burdens for residents of a number of American cities, including Houston, are

Taxation and Spending 277

Table 13-6 | **Estimated state and local taxes paid by a family of four in selected large cities, 1984**

| City | Total Taxes (and Taxes as Percentage of Total Income) for Family Income of | | |
	$15,000	$35,000	$75,000
Atlanta	$995 (6.6%)	$2,715 (7.8%)	$6,238 (8.3%)
Boston	$1,177 (7.8%)	$3,045 (8.7%)	$7,161 (9.5%)
Chicago	$1,268 (8.4%)	$2,971 (8.5%)	$6,160 (8.2%)
Denver	$896 (6.0%)	$2,433 (7.0%)	$5,518 (7.4%)
Houston	$670 (4.5%)	$1,384 (4.0%)	$2,596 (3.5%)
Los Angeles	$908 (6.1%)	$2,454 (7.0%)	$7,650 (10.2%)
Memphis	$1,036 (6.9%)	$1,953 (5.6%)	$3,494 (4.7%)
New York	$1,603 (10.7%)	$4,791 (13.7%)	$12,640 (16.9%)
St. Louis	$1,371 (9.1%)	$3,257 (9.3%)	$6,874 (9.2%)
Average for all states and the District of Columbia	$1,182 (7.9%)	$2,940 (8.4%)	$6,730 (9.0%)

Source: Department of Finance and Revenue (1985).

given in Table 13-6. Because the general pattern of taxation is so similar within each state, it is reasonable to use the Houston figures as representative of tax burdens in other major Texas cities.

It is clear, first, that the state and local tax burdens borne by Houstonians are quite regressive. High-income Houstonians, in other words, may pay a larger amount of taxes than that paid by their lower-income fellow residents, but they pay a smaller proportion of their total income in taxes. Second, although Houston and Texas are not alone in having a regressive system, many other major American states have tax systems that are uniformly progressive or are at least progressive through most of the income scale. In the latter states some version of an ability-to-pay tax system exists. Thus it is not simply one or another single tax in Texas that is regressive; the overall Texas tax system has that character. Such regressivity, though it does characterize certain other states' tax systems as well, is certainly not typical of them all.

The figures in Table 13-6 also underestimate the degree of regressivity in Texas's tax system today. The state's major tax increases in 1984, 1985, 1987, and 1991 were mostly in regressive taxes and user fees (the general sales tax; selective sales taxes on gasoline, tobacco, and alcoholic beverages; and auto inspection and licensing fees). Thus current estimates would indicate an even higher relative tax burden for low-income Texans and, hence, an even more regressive system.

We should also note some of the other tax-load comparisons in Table 13-6. Both low-income and high-income Houstonians pay percentage tax rates that are quite low in comparison with the relevant national averages. However, the tax load of wealthy Houstonians is especially low in comparison with the national average for high-income taxpayers. As we indicated earlier in this chapter, Texas is, indeed a low-tax state. But it is far more a low-tax state for the wealthy than it is for the poor.

A second way in which we might evaluate relative tax burdens is by comparing them with the benefits citizens get in return for the taxes they pay. Several patterns—and justifications for those patterns—are possible here. For example, some states with progressive tax systems might also provide more public services to their high-income citizens than to their low-income citizens. In such instances we might conclude that the overall system is **proportional**: those who bear relatively higher tax burdens get relatively more services and vice versa. Alternatively, some progressive-tax states might actually provide more services and programs for their relatively poor citizens than their better-off ones. In this case the net results would be even more progressive than the tax burden alone would suggest. The poor would be paying relatively lower taxes and getting relatively more public services.

Turning explicitly to Texas, one could also imagine several theoretical possibilities for the total benefit/burden ratio in the state. If Texas provided relatively high services for its low-income citizens, then the high tax load of such people might be justified on the basis of benefits received. Alternatively, public services proportional to income would simply leave unaffected the regressivity produced by the tax system, and services that favored high-income people would make the overall system even more regressive.

A good deal of the information already provided in this chapter hints at the distribution of benefits and burdens in Texas. The tax system itself is highly regressive. Several of the public expenditure comparisons in earlier tables indicated that Texas provides especially limited public welfare services in comparison with the other states. The combination of regressive taxes and very limited assistance to low-income citizens indicates that the overall Texas system is even more regressive than the tax burden information alone suggests. In other words, low-income Texans pay more taxes as a percentage of their income than do their higher-income neighbors, yet they get no more—in fact, they probably get less—back from the state in services than better-off individuals do.

The conclusions we have drawn about relative benefits and burdens from the preceding information are supported by a comprehensive study of the extent to which state government programs redistribute income and services to their poorer citizens. In examining the extent to which state and local government expenditures and services either benefited or burdened the lowest-income groups in each state, Booms and Halldorson (1973) found that Texas had the second most regressive system in the continental forty-eight states.

| Conclusion |

The first major conclusion of this chapter was that Texas is a low-tax state. Surely the majority of Texans, if not all of them, would be delighted by that fact. Rare indeed are citizens who would volunteer to pay more taxes than they already do or who would not gloat over paying lower taxes than the citizens of most other states pay.

The second major finding was that Texas is, as well, a low-service state. One must suspect that many Texans would also applaud that fact. The strong strain of individualism in the state's political culture—described at length in Chapter 3—helps explain why many Texans would be happy to forgo many state services or programs, or better services than they now get, for the sake of independence. Yet one might suspect that not all Texans would take that position. Some of them might criticize the quality of certain public services provided by the state or their local city government. One must suspect that some of that criticism would come from citizens who desire better services but at no more cost than they now pay. The sophisticated citizen, however, knows that there is some truth in the adage, You get what you pay for. Thus some citizens might well criticize the current benefits they receive from government and be willing to pay higher taxes to secure better services.

The state's low-service approach also has important social consequences. Texans with sufficient personal income can buy at their private expense additional goods and services—educational, health, police, recreational, library, and so on—to supplement what the state provides. Thus some people send their children to private schools because they believe the education provided there is better than that of the public schools. Many wealthy and even middle-class neighborhoods in Texas cities hire supplementary constables or security services to augment the services provided by the municipal police. We could offer a long list of additional examples of this sort, but even without a longer list, the implications are obvious.

Those who must rely on public services—because they cannot afford the cost of private supplements—must depend upon relatively low service and benefit levels. It is not simply the poor who are typically relegated to this position. Most middle-income Texans send their children to public schools and colleges. Most middle-income Texans do not have private security services in their neighborhoods, nor do they belong to private country clubs or other private recreational facilities. Across the range of public services provided by state and local governments, in other words, the majority of Texans must rely on services of below-average quality in comparison with those provided nationally.

The third major finding of this chapter was that—because of the state's governmental system and tax system—Texas fares poorly in attracting federal assistance. This circumstance, too, may be an instance of getting what one pays for. It is probably a circumstance about which the majority of Texans would not be happy to learn. Most Texans presumably would agree that, because they pay what they believe to be their share of federal taxes, their state should reap its fair share of federal benefits. Yet such does not appear to be the case in Texas. And the reasons for the poor success in attracting federal funds are linked to the independent, low-service, "cheaper is better" character of Texas government.

Finally, this chapter has explained how the overall public taxation and expenditure policies of the state of Texas are quite regressive with respect to the benefits enjoyed and burdens borne by citizens of different income classes. In fact, these circumstances constitute a part of the low-tax myth of Texas government (Hill, 1986). The relatively modest public efforts to aid the poor of the state make the overall effects of the tax and spending systems even more regressive. This last circumstance, one must suspect, is not one even a majority of Texans would applaud. This characteristic of Texas public policies means that income is transferred from the relatively poorer citizens of the state to the wealthy. Thus the state does not have simply a free-choice system in which citizens may supplement state services with private expenditures if they want and can afford to do so. Instead it is a system that penalizes the poor to benefit the wealthy—and does so to a degree greater than almost any other state. Once again, one must suspect that the majority of Texans, if they were aware of this circumstance, would not approve of it. Even those who did not favor a progressive system that benefited the poor more than the wealthy would presumably opt for a proportionate system in which benefits and burdens were borne in some sense on an equal basis.

Notes

1. One other perspective illustrates the low level of state and local taxes in Texas. The U.S. Advisory Commission on Intergovernmental Relations (ACIR) estimates the tax effort implied by each state's existing tax system. **Tax effort** is defined by the ACIR as the ratio of actual tax collections in a given year to the amount of taxes that could have been raised if the state had based its collections on the average tax rate among the states (applied to the various taxable aggregates such as income, retail sales, property values, and so on in the state). According to those calculations, Texas had the lowest tax effort of all fifty states throughout the late 1960s and the 1970s (U.S. Advisory Commission on Intergovernmental Relations, 1983:7).
2. Public welfare receives particularly little state and local government support in Texas. Take, for example, the Supplemental Security Income program, a federal program that provides monthly cash allotments to poor adults who are blind, disabled, or over the age of 65. The federal government provides the bulk of the funds for the program, including a base monthly allotment for qualified recipients. The state governments implement the program and dispense the monthly benefits. The states are also allowed to supplement the monthly allotments provided by the federal government if they believe the support levels are too low. Texas is the only state that does not supplement those benefit levels.

   Moreover, many states have developed "general assistance" welfare programs of their own that help poor people who are not eligible for assistance under the various federal programs. However, until the Texas Legislature enacted such a program in its 1985 special session, Texas was one of only nine states that had no substantial program of this kind.

   These examples are not meant to imply that Texas should have such programs or that it should provide more-generous public welfare. Such matters ought to be settled in a democratic system by the will of the majority. What is important about these examples is the information they provide about the true priorities of Texas government.
3. The state and local expenditure figures cited earlier in this chapter, it should be noted, were based on revenues from all sources. Thus federal support for service levels in different policy areas is already reflected in those figures.

References

Anderson, Lynn F., and McMillan, T. E., Jr. 1953. *Financing State Government in Texas.* Austin: Institute of Public Affairs, University of Texas.

Booms, Bernard H., and Halldorson, James R. 1973. "The Politics of Redistribution: A Reformulation." *American Political Science Review* 67 (September): 924–933.

Department of Finance and Revenue, Government of the District of Columbia. 1985. *Tax Rates and Tax Burdens in the District of Columbia: A Nationwide Comparison.* Washington, D.C.

Fossett, James W. 1984. "The Politics of Dependence: Federal Aid to Big Cities." In Lawrence D. Brown, James W. Fossett, and Kenneth T. Palmer (eds.), *The Changing Politics of Federal Grants.* Washington, D.C.: Brookings Institution.

Hill, Kim Quaile. 1986. "The Low-Tax Myth." *Texas Observer* (June 27): 6–7.

Musgrave, Richard A., and Musgrave, Peggy B. 1980. *Public Finance in Theory and Practice.* 3rd ed. New York: McGraw-Hill.

Penniman, Clara. 1965. "The Politics of Taxation." In Herbert Jacob and Kenneth N. Vines (eds.), *Politics in the American States: A Comparative Analysis.* Boston: Little, Brown.

Skove, Cindy. 1987. "Housing Rehab Programs Finally Take Hold in Bryan." *Bryan–College Station Eagle*, September 29, p. 1B.

Stein, Robert M. 1981. "The Allocation of Federal Aid Monies: The Synthesis of Demand-Side and Supply-Side Explanations." *American Political Science Review* 75 (June): 334–343.

U.S. Advisory Commission on Intergovernmental Relations. 1983. *Fiscal Capacity as a Method of Allocating Federal Grant Funds.* Washington, D.C.

U.S. Bureau of the Census. 1990. *Government Finances in 1987–1988.* Washington, D.C.

―――. 1991a. *Government Finances: 1988–1989.* Washington, D.C.

―――. 1991b. *Public Education Finances: 1988–1989.* Washington, D.C.

―――. 1991c. *Statistical Abstract of the United States, 1991.* Washington, D.C.

U.S. Department of Justice. 1991. *Correctional Populations in the United States, 1988.* Washington, D.C.

U.S. Social Security Administration. 1990. *Social Security Bulletin: Annual Statistical Supplement, 1990.* Washington, D.C.

Chapter 14

The Future of Government and Public Policy in Texas

Like other textbooks on Texas government, this book has covered a host of topics in detail. There is always the risk that such a book will leave the reader a bit unsatisfied at the end. Survey textbooks like this one typically just stop at the end of a series of discrete chapters, without offering a conclusion or summary of the inevitably broad terrain they have covered.

We would be unsatisfied, as well, with so routine an ending. We have laid out and explored several key themes in this book, and we will now take the opportunity to return to their broad implications, free of the details that were necessary for their explanation in the preceding chapters. Other observations occur to us now, too, that did not have a good place in earlier chapters. And we are compelled to engage in the inevitably risky business of forecasting. What might the future hold for Texas governments? Can the ideas presented earlier in the book help us answer that question? In the present chapter we will summarize our earlier points and make predictions for the future, based on what has come before.

A Time of Change and Challenge

The state of Texas is experiencing a period of remarkable change that presents, as well, equally remarkable challenges for its residents and governments. Recall, as one element of that change, the dramatic transformation the state's economy is experiencing, as described in Chapter 1. The old industrial economy, rooted in oil and gas and in manufacturing, is giving way to what has been loosely called the postindustrial economy, the specifics of which are still in doubt. Early in this book we also described notable population changes—rapid growth in general, the particular growth of the Hispanic population, urbanization, and suburbanization. And we discussed how the political cultures of the entire state and of some of its ethnic subgroups are evolving. Substantial challenges for government grow out of

286 *Chapter 14*

the economic and population changes, and new expectations for government arise out of the political culture changes.

What we have sketched in the above paragraph is a broad portrait of the implications of this period of change. We could elaborate that portrait with numerous examples. Under the topic of economic change, we could discuss the decline of the crude oil and natural gas industries and the specific problems that the decline poses for the state. Alternatively, we could discuss the wooing of high-tech industries by the state and the policy problems inherent in that effort.

Our comments about population and cultural changes could also be extended. As one example, urbanization creates a lengthy list of policy problems unique to large metropolitan areas. Similarly, the growth of the Hispanic population has raised the political power of an ethnic subgroup that has long been underserved by state and local governments. And the adoption of individualistic and moralistic political cultures by the state's ethnic minorities has particular implications for their expectations of government. We could, then, expand our general remarks about this period of change to illustrate specific implications for government in great detail, but such elaboration should not be necessary. Our goal is not to provide a laundry list of problems government faces but to describe the general character of the times.

These remarks suggest, as well, that the future of government and public policy in the state could be difficult to predict. Dramatic socioeconomic changes like those Texas has experienced create great disagreement and social discord. Some individuals and groups are the happy beneficiaries of such changes; others are the unfortunate victims. Thus there is inevitably wide disagreement about the implications of such changes for both individuals and governments. Appropriate government policy responses to such changes are equally controversial for that reason, and because they are controversial, they are less predictable. But living in such times makes a concern with the future of government all the more important. Texans and their governments will face out-of-the-ordinary problems for the next few decades. Thus a concern with those problems and their implications for government is important to all Texans.

History, Tradition, and Traditional Attitudes Toward Government

As is evident from other parts of this book, we believe that an understanding of the future—or of the present, for that matter—must begin with an understanding of the past. In Texas history we can discover values, traditions, and attitudes— as well as present-day government policies shaped by those forces—that will also influence future policy choices.

The Future of Government and Public Policy in Texas 287

For the overwhelming part of its history, Texas has been dominated by the land and its resources—by farming and ranching and oil. Societies that are tied to the land are inevitably conservative. Their natural rhythms are attuned to the harvest, the seasons and the weather, and great calamities such as droughts and epidemics. The emphasis in agrarian societies is upon the individual and the family rather than the group and the mass. The sacred values are self-reliance, hard work, and inventiveness. Government is not to be trusted. Public service levels are minimal. Government's role is limited to absolute essentials: fighting invaders or criminals, building and repairing roads, educating children.

In societies that are tied to the land, individual freedom is of paramount importance. But that freedom is primarily the freedom to be left alone. Government has no obligation to intervene when some people have more freedom than others or when one group denies opportunities to another. The winners are the strong, the lucky, the stubborn, the ambitious. The unfortunate, the meek, the disadvantaged, and the less determined are shunted aside.

One great contradiction in attitude and policy that results in landed societies such as Texas emerges from the conflict between freedom and conformity, for the vaunted freedom of the individual can exist only within certain well-defined limits. Agrarian societies exert great pressures to ensure conformity within the larger community of individuals. The group is highly intolerant of most forms of unorthodox behavior. Freedom has the greatest meaning for the individual acting alone. The group carefully defines behavior and punishes deviants who challenge established norms.

But early Texas was more than just a landed society. To the natural conservatism and insulation of an agricultural state was added the powerful element of the frontier. Agricultural communities are stable, established, and settled. Their patterns and rhythms are set, predictable, and resistant to change. Texas had the farm, but for most of the nineteenth century it also had the newness and harshness of unsettled territory. To the myth of the self-reliant small farmer was added the myth of the rugged and isolated individualist—the cowboy, the Indian fighter, the Texas Ranger.

And the frontier was dangerous. Violence was an integral part of Texas history from the beginning. There was the war with the Mexicans for independence. Before that, and long after it, and for most of the rest of the nineteenth century, there were the Indians. Comanches—the name struck terror in the heart of the settler. The Comanche moon was a full moon on the frontier, when Comanche raiding parties hunted horses, hostages, and Texan scalps.

The Comanches followed the great buffalo herds down from Kansas and Oklahoma into Texas, and they fought the Texans essentially to a standstill. The Texas frontier did not close until the 1890s, a fact that can be largely attributed to the ferocity of the Comanches. Widely recognized as the finest light cavalry the continent has ever seen, the Comanches resisted settlement of the state west of Austin and San Antonio for decades.

There was other violence too. The Civil War imposed a pervasive defeat on Texas, and Reconstruction made the bitterness last. The violence of whites against blacks, cattlemen against farmers, cowboys against rustlers, and Rangers against outlaws would come later.

Although public policy in Texas is not directly attributable to the state's frontier and agrarian heritage, that heritage has exerted an influence. It can be seen in several ways. For example, the frontier, the farm, and the ranch emphasized the individual rather than the group. Although a sense of community certainly existed, it was a narrow conception of community that prevailed. The individual relied upon family and neighbors for help in time of need. The notion that the community was relevant to the individual and his or her needs was an alien one. As a result, there is still a sense in Texas today that the crucial social and political unit is the family and the immediate neighborhood. Little group action is evoked to solve common political and social problems. Therefore, political action tends to be fragmented and short-lived.

Another effect of the frontier and agrarian heritage can be seen in public attitudes toward government. Texans have been traditionally suspicious of government. The emphasis on individualism meant that they placed little value on collective, community action as is provided by government. Instead, the virtues of hard work, self-reliance, and rugged individualism were accorded special status. Further, Texans in general had little sympathy for the poor and the disadvantaged. Texans who were successful in life were typically thought to have earned their status through hard work and merit. The poor and the needy, in contrast, were simply the losers in the competitive struggle. And they were often thought to deserve their fate for lack of effort and initiative. Thus few Texans would support governmental assistance to such people, and social welfare programs were virtually nonexistent.

Because of such attitudes, rural states also provide low levels of public service generally. Few of the services required for life in large urban areas are necessary. Many of the social problems of rural areas—crime, pollution, traffic—are also more modest and require less vigorous government action. Expectations for governmental services are lower, as well. People demand less of government, whether it is in the quality or in the breadth of public services and programs.

These attitudes about the role and functions of government were nurtured throughout most of the history of Texas. As a result, the tremendous socioeconomic changes the state is now experiencing are destined to create serious political conflicts. The problems wrought by those changes require governmental action that clashes with traditional beliefs and expectations. Many Texans will want to cling to those traditional views. Existing policies created with respect for those views will also be an impediment to the resolution of contemporary problems, and advocates of those existing policies will oppose their elimination.

| Contemporary Attitudes Toward Government |

Many Texans still hold some traditional attitudes toward government. Indeed, some Texans are thoroughgoing traditionalists, although we suspect that the number of such people is declining. Newer attitudes, which are at times not even fully recognized by the people who hold them, are becoming commonplace. We have explained a number of the reasons for these new attitudes in earlier chapters.

Attitudes Toward Current Policy Problems

The specific list of problems the state faces today induces many Texans to demand that government take on new responsibilities to solve one or another of those problems. The economic challenges the state is facing, for example, have led many Texans to demand that government take responsibility for the economic future. Ethnic minorities demand their share of the benefits of state policies, which they argue has long been denied them. The residents of urban areas demand good schools, well-paved streets, less crime, and on and on.

New problems are forced onto the agenda, too, from a variety of sources. Texans want government to stem the flow of illegal drugs from around the world, and the flow of illegal aliens from south of our border. Some would have Texas governments outlaw abortions; others would have the right to abortions guaranteed by government. The federal courts from time to time have been a forum where people who have been denied their rights by state government have gotten justice—and a new set of responsibilities for the state.

In sum, Texans are no longer wedded to their parents' bare-bones philosophy of government. Instead, Texans today are often ready to turn to government for solutions to the major problems of their lives. In good part, that dependence on government is inevitable. Urban dwellers cannot live the independent, self-sufficient life of their rural forebears. Modern life—in large metropolitan areas that are heavily dependent on particular economic and social relations—requires collective, instead of individual, action for its smooth functioning. Government is the vehicle that citizens typically choose to provide appropriate collective responses to achieve that end.

The Attitudes of Political Conservatives

Even political conservatives demand aggressive government action on a number of issues. In fact, conservatives in both major political parties have a number of common interests in active state and local government policy. One could even argue that in states that are experiencing rapid socioeconomic change, as Texas is, political conservatives are as supportive of high service levels as liberals are. In fact, conservatives frequently take the lead in developing new public programs, projects, and services. The important point on which conservatives and liberals

290 *Chapter 14*

disagree is not the size of government. Instead, the major issue of contention is which programs government will spend money on. When public policy in Texas is viewed in those terms, it becomes more understandable.

Conservatives do not oppose all government programs and services in principle. They are not even necessarily opposed to higher taxes. What they are opposed to are government services that they do not perceive as beneficial to economic growth. To many business people, wasteful and inexcusable government programs include social welfare services of all types. Efforts to expand and fund such programs inspire attacks that center around "big government," "handouts," and higher taxes. The same people, however, will support other government expenditures as absolutely essential to the economic health of the state.

Conservatives are among the most forceful advocates of quality education in the state, for example. Yet their reasons for supporting education differ from the arguments advanced by liberals. A liberal might say that a superior education is crucial to the full development of human potential. As such, it should not be evaluated in dollars and cents. Instead, it should be supported because it contributes to the eradication of discrimination and injustice, because it breaks down barriers to equality of opportunity, and because it enhances the dignity and worth of the individual citizen. In short, a civilized society requires that the education of the citizen be accorded first priority.

Conservatives, on the other hand, would justify support of education in economic terms. High-quality education is seen as crucial to the economic future of the state. Many business people support higher levels of funding for both the public schools and higher education because they fear that Texas will begin to lose the battle for industry if the quality of its education declines. It is frequently noted that Texas is ill-equipped to compete in the long run for high-tech industry because its university system cannot compare to the universities found in California and Massachusetts. Business and industry require highly skilled technicians and professionals as well as an institutionalized research capacity. Consequently, a superior university system is needed to secure the state's position in the highly competitive struggle for high-tech firms. Conservatives support a variety of other government-funded services and projects. An adequate transportation system, for example, is seen as essential to continued economic growth and development. Thus there is widespread support among conservatives for airports and freeways. An adequate supply of water is similarly viewed as vital to a robust economy. Thus government programs to provide sufficient water for the state's needs also enjoy strong support.

Conservatives do not support high levels of funding for all government services, however. Unless a direct relationship is apparent between the service and a benefit to business and industry, they are likely to oppose the service. A careful distinction is drawn between government programs that will stimulate economic growth and create jobs and those that are perceived as handouts to the lazy and undeserving. That distinction can be seen with respect to the current major policy issues in the state. There is widespread support for greater governmental expenditures for education, water, and highways. Program expenditures to improve the prison system, however, have aroused widespread opposition. In fact, prison reform was forced upon the state by the federal courts. The differences in the levels of support for these various programs can be attributed to the idea that highways, education, and water are essential to continued economic growth but prison improvements are not.

One should not infer, however, that conservatives and liberals have reached a consensus with respect to these policy areas. They continue to disagree over the content, funding, and control of programs designed to address various problems. The important point is that the powerful conservative ideology of Texas politics exalts the virtues of limited government, self-reliance, and rugged individualism. Already that ideology has begun to clash with the demands for expanded public services imposed by industrialization and urbanization. Government not only begins to spend more but also assumes a much more active role in the regulation of economic and social activities. Land-use and zoning ordinances have to be developed, tax assessments have to be revised, and civil and criminal codes require expansion. Further, various occupational groups demand regulation of their professions, and insurance, housing, public utilities, and other industries have to be regulated.

Contradictory Attitudes

We have argued that Texans of all ideological types have some desires for expanding the responsibilities for government. Equally notable, however, is that many individual Texans also hold some contradictory attitudes about the responsibilities of government. Two particular contradictions are especially common and important with regard to the concerns of this chapter.

Some Texans, first, assert that they want limited government when they think of such matters in the abstract. But when faced with some particular situations and problems, they expect active, aggressive governmental policies. They have not reconciled the conflict between their own traditional and contemporary attitudes toward government. For that reason they are likely to make contradictory demands on government—at times in favor of expanded programs and policies and at times opposed to them.

Of equal concern are the many Texans who want strong government response to one or more policy problems but do not want to bear the tax burden of such efforts. They want good roads, many police officers to respond to crime, well-equipped schools, well-educated teachers, and so on, but they also want a minuscule tax burden. They want modern government for the price of nineteenth-century government. Because they have lived for generations with a low tax burden (as was described in Chapter 13), some Texans may assume such a system can last forever. Such Texans have not faced the reality that the government they desire will inevitably be expensive—at least compared with what they have paid in taxes in the past.

292   *Chapter 14*

The Future of Public Policy

The preceding discussions of attitudes toward government, supplemented with material from several earlier chapters, suggest some of the most likely attributes of future public policies in Texas. Despite the inevitable risks of forecasting the future, we have considerable confidence in our predictions.

A Growing Governmental Agenda

Given that many Texans want government's responsibilities to grow—or unwittingly force those responsibilities to grow by making new demands on government—we can make one easy prediction for the future of Texas government. The positive state, in which government takes on many social and economic responsibilities, is here to stay in Texas. Indeed, it will likely even expand in the future.

The selective attitudes about growth held by political conservatives in the state mean that governmental growth will not be uniform across all policy areas, however. Government expenditures will, indeed, increase. Public programs will expand, and government's regulatory role will grow. But the great driving force shaping public policy in Texas during the next few decades will be economics. All major policy proposals will be evaluated in terms of their contribution to furthering economic development and creating jobs. The current fascination with high tech is likely to continue. If high-tech and service industries do come to dominate the American and Texas economies, then the role of government in the state will probably expand even faster than anticipated. As we discussed in earlier chapters, high-tech firms employ few blue-collar workers. Instead they are top-heavy with highly trained and well-educated professionals. The same situation is generally true for the various support service occupations. Service industries employ large numbers of lawyers, accountants, bankers, medical doctors, economists, and researchers. The significance of all of these engineers, computer analysts, scientists, lawyers, and accountants for public policy in Texas is that they will demand a wide array of services. A superior public school and university system will be a major priority. Other major service demands will be for parks and recreation and police protection.

Thus several developments in the economy have exerted, and will continue to exert, major influence upon public policy in Texas. The recent and rapid industrialization and urbanization of the state have placed heavy demands upon government for education, water, transportation, and police and fire services. The conservative business community has strongly supported these expanded services as essential to the continued economic growth and development of the state. Not all government programs have received that kind of support, however. Public services that are perceived as handouts to the poor and the otherwise undeserving are vigorously resisted. Consequently, welfare services and efforts to improve the prison system are greeted with strong opposition. The state government's role in the regulation of land use, occupations, housing, insurance, and utilities has also expanded.

This trend toward bigger government and greater expenditures for programs favorable to economic growth began in the 1960s and should be expected to continue. In fact, major policy proposals in the future will probably be even more carefully evaluated in terms of their contribution to economic development. The competition among the states for business and industry is much stronger today than it was several years ago. Today, state and local governments offer a variety of tax inducements and economic incentives to attract industry. This intense competition will cause policy proposals to be assessed according to their relevance to economic growth.

The conservative ideology emphasizes limited government, self-reliance, private-sector solutions to problems, and no government handouts. There is a great irony, then, in the concerted efforts of the business community to lure high-tech firms to the state by attempting to improve the education system and transportation network with government monies. What is arising is a three-way partnership among government, the business community, and prospective business firms. That relationship involves a fundamental change in Texas politics. Previously the relationship between state government and the dominant sectors of the economy—oil and gas and agriculture—was more passive. Those industries were not indifferent to government, and they surely had enormous political influence, but they sought to limit government's role. They used their political clout to restrict government regulation of their economic activities and interests. They also worked effectively to keep services, expenditures, and taxes low.

Significantly, however, no partnership existed among oil, agriculture, and government in a positive sense. That is, industry leaders and public officials did not actively seek to fashion a set of new policies that would attract business and jobs to the state. Oil and agriculture were already there, and they worked to maintain the status quo. The partnership, then, was essentially limited and negative. Industry did not need high service levels. Neither did its workers; roughnecks and sharecroppers are little concerned with the urban service amenities that high-tech yuppies expect. What the oil and agriculture industries wanted was for government to leave them alone so they could explore and drill for oil and raise their cattle and crops. They sought to avoid extensive regulation and high taxes. Beyond that, they did not contemplate a positive vision for the state.

The emerging partnership in Texas between government and business today is active and forceful. It seeks to develop a service infrastructure that will lure business and industry to the state and stimulate economic development. As a result, government will continue to grow. This active partnership between business and political leaders in the state represents one of the most significant developments in Texas during the past several decades.

Conflict over Government's Agenda

Because many Texans hold contradictory attitudes about the role of government, each new increment to government's power, inevitable though it might be, will be controversial and hotly debated. Even new governmental efforts directed at economic growth will be opposed by some Texans. Demands for improved urban services will be criticized by those who cling to the desire for limited, cheap government. And many of the demands of black and Hispanic Texans, which will often reflect a desire for social welfare services, will be especially controversial. For all these reasons, then, although the expansion of the positive state may be inevitable, it will not follow an easy path.

Contemporary Governmental Realities

Future governmental policies in Texas will doubtless be shaped in good measure by some combination of elite and general public attitudes like those discussed above. (We should remind the reader that, based on the material in a number of earlier chapters, we would expect elite attitudes to be more influential than attitudes of the general public.) Yet government policy does not change rapidly in the face of new public expectations—regardless of which portion of the public expresses those attitudes. Governments always have a set of well-established policy commitments that have evolved slowly over time and are difficult to change for many reasons.

Change alone is frequently controversial, and we have offered reasons why changes of the kind we are considering here will be especially controversial. Existing policies also typically have many supporters, some of whom reap significant benefits from them and thus have material, personal reasons to resist change. Existing policies are also typically implemented by well-established bureaucratic organizations in the executive branch that are themselves sources of inertia. Bureaucracies often resist change, and they can require considerable time and effort to change, even when they do not resist it. Indeed, a major strength of bureaucratic organization is that it can bring a high degree of concentrated, selected resources to bear on a given problem or to carry out a given policy. Yet that very strength can be a disadvantage at times when citizens wish to alter government policy. It can be quite difficult to dismantle such organized entities and redirect their efforts.

For all the preceding reasons, we should expect that future public policies in Texas will be shaped, in part, by current ones and by the current structure of state and local government, which implements those policies. In addition, what we have learned in prior chapters suggests that contemporary governmental structures and policies in Texas are complex, ill-coordinated, parochial, and resistant to change.

Governmental Structure

For a number of reasons the system of governance in Texas is highly fragmented and ill-designed, at least from a rational perspective of what might be the preferred system for a modern, postindustrial society. The state constitution mandates a creaky, fragmented state government of limited powers that was well suited to the late nineteenth century but hardly to the dawn of the twenty-first one. The governor is a figurehead and a cheerleader for policy change who has few of the powers of a true chief executive or policymaker. The legislature is structurally frozen in the past—constitutionally restricted to the powers such a body might need in the 1870s. The executive branch is highly decentralized and essentially leaderless. At the same time, it is ill-financed and therefore often ineffective, as well as being uncoordinated and therefore inefficient because of the overlapping and sometimes contradictory efforts of different agencies.

Every component of the system of local governance exhibits similar characteristics and problems. City and county governments are limited by constitutional and statutory strictures on their powers. Special districts have flourished because of those limits, thereby exacerbating the problem of coordinating government policy and ensuring efficient delivery of policy and services. The system of independent school districts has preserved the goal of local autonomy over the goals of efficiency and effectiveness—even when autonomy was meaningless because of the modest resources of many school districts.

Most of Texas government is relatively amateurish, as well. The legislature is a part-time activity of the bulk of its members. Most elected officials in local government must sharply limit their official duties because theirs, too, are part-time positions. Although the executive branch of state government has a number of agencies with highly professional staffs, such agencies are more exceptional than typical. Professional requirements are often not very high, and political favoritism, opportunism, and good-old-boy networks are often more important for securing state jobs.

Existing Policy Commitments

Texas state and local governments have long-standing commitments to a number of policies that are ill-designed with respect to future needs and that clash with efforts to respond effectively to the major problems of the day. Two examples illustrate this far-too-common problem.

First, by virtually every account, the present-day tax system is both highly inequitable and insufficient for the state's needs. The system of taxes on individuals in highly regressive and, hence, unfair. The out-of-date system of business taxes is equally unfair—imposing high burdens on some kinds of business and quite modest burdens on others—because it is not compatible with the modern economy. Equally important, the tax system fails to provide adequate revenues to fund state programs. Even in recent years when the economy of the state has been sound and indeed thriving, the tax system has not generated equivalently healthy levels of revenue. Yet

Chapter 14

the present tax system has its staunch defenders—those whose material interests are well served because they now pay low taxes and those who fear any change because it might lead to higher taxes. For this reason, reform of the tax system has proven difficult. Because the state lacks an adequate revenue-generating tax system, it has been unable to move ahead effectively on many of its most pressing policy problems. Progress has been stalled in many areas for lack of resources.

The public education system, as we have noted in earlier chapters, is another state structure in which policy commitments inhibit meaningful responses to future and even present-day problems. The state's school system prizes local control, football, and plain cheapness over providing forward-looking educations to Texas schoolchildren. The school system is especially deficient with respect to the needs of the state's ethnic minorities—and, for that matter, with respect to the needs of the state itself for well-educated minorities in the future. The high school dropout rates of blacks and Hispanics are remarkably higher than those of Anglo students, and the enrollment of blacks and Hispanics in the state's colleges and universities is embarrassingly low. This situation shortchanges not only minority-group individuals but also the state's future economic potential. To be competitive in the high-tech race and related economic development endeavors, the state needs a well-educated work force that includes all its ethnic groups. Texas cannot afford to have a large portion of its work force be ill-educated and hence ill-prepared for the postindustrial economy. Given that Hispanics and blacks will soon constitute the majority of the state's population, fulfilling their educational needs is critical. Because Hispanics are emerging as a political force, the deficiencies of the Texas educational system have now become controversial political problems with which the state and its school districts must contend. However, these problems will not be quickly addressed and easily resolved. Instead, they will be added to a crowded agenda of other controversial—and expensive—problems the state must struggle with. How—and how well—the state will tackle them is less certain.

As the two preceding examples illustrate, Texas has a hodgepodge of policy commitments that can affect its response to the major social and economic challenges of the day. In the best of cases, the state has well-developed policies that are compatible with emerging efforts to expand the economy in a way that is fair for all Texans. In the worst of cases, existing policies favor one or another special interest or outdated political value while posing a barrier to contemporary economic and social goals. In a fragmented governmental system—like Texas's—that has been long dominated by select economic elites, there will doubtless be numerous examples of the latter policies. In addition, the rigidities and other limitations of the existing governmental structures make it even more difficult to root out and eliminate such policies.

In sum, Texas does have big government—the positive state—but that government is hardly a well-coordinated system. Instead, it is chaotic, and because so many special interests have ensured their own benefits in that system, it is especially resistant to change or rationalization.

Index

Abilene, 26
Adjutant general, 170
Advisory Commission on Intergovernmental Relations (ACIR), 281
AFL-CIO, 99
Afro-Americans. *See* Blacks
Agencies, state, 167–173. *See also* Bureaucracy; Executive branch of government; *specific agencies*
   appointed department heads, 170
   boards and commissions, 171–172
   election of agency heads, 146, 168, 170
   Sunset Advisory Commission review of, 181–183
   termination of, 182
Agrarian protest movements, 77
Agriculture, 60, 96, 168
   boards and commissions, 171
Agriculture commissioner, 168
Aliens, illegal, 20–21
Amarillo, 26, 239
Amendment. *See* Constitution (U.S.)
American Civics, 38–39
American Federalism, 41
Anglo-Americans:
   in city government, 230–231
   education levels, 31
   income and poverty levels, 30
   migration of, 16–18
   occupational categories of, 32
   percentage of, 15, 24
   political subculture of, 46–47
   population growth (1850–1990), 16
   school districts and, 258
   Southern, 17–18, 22, 23, 46–47
   suburbanization and, 213–214
   in Texas legislature (1991), 127
Annexation by cities, 218–219
Appellate courts, 190, 201–203
Appointive powers of governors, 143, 146
Apportionment, 86
Arlington, 232, 239
Asians, 15, 24, 231
Assessor and collector of taxes, 247
Attorney general, 168
Austin, 6, 25, 26, 161, 193, 208, 211, 214, 216, 239

Baker v. *Carr*, 86
Ballot, long, 91–92

Bean, Roy, 187
Beaumont, 27
Bench trial, 196
Bexar County, 216, 249, 250
Beyle, Thad L., 143, 146
Bill of Rights, 56
Biotechnology, 5
Blacks:
   Bourbon Coup and, 78
   in city government, 230–231
   education levels, 31
   educational reform and, 296
   income and poverty levels, 30
   migration of, 18–19
   occupational categories of, 32
   percentage of, 15, 24
   political subculture of, 49–50
   population growth (1850–1990), 16
   Republican party and, 77, 78
   school districts and, 258
   suburbanization and, 213–214
   in Texas legislature (1991), 127
   urbanization and, 27
   voting by, 77, 78–80, 87
Blake, Roy, 120–121
Blanco County, 193, 194
Board of education. *See* State Board of Education
Board of Examiners of Social Psychotherapists, 182
Board of Library Examiners, 182
Board of Tuberculosis Nurse Examiners, 182
Boards, 171–173. *See also specific boards*
Booms, Bernard H., 279
Border Patrol, U.S., 20
Bourbon Coup, 78–79, 80, 100
Brazoria, 232
Brazos County, 251
Bribery of legislators, 130
Briscoe, Dolph, 155
Bryan, 275
Bryan-College Station, 6
Budgets:
   city government, 238–240
   gubernatorial powers, 143, 146–147
   Legislative Budget Board, 147, 173, 174
Bureaucracy. *See also* Executive branch of government; Government employees
   accountability vs. professional independence of, 164

Index

298

Bureaucracy (*continued*)
  change resisted by, 294
  in city government, 226
  clientele groups of, 166–167, 180
  contradictions of, 163–164
  cost of, 173–174
  efficiency vs. effectiveness of, 164
  evolution of, 165
  fairness vs. responsiveness by, 163–164
  philosophical perspectives toward, 162–163
  power of, 161–162, 165–167
  privatization and, 173–174
  public expectations about, 163–164
  reform of, 175–181
  role of, 162–165
  Sunset Advisory Commission review of, 181–183
Burial Association Rate Board, 182
Bush administration, 214, 276
Businesses:
  attracting, 5–7
  corporate franchise tax, 266
  government partnership with, 293
  interest groups and, 235

California, high-tech competition from, 6–7
Campaign costs:
  of governors, 153–154
  interest group contributions, 132
  of legislators, 100, 126, 132
Capitol building, 105
Carp, Robert A., 196
Carrasco, Jorge, 161
Cities. *See also* City government; Suburbanization; Urbanization
  annexation powers, 218–219
  automobiles' impact on, 211, 212
  budgets of, 238–240
  central-city problems, 213, 217–218, 219–221
  city-state relations, 219
  developmental policies of, 220, 221
  extraterritorial jurisdiction of, 218
  federal aid and, 214–216
  policy priorities, 219–221
  political economy, 211–222
  redistributive policies of, 220–221
Citizen, role of, 38–40, 41
Citizens Conference on State Legislatures, 112–113, 114–115, 118, 119, 121, 123, 124
City government, 216–219, 225–241
  annexation powers of, 218–219
  budgets, 238–240
  character of elected officials, 230–231
  city-state relations, 219
  commission form of, 228–229
  conservatives and, 233–234, 240–241
  council-manager plan (reformed), 227, 229–230
  effectiveness of participation, 237–238
  exit as participation, 237, 238
  forms of, 227–230
  fragmentation of, 216–218, 221–222
  home rule, 219
  interest groups and, 234–236, 237–238
  mayor-council plan (unreformed), 228, 229–230
  municipal courts, 194, 204, 206, 208
  policy priorities, 219–221
  protest, 235, 236–237, 238
  public services provided by, 225–226
  state government compared to, 225–227
  voter participation, 231–234, 237
City manager, 227, 229–230
Civil War, 17, 58, 76–77, 288

Clements, Bill, 85, 99–100, 153, 154, 155, 156, 269, 270
Clientele groups, 166–167, 180
College Station, 232
Comanches, 287–288
Commissioner of agriculture, 168
Commissioner of the General Land Office, 168
Commissioners' court, 245–246
Commissions, 171–173. *See also specific commissions*
Committee system of Texas legislature, 113, 116–118
Communities Organized for Public Service (COPS), 235–236
Comptroller of Public Accounts, 9, 168. *See also* Texas Performance Review
Connally, John, 138, 153, 155
Connor, Seymour V., 47
Conservatives:
  attitudes of, 289–291
  city government and, 233–234, 240–241
  governmental agenda and, 292–293
Constable, 247
Constitution (Texas), 55–72
  functions of, 55–57
  history of, 58–62
  revision of, 62–68, 71
Constitution (Texas) of 1845, 58, 140
Constitution (Texas) of 1861, 58
Constitution (Texas) of 1866, 58
Constitution (Texas) of 1869, 58–59, 140
Constitution (Texas) of 1876, 55, 58–71
  amendment results, 65–68
  amendments proposed and adopted (1880–1991), 63
  blueprint for government in, 60–61
  character of, 57, 65
  county government provisions in, 244–245
  impact of, 68–70
  intent of 1875 convention, 58–60
  judicial system and, 70, 187, 192
  positive state and, 71
  ratification of, 61–62
  representativeness and, 140
  revision of, 62–68, 71
  U.S. Constitution vs., 57, 64, 68
  voter turnout for amendments, 64–65, 66
Constitution (U.S.):
  Fifteenth Amendment, 55, 85–86
  Fourteenth Amendment, 87
  state constitutions and, 55–56
  Texas Constitution vs., 57, 64, 68
  Twenty-fourth Amendment, 86–87
Constitutional Convention of 1875, 58–60
Constitutional Convention of 1974, 57, 62–64
Constitutions, state, functions of, 55–57
Coordinating Board, Texas College and University System, 171
COPS (Communities Organized for Public Service), 235–236
Corporate franchise tax, 266
Corpus Christi, 26, 239
Corrections. *See also* Judicial system (Texas)
  Court of Criminal Appeals, 193, 199, 202–203
  department reorganization, 180
  government spending on, 272, 273
  Ruiz v. Lynaugh impact on, 188
County attorney, 247–248
County auditor, 248
County clerk, 247
County government, 243–251
  appointed officials, 248
  commissioners' court, 245–246

Index

299

constitutional provisions for, 244–245
courts, 192, 194, 204, 206, 208, 245–246
elected officials of, 246–248
expenditures of, 244–245, 246, 250–251
fragmentation of, 248, 260
home rule, 244
judge, 246–247
legal responsibilities of, 243–244
offices, 245–248
policy priorities of, 249–251
powers of, 244–245
problems with, 248
public services of, 248–251
structure and functions of, 244
urban vs. rural counties, 249
Court of Criminal Appeals, 193, 199, 202–203, 204, 206
Court system. *See* Judges; Judicial system (Texas)
Courts of appeals, 192–193, 194, 202, 204, 206
Courts of limited original jurisdiction, 190, 192
Courts of original jurisdiction, 190, 193–194, 197
Courts of record, 192
Crime, urban, 217–218
Culberson, Charles, 82
Cultural diversity, 22–23
Curry, Landon, 183

Dallas, 6, 21, 25, 26, 27, 85, 204, 205, 211, 213, 214, 216, 239
   city government, 230, 232
Dallas County, 216, 249, 250
Dalton, Robert, 143
Daniel, Price, 155
Davis, E. J., 59, 140
Davis, J. William, 121–122, 137
Delegate, defined, 110
Democratic party. *See also* Political parties
   economic change and, 12
   internal struggles of, 101
   as one-party system, 76–88
Demographics, 24–33, 89–90
Department of Community Affairs, 170
Department of Corrections, 180
Department of Criminal Justice, 180
Department of Mental Health and Retardation, 171
Dewey, Thomas, 84
Director, Department of Community Affairs, 170
Director, Office of State-Federal Relations, 170
District attorney, 247–248
District courts, 192, 194, 197–201, 204, 206, 208
Districts, school. *See* School districts
Districts, special. *See* Special districts

Economy, 1–13
   diversification of, 1–3
   employment breakdown by industry, 3
   future of, 9–10
   high-tech industries' emergence, 5–9
   income and poverty levels, 27–30, 32–33
   interest groups and, 95–96
   oil and gas industries' decline, 3–5
   politics and, 2, 10–13
   public policy and, 292–293
   service industries' importance, 8
   social changes and, 11–12
   transformation of, 9–10
   twenty-year forecast, 9–10
Edgewood v. *Kirby*, 188
Education. *See also* State Board of Education
   board election controversy, 141
   boards and commissions, 171

city government and, 227
in civics, 38–39
conservatives' attitude toward, 290
Constitutional Convention of 1875 and, 61
courts' impact on, 188–190
economy and, 11
ethnic groups and, 31
government spending on, 272–273
high-tech race and, 7
of judges, 203
levels of, 31
politics of, 256–258
recent trends, 32
reform struggles, 11, 296
school districts, 255–260
of Texas legislators, 127
Effectiveness, 164, 180–181
Efficiency, 164, 180–181
Eisenhower, Dwight, 84
El Paso, 26, 27, 208, 228, 239
El Paso County, 249, 250
Elazar, Daniel, 41–42, 43, 46–47, 50, 51
Eldersveld, Samuel J., 76
Elected officials. *See also* Bureaucracy
   city officials, 227–228
   county officials, 246–248
   influence on political culture, 40
   judges, 194–195, 204–205
   legislators, 124–129
Election calendar, 40, 92–93
Elections, 75–102. *See also* Voting
   of agency heads, 146, 168, 170
   campaign costs, 100, 126, 132, 153–154
   city, 227–228
   federal government intervention, 85–87
   gubernatorial, 79, 81, 93
   interest groups and, 99–100
   of judges, 194–195, 204–205
   of legislators, 124–126
   long ballot, 91–92
   obstacles to two-party competition, 90–94
   one-party system, 76–88
   political culture and, 39–40
   primaries, 81, 85–86
   public participation in, 64–65, 66, 79–81, 87–90, 92–93
   special elections, 64
   State Board of Education election controversy, 141
Employment:
   breakdown by industry, 3
   in high-tech industries, 7–9
   occupational categories by ethnic group, 31–32
   recent trends, 32–33
   regulatory boards and commissions, 172–173
   in service industries, 8
   Texas' rank by workforce size, 3
   twenty-year forecast, 9–10
Equal Protection Clause of Fourteenth Amendment, 87
Europeans, migration of, 22, 23
Executive branch of government, 161–184
   bureaucratic power, 161–162, 165–167
   bureaucratic role, 162–165
   fragmentation in, 175
   impact of Constitution on, 69
   oversight by legislature, 107, 109–110
   reform of, 175–181
   size of, 173–174
   Sunset Advisory Commission review of, 181–183
   Texas state agencies, 167–173
Executive leadership, 142, 157, 165
Extraterritorial jurisdiction, 218

300 *Index*

Farenthold, Frances "Sissy", 84
Farmers, 60
Farmers Alliance party, 77
Federal aid:
    cities and, 214–216
    state taxes and, 269
    in Texas, 273–276
Ferguson, "Farmer Jim" ("Pa"), 62, 81
Ferguson, Miriam "Ma", 81, 82
Fifteenth Amendment, 55, 85–86
Finer, Herbert, 162, 165
Formal powers, defined, 143
Fort Worth, 6, 25, 26, 27, 214, 216, 239
Fourteenth Amendment, 87
Frankel, Marvin E., 196
Friedrich, Carl, 162–163

Galveston, 228–229
Game of Texas, The, 267–268
Gantt, Fred, 69, 151
Garland, 239
Gas industry. *See* Oil and gas industries
General elections, 64, 79
German Americans:
    migration of, 22
    political subculture of, 50–51
Glick, Henry Robert, 200–201
Golden Triangle, 27
Government. *See also* City government; County government
    agenda of, 292–294
    attitudes toward, 286–291
    business partnership with, 293
    city and state governments compared, 225–227
    contemporary realities, 194–196
    economic development responsibilities of, 10–11
    fragmentation of, 216–218
    impact of Constitution on, 68–70
    as positive state, 70–71
    professionalism of, 97–98, 106, 122, 133, 164, 195, 275
    role of, 38, 40–41
    spending, 270–279, 292–294
    structure of, 295
Government employees. *See also* Bureaucracy
    agency heads, 146, 168, 170
    boards and commissions, 171–173
    city government, 230–231
    county government, 246–248
    governor of Texas, 137–158
    judges, 203–207
    legislators, 124–129
Governor of Texas, 137–158
    appointive powers of, 146, 206–207
    budget powers of, 146–147
    campaign costs of, 153–154
    as chief of state, 151, 157
    gubernatorial elections, 79, 81, 93
    image of, 137–139
    impact of Constitution on, 69
    intergovernmental relations powers of, 148–149
    legislative powers of, 149
    military powers of, 148
    organization powers of, 147
    as party head, 151–152
    personal backgrounds of governors, 154, 155
    plural executive and, 69
    political personality of, 152
    postgubernatorial careers of, 154, 156
    powers of (formal), 138, 143–149
    powers of (informal), 150–152

    requirements for office, 153–154
    salary of, 153
    staff of, 149–150
    tenure potential of, 146
    term of office, 153
    veto powers of, 147–148
Governors of states:
    appointive powers, 143, 144–145
    budget powers, 143, 144–145
    as chief of state, 151
    functions of, 139–142
    organization powers, 143, 144–145
    as party head, 151–152
    political personality of, 152
    powers of (formal), 143–149
    powers of (informal), 150–152
    tenure potential, 143, 144–145
    veto powers, 143, 144–145
Gramm, Phil, 84–85
Grand juries, 195–196
Grand Prairie, 232
Grange (Patrons of Husbandry), 60, 61, 98
Great Depression, 19–20
Greenback party, 77
Gregg County, 251
Gross state product, 2

Halldorson, James R., 279
Hamm, Keith E., 99
Harris County, 192, 193, 194, 196, 216, 244–245, 249, 250
Hartley, William H., 38
Health:
    administrative system proposed for, 178
    agencies, 176
    boards and commissions, 171
    R.A.J. v. *Jones* impact on, 188
    welfare programs, 272, 273, 281, 294
Health and Human Services Commission, 176–178, 180
Health officer, 248
Henderson, Bancroft C., 205, 208
High-tech industries, 5–9
    competition for, 6–7
    defined, 5
    economic stratification due to, 8–9
    educational system weaknesses and, 7
    emergence of, 5–6
    employment opportunities in, 7–9
    future of, 6–9
    twenty-year forecast, 10
Hill, John, 195
Hispanics. *See* Mexican Americans
History:
    of bureaucratic role, 165
    of Constitution of Texas, 58–62
    of population growth, 15–23
    public philosophy eras, 139–142
    of Texas, 286–288
Hobby, Bill, 120–121, 195
Home rule, 219, 244
Hospitals. *See also* Health
    boards and commissions, 171
    R.A.J. v. *Jones* impact on, 188
House of Representatives (Texas). *See also* Legislature (Texas)
    characteristics of members, 127, 129
    eligibility requirements, 124
    size of, 113
    standing committees (1991), 116
    terms, 124

Index

301

Houston, 6, 21, 25, 27, 85, 196, 204, 205, 208, 211, 213, 216, 218, 239
  city government, 228, 229, 230, 232
  federal funding for, 214–215
  taxes, 276–277
Houston Post, 119, 120–121
Houston Ship Channel, 214–215
Human services, 176, 178
Hurt, Harry, 5

Immigration Reform and Control Act, 20
Immigration Service, 20
Income levels, 27–30, 32–33
Income taxes, 265–266, 268–269
Independent Oil and Gas Producers Association, 99
Individualistic political subculture, 51
  defined, 42–43
  distribution of (U.S.), 44–45
  of southern Anglo-Americans, 46–47
Industrialization, 1, 51–52, 211
Industry, employment breakdown by, 3
Interest groups:
  bribery by, 130
  business interests and, 235
  campaign contributions by, 132
  checks on power of, 95–98
  city government and, 234–236, 237–238
  democratic polity and, 94–95
  elections and, 99–100
  legislature and, 106, 130–133
  power in Texas, 98–99
  presiding officers influenced by, 133
  as research sources, 132–133
  social lobby by, 130–131
Intergovernmental relations, 148–149, 281
Ivins, Molly, 172

Jester, Beauford, 155
"Jim Crow" laws, 49
Johnson, Lyndon, 84
Jordan, Terry G., 46, 50
Judges, 203–207
  bench trials by, 196
  characteristics of, 205–207
  county judge, 246–247
  in Court of Criminal Appeals, 193
  in courts of appeals, 192–193
  in district courts, 198
  legal requirements for office, 203
  salaries of, 203–204, 208
  selection of, 194–195, 204–205
  in Texas Supreme Court, 193
Judicial system (Texas), 187–209
  appellate courts, 190, 201–203
  caseloads of courts, 197–203
  commissioners' court, 245–246
  constitutional impact on, 70, 187, 192
  county courts, 192, 194, 204, 206, 208, 245–246
  Court of Criminal Appeals, 193, 199, 202–203, 204, 206
  courts of appeals, 192–193, 194, 202, 204, 206
  courts of limited original jurisdiction, 190, 192
  courts of original jurisdiction, 190, 193–194, 197
  courts of record, 192
  disposition of district court cases, 199–201
  district courts, 192, 194, 197–201, 204, 206, 208
  geographic distribution of courts, 193–194
  grand juries, 195–196
  image of, 189–190, 201
  justices of the peace, 194, 204, 206, 247
  municipal courts, 194, 204, 206, 208
  organization of, 190–197
  petit juries, 197
  public policy process and, 188–189
  Supreme Court, 193, 202–203, 204, 206, 257–258
  trial juries, 196–197
Judicial systems of states, functions of, 187–188
Justices of the peace, 194, 204, 206, 247

Kaufman, Herbert, 139, 141, 142, 165
Key, V. O., 80
Kingsville, 232
Kuttner, Bob, 8

Laissez-faire philosophy, 42, 109, 141
Land commissioner, 168
Lanham, S. W. T., 82
Laredo, 26, 232
Last Picture Show, 212
Law:
  attorney general's functions, 168
  gubernatorial lawmaking function, 149
  legislature's lawmaking function, 107
  ordinary vs. constitutional, 56–57, 65–66
  Texas lawmaking process, 108
Law Enforcement Assistance Administration, 244
League of United Latin American Citizens v. Richards, 188–189
Legislative Budget Board, 147, 173, 174
Legislature (Texas), 105–134
  calendar of, 118–119, 120–121
  campaign expenses, 100, 126, 132
  characteristics of legislators, 127, 129
  committee system in, 113, 116–118
  election requirements, 125–126
  eligibility requirements, 124
  evaluation of, 105–106, 112–122, 123–124
  image of, 105–106
  impact of Constitution on, 69–70
  interest groups and, 97–98, 106, 130–133
  lawmaking function of, 108, 109–110
  legislators, 124–129
  oversight function of, 109–110
  presiding officers' power, 116–118, 119, 123, 133
  professionalism of, 97–98, 106, 122, 133
  representation function of, 110–111
  salaries, 119–120, 125
  seniority system in, 116–117
  sessions of, 113
  staff support for, 121
  standing committees (1991), 116
  terms, 124
  Texas Monthly assessment of legislators, 106
  turnover of legislators, 122, 126–128
Legislatures of states:
  Citizens Conference rankings, 114–115
  evaluation criteria, 112
  functions of, 106–111
  professionalism of, 97
Lelsz v. Kavanagh, 188
Lewis, Gib, 117
Licensing fees, 266–267, 268
Lieutenant governor (Texas Senate), 116–117, 119, 120, 121–122, 123, 133
Light Crust Doughboys, 81
Lobbying. *See also* Interest groups
  clientele groups, 166–167
  research sources provided by, 132–133
  social lobby, 130–131
Local government. *See* City government
Long ballot, 91–92
Longview, 208

Index

Lotteries, 267–268
Lubbock, 26, 208, 239
Lubbock County, 193, 194

McMurtry, Larry, 212
McWilliams, Cary, 19
MADD (Mothers Against Drunk Driving), 94
Manned Spacecraft Center, 215
Manufacturing:
   Texas' rank by dollar value, 3
   twenty-year forecast, 9
Marshall, 208
Marshall, Ray, 8
Massachusetts, high-tech competition from, 6–7
Mayor, 228, 229–230
MCC (Microelectronics and Computer Technology
   Corp.), 6
Meier, Kenneth, 180
Meinig, D. W., 18, 37
Mental health, 171
Mexican Americans:
   in city government, 230–231
   educational reform and, 296
   education levels, 31
   income and poverty levels, 30
   League of United Latin American Citizens v. Rich-
      ards, 188–189
   occupational categories of, 32
   percentage of, 15, 24
   political subculture of, 47–49
   population growth (1850–1990), 16
   San Antonio interest group, 235–236
   school districts and, 258
   suburbanization and, 213–214
   in Texas legislature (1991), 127
   urbanization and, 27
   voting by, 80, 87
Mexicans, migration of, 19–22, 23
Microelectronics and Computer Technology Corp., 6
Midland, 26, 208
Midland County, 251
Migrants, 16–22
   Anglo-Americans, 16–18
   Asian, 15
   blacks, 18–19
   distribution of political subcultures and, 43–45
   Europeans, 22, 23
   German, 22
   illegal, 20–21
   Mexicans, 19–22, 23
   Middle Eastern, 15
   Native American, 15
   origins in state regions, 23
   Southern, 17–18, 22, 23
   Sunbelt, 18, 52
Military, gubernatorial powers, 148
Miller, Lawrence W., 125, 127, 128
Minorities. *See specific minority groups*
Moody, Dan, 138
Moralistic political subculture, 51
   defined, 41–42
   distribution of (U.S.), 44–45
   voter turnout and, 80–81
Morehouse, Sarah McCally, 99
Mothers Against Drunk Driving (MADD), 94
Municipal courts, 194, 204, 206, 208
Municipalities. *See* Cities
Municipal utility districts (MUDs), 252, 253, 254

Naftalis, Gary P., 196
Native Americans, 15, 231, 287–288

Natural resources, boards and commissions, 171–172
Neutral competence, 140–142, 156, 165
New Deal, 83–84
Nixon, Richard, 84
No bill, 196

Obnoxious Acts, 58, 59
Occupations. *See* Employment
O'Daniel, W. Lee "Pappy", 81–82, 84, 138, 156
Odessa, 26
Office of State-Federal Relations, 170
Office of the Governor, 149–150
Oil and gas industries:
   declining importance of, 3–5
   in Houston, 215
   tax revenues from, 4–5, 269
   twenty-year forecast, 9
One-party system, 76–88. *See also* Democratic party;
   Political parties
   consequences of, 79–82
   formation of, 76–79
   interest groups and, 97
   obstacles to two-party competition, 90–94
   voter turnout and, 89
   weakening of, 82–88
Orange, 27
Organization of Petroleum Exporting Countries
   (OPEC), 4
Organization powers of governors, 143, 147

PACs (political action committees), 100, 132
Panic of 1873, 50
Patrons of Husbandry (The Grange), 60, 61, 98
Peterson, Paul, 220, 221
Petit juries, 197
Pharr, 228
Pink Bollworm Commission, 182
Plural executive, 69
Political action committees (PACs), 100, 132
Political culture, 37–53
   of blacks, 49–50
   "civics text" concept of, 38–39
   components of, 38–41
   defined, 38
   distribution of (U.S.), 44–45
   of Germans, 50–51
   individualistic, 42–47, 50, 51
   interest group power and, 96
   of Mexican Americans, 47–49
   moralistic, 41–42, 43–46
   patterns of, 41–46
   of southern Anglo-Americans, 46–47
   stereotype of Texans, 37–38
   subcultures in Texas, 46–51
   traditionalistic, 43–48, 49–50, 51
Political economy, 1–12
   of cities, 211–222
   defined, 2
   high-tech industries' importance, 5–9
   oil and gas industries' decline, 3–5
   service industries' growth, 8
Political efficacy, 89
Political parties. *See also* Democratic party; One-party
   system; Republican party
   democratic polity and, 75–76
   federal government intervention, 85–87
   governor as head of, 151–152
   individualistic view of, 42–43
   influence on political culture, 40
   interest group power and, 96–97
   long ballot and, 91–92

Index   303

moralistic view of, 42
New Deal impact on, 83–84
obstacles to two-party competition, 90–94
one-party system, 76–88
socioeconomic change and, 83
traditionalistic view of, 43
Poll tax, 86–87
Poor:
government spending on, 272, 273
school districts and, 258
suburbanization and, 213–214, 220–221, 222
as voters, 89, 234
Population, 15–34
cultural diversity, 22–23
demographic characteristics of, 24–33
future trends of, 24
growth of, 15–24
migration of, 16–22
Texas' rank among states, 15
urbanization, 25–27, 33
Populist party, 77
Port Arthur, 27
Positive state, 71, 109–110, 141–142, 294, 296
Postindustrial era, 9
Potter County, 251
Poverty levels, 27–30, 32–33
Primary elections, 81
all-white primaries, 85–86
Prisons. *See* Corrections
Privatization, 173–174
Professionalism:
of bureaucracy, 164
federal aid programs and, 275
of Texas government, 295
of Texas legislature, 97–98, 106, 122, 133
Progressive taxation, 265–266, 268–269, 278
Property taxes, 264–265, 268
Protest, city government and, 235, 236–237, 238
Public philosophy, 139
bureaucratic role and, 165
executive leadership as, 142, 157, 165
neutral competence as, 140–142, 156, 165
representativeness as, 139–140, 156, 165
Public services:
city government and, 225–226
conservatives' attitude toward, 289–291
county government and, 248–251
spending on, 270–273, 279–280
taxes and, 12, 270–273, 279–280
welfare programs, 272, 273, 281
Public Utility Commission (PUC), 167
Public welfare spending, 272, 273, 281
Puritans, 42

R.A.J. v. *Jones*, 188
Radical Republican regime, 58–59
Railroad Commission, 170
Ransone, Coleman B., 143
Reagan administration, 84, 214, 276
Reconstruction, 288
Democratic party and, 77
ending of, 58–60
Redford, Emmette S., 69
Redistributive policies, 220–221
Regressive taxation, 265, 268, 276–279, 280
Regulation of occupations, 172–173
Representativeness, 139–140, 156, 165
Republican party. *See also* Political parties
black support for, 77, 78
economic change and, 12
German support for, 50–51

increase of power by, 84–85
judicial elections and, 205
obstacles to two-party competition, 90–94
Reconstruction and, 77
Retail trade:
Texas' rank by dollar volume, 3
twenty-year forecast, 10
Reynolds v. *Sims*, 86
Richards, Ann, 100, 148, 149–150, 154, 155, 267, 269
Richland Hills, 232
Richmond, 232
Rights of citizens, 56
Robstown, 232
Roosevelt, Franklin, 83–84
Ruiz v. *Lynaugh*, 188

Sales taxes, 265, 268
San Angelo, 25, 26
San Antonio, 21, 26, 27, 208, 211, 213, 214, 216, 229, 235
and high-tech industry, 5, 6
San Jacinto Monument, 22
Sayers, Joseph D., 82
Schlesinger, Joseph A., 143
School districts, 255–260
governance of, 256
number and variety of, 258–260
politics of, 256–258
Schumpeter, Joseph, 163, 165
SCSA (Standard Consolidated Statistical Area), 28–29
Secretary of state, 170
Select Committee on Tax Equity, 269
Senate (Texas). *See also* Legislature (Texas)
characteristics of members, 127, 129
eligibility requirements, 124
lieutenant governor's power, 120, 121–122
standing committees (1991), 116
terms, 124
Seniority system, 116–117
Service industries' employment, 8
Services, public. *See* Public services
Severance taxes, 267
Sharp, John, 267, 269
Sheriff, 247
Shivers, Allan, 69, 84, 138, 155
Sinclair, T. C., 205, 208
Skunk removal, 161
Slavery, 49, 50
Smith, Preston, 155
Smith v. *Allwright*, 85–86, 87–88
SMSAs (Standard Metropolitan Statistical Areas),
25–26, 28–29
Social change, economic change and, 11–12
Social lobby, 130–131
Southerners. *See also* Anglo-Americans
migration of, 17–18, 22, 23
political subculture of, 46–47
Space industry, 5–6
Spanish-surnamed Americans. *See* Mexican Americans
Speaker of the House, 116–118, 119, 123, 133
Special districts, 252–255
growth of, 252, 253–254
nomenclature for, 252–253
problems with, 255
in Texas (1987), 252
Special elections, 64–65
Special interest groups. *See* Interest groups
Spending, governmental, 270–279
distribution of, 270, 276–279
federal aid, 273–276
growing agenda, 292–294
state and local, 270–273

304 Index

Standard Consolidated Statistical Area, 28–29
Standard Metropolitan Statistical Areas, 25–26, 28–29
State Board of Barber Examiners, 172
State Board of Education:
  described, 170, 256
  election of members, 141, 146
State Board of Medical Examiners, 172
State Board of Morticians, 172
State constitutions, functions of, 55–57
State Legislatures: An Evaluation of Their Effectiveness, 112
State treasurer, 170
Statutory law, constitutional law vs., 56–57, 65–66
Stevenson, Coke, 155
Stonewall Jackson Memorial Board, 182
Student Lawyer, 204
Suburbanization, 26, 213–214, 215–219, 221, 237
Sunbelt migrants, 18, 52
Sunset Advisory Commission, 181–183
Supreme Court (Texas), 193, 202–203, 204, 206, 257–258
Supreme Court (U.S.), 85–86
Sweetwater, 208

Tarrant County, 216, 249, 250
Tax effort, 281
Taxes, 263–270
  assessor and collector, county, 247
  corporate franchise, 266
  corporate income, 266, 268–269
  individual income, 265–266, 268–269
  licensing fees, 266–267, 268
  lotteries, 267–268
  national averages compared to Texas, 263–264
  oil and gas industry revenues, 4–5, 269
  progressive taxation, 265–266, 268–269, 278
  property, 264–265, 268
  proportional services for, 278
  public services and, 12
  reform of system, 295–296
  regressive taxation, 265, 268, 276–279, 280
  sales, 265, 268
  school districts and, 258–259
  severance, 267
  sources of revenues, 264–268
  special districts and, 254
  tax effort, 281
Taylor County, 249, 251
Technology. *See* High-tech industries
Tenure, gubernatorial, 143, 146
Texan, stereotype of, 37–38
Texas Air National Guard, 170
Texas Animal Health Commission, 171
Texas Army National Guard, 170
Texas Association of Business, 99
Texas Association of Realtors, 99
Texas Chamber of Commerce, 11
Texas Chemical Council, 99
Texas City, 228
Texas Education Agency, 170, 256, 258, 259
Texas Employment Commission, 8
Texas Health Facilities Commission, 182
Texas Judicial Council, 205
Texas Legislative Council, 93
Texas Medical Association, 99
Texas Medical Center, 215
Texas Mid-Continent Oil and Gas Association, 99
Texas Monthly, 106, 212

Texas Motor Transportation Association, 99
Texas Navy, 182
Texas Performance Review, 174, 175, 177, 269–270
Texas Railroad Commission, 170
Texas Savings and Loan League, 99
Texas State Guard, 170
Texas State Teachers Association, 99
Texas Trial Lawyers Association, 99
Texasville, 212
Texas Water Commission, 171–172
"Them Hillbillies Are Politicians Now," 82
Thiele, Mrs. Harold, 161
Tomball, 232
Toombs, Dennis L., 208
Tower, John, 84–85
Traditionalistic political subculture, 51
  of blacks, 49–50
  defined, 43
  distribution of (U.S.), 44–45
  of Mexican Americans, 47–49
  of southern Anglo-Americans, 46–47
Travis County, 216, 249, 250
Treasurer:
  county, 247
  state, 168, 170
Trial juries, 196–197
Truman, Harry, 84
Trustee, defined, 110
Twenty-fourth Amendment, 86–87

Urbanization, 25–27, 33, 51–52, 213, 219
Utility companies, 167

Veterans Land Program, 168
Veto powers of governors, 143, 147–148
Vice president (U.S.), lieutenant governor compared to, 121–122
Vincent, William S., 38
Vines, Kenneth N., 200–201
Voter registration, 40, 87
Voting. *See also* Elections
  all-white primary, 85–86
  by blacks, 77, 78–79, 85–86, 87
  in city politics, 231–234, 237
  on constitutional amendments, 64–65, 66, 68
  federal government intervention, 85–87
  "one-man, one-vote" apportionment, 86
  political culture and, 39–40
  turnout, 64–65, 66, 79–81, 88–90, 92–93, 231–234
  Voting Rights Act of 1965, 87
Voting Rights Act of 1965, 87

Water control and improvement districts (WCIDs), 252–253
Water Development Board, 171–172
Welfare programs, 272, 273, 281, 294
West, Felton, 120
White, Mark, 99–100, 150, 154, 155
Wholesale trade, 10
Wichita County, 249, 251
Wichita Falls, 208
Wiggins, Charles W., 99
Williams, Clayton, 154
Women in government, 127, 206, 231
Woodward, C. Vann, 78
Wright, Ruth Cowart, 137

Yankees, 18
Yarborough, Ralph, 84

TO THE OWNER OF THIS BOOK:

We hope that you have found *Texas Government: Politics and Economics*, Third Edition, by Hill and Mladenka, useful. So that this book can be improved in a future edition, would you take the time to complete this sheet and return it? Thank you.

Instructor's name: _____

Department: _____

School and address: _____

_____

1. The name of the course in which I used this book is: _____

_____

2. My general reaction to this book is: _____

_____

_____

3. What I like most about this book is: _____

_____

_____

4. What I like least about this book is: _____

_____

_____

5. Were all of the chapters of the book assigned for you to read?   Yes   No

   If not, which ones weren't? _____

6. Do you plan to keep this book after you finish the course?   Yes   No

   Why or why not? _____

_____

7. On a separate sheet of paper, please write specific suggestions for improving this book and anything else you'd care to share about your experience in using the book.

Optional:

Your name: _____ Date: _____

May Wadsworth quote you, either in promotion for *Texas Government: Politics and Economics*, Third Edition, or in future publishing ventures?

Yes: _____   No: _____

Sincerely,
Kim Quaile Hill
Kenneth R. Mladenka